THE NEWEST
CORVETTE
CORVETTE
CORVETTE
CORVETTE
CORVETTE
BY MICHAEL LAMM

CORVETTE
FROM A THROUGH Z-51

For Charlie

Lamm-Morada Publishing Co. Inc.

Post Office Box 7607
Stockton, California 95207
Telephone (209) 931-1056

First Printing, August 1983
ISBN 0-932128-04-1
Library of Congress Card Catalog Number 83-081471

CONTENTS

Chapter 1

Something Old, Everything New

Corvette development never ceases. Throughout the 15-year life of the 1968-82 Corvette, at least one group inside Chevrolet's engineering section, along with one studio at GM Design Staff, worked continuously on a replacement. Experimental models surfaced occasionally as showcars — the Astro II, the 2- and 4-rotor Wankel prototypes, and finally the Aerovette of 1977.

For years, the old master, Zora Arkus-Duntov, had been in overall charge of Corvette development. Duntov, in fact, had charge of engineering all Corvettes from 1956 through 1974.

Over the years, Zora had orchestrated each annual model change, had come up with most of the Corvette's RPO's (regular production options), and had also shouldered the never-ending responsibility of peering into the future—of proposing each new generation. Even after his retirement in Jan. 1975, Duntov continued to visit Corvette headquarters in Warren, Mich., once a month or so.

In recent times, however, the "next" generation found itself delayed time and again, mostly because the 1968-derived car kept selling so well. No other General Motors passenger vehicle had—or has ever—enjoyed such a long, healthy life. The package that eventually ended up being the '84 Corvette was originally projected as the 1982 model. But Corvette sales remained so strong through the early Eighties that, despite the 1981-82 recession, Chevrolet couldn't justify introducing the new car until Mar. 24, 1983 in California and Apr. 21 nationwide.

Another reason for this decision involved the new Corvette assembly facility at Bowling Green, Ky. GM thought it wiser to start up the new plant 18 months ahead of building an all-new car in it. It didn't seem prudent to launch both at exactly the same time. As we'll see in Chapter 7, Bowling Green began producing 1981-82 cars in June 1981.

McLellan Takes Over From Zora. When Duntov retired on Jan. 1, 1975, David R. McLellan became his successor as Corvette chief engineer. McLellan told me matter-of-factly that there wasn't a specific date or event that marked the birth of the 1984 Corvette. The car evolved during 1978 from a careful analysis of the market plus an evaluation of the Corvette's antecedants, both production and experimental.

Reflecting on the thought and work that went into creating the 1984 Corvette, Dave McLellan emphasized the new car's philosophy. "Above all," he said, "the Corvette is a sports car meant for the enjoyment of driving. The major points of the Corvette remain important in absolute terms. Acceleration, top speed, handling, and braking have to be absolutely the best—second to none. We felt committed to make the Corvette so superior that nothing could touch it at a stop light or on a California mountain road or even on the race track. By recognizing the importance of performance, and by its exciting, contemporary styling, the Corvette also turns out to be a car to be seen in—proudly. It's a statement of lifestyle."

McLellan's idea, simply put, was to make a quantum leap in the front-engined automobile; to bring it to its ultimate potential. This approach cut through some lobbying by a few members of Chevrolet Engineering and a group of designers at GM Design Staff; factions that, early on, would have preferred a mid-engined car.

We'll go into that more deeply in our chapter on the '84 Corvette's design evolution, but for the moment, suffice it to say that McLellan did look into several midship designs and built one midship mule. With due respect, he recognized and appreciated Duntov's predilection for a mid-engined Corvette. In a 1978 conversation, Zora acknowledged to McLellan that Chevrolet wasn't committed to the mid-engine concept, although when I questioned Duntov in late 1982, he expressed some disappointment that the new car had abandoned the midship layout. The strongest support,

Chief engineer David R. McLellan acknowledges that a mid-engined Corvette could have been done, but it showed no advantages over conventional layout.

Long series of mid-engined prototypes culminated in radical 1977 Aerovette, which at various times carried rotary engines or the 400-cid Chevrolet V-8.

Aerovette's creator, Zora Arkus-Duntov, favored the mid-engine layout, and the car's interior designers gave it a well shrouded LED instrument panel.

Despite Aerovette's obvious appeal, drivetrain complexity, noise, plus space and air conditioning limitations led McLellan back to traditional engineering.

though, for the mid-engine idea came from Design Staff where the lower, more forward-raked silhouette would have given the stylists new proportions to work with.

McLellan continues: "The Stingray kept selling very robustly even into the early Eighties, and this trend made it harder to sell management on any new Corvette program, front- or rear-engined. Given our limited manufacturing capacity at St. Louis; given that you couldn't market any more cars of the more expensive mid-engine configurations — at that time management wasn't interested in these other sides of the game."

Dave McLellan and his top aides drove and analyzed many of the major mid-engined sports cars from around the world, and Dave finally concluded — for reasons we'll discuss at greater length in Chapter 4 — that a front-engined, rear-drive Corvette was clearly the way to go.

"The engineering advantage of a mid-engined car," explains McLellan, "is its driving-axle traction. This is a plus, though, only when the weight-to-horsepower ratio goes beyond what's achievable in a modern road car; that is, over about 10:1. Its disadvantages lie in the much more difficult integration of handling, braking, and acceleration — the difficulty of keeping the car stable under very hard cornering conditions when much more than 50% of the vehicle's weight is on the driving wheels."

And Paul J. King, Chevrolet's director of engineering, adds, "The background work we'd been doing centered very much around mid-engined vehicles, because the midship configuration was a new and dramatic concept in the sports-car world. It still is. All the forward thinkers were talking about that configuration.

"But you know, in a real exotic car, you don't need anything except what you've got on and a bathing suit; maybe not even the bathing suit. Yet in a practical sense, particularly in the U.S., the Corvette is a car that you still do want to put some luggage and personal effects into. That became a factor in the packaging. I think Dave was selling front-engine/rear-drive before I was ready to accept it," concludes King.

A World Up in the Air. And McLellan reminds us of the uncertain world the 1984 Corvette would be born into. "Back in 1978, when we were dealing with the 55-mph speed limit, tremendous oil-price fluctuation, airbags or passive restraints, the spectre of a gas-guzzler tax — all those factors took some sorting out.

"One of the ideas we seriously looked at was to do the Corvette a lot like the P-Car — not in terms of body panels and such details, but we seriously thought about using our X-Car suspension and unit powertrain assemblies to build a mid-engined Vette.

"However, we ran up against the torque-capacity limitations of these powertrains. If we turbocharged, say, the Citation X-11 V-6 and threw a lot of extra horsepower at the transaxle, we'd break it. A lot of that has changed since then — I'm not putting down the P-Car — but that idea gave us a very uncertain future back in 1978.

"And then along came the decision to do the 1982 F-Cars — the new Camaro and Firebird — as front-engined, rear-drive vehicles, *with a V-8 engine*. Earlier on, General Motors had been looking at fwd versions of the F-Car, but when they decided to go rear drive for handling, here was just one more voice that said there was no way we could get the relative performance superiority from a Corvette with a V-6 powertrain.

"You'll recall that there was talk back in 1978 about the imminent demise of the V-8 engine. Our analysis, though, told us we could meet the expected (and now real) gas-guzzler-tax threshold that stairsteps to 22.5 mpg in 1986 by designing a lighter, more aerodynamic Corvette and applying all the known engine and transmission technology.

"So I said to myself back in 1978, Let's take another run at what we've got. We then spent some time just rethinking the front-engine/rear-drive car as a package concept and found that, in fact, we could pull a lot of size out of it, yet retain the V-8

McLellan modified several '78 Vettes to become mules for the new car. He chopped wheelbases and installed aluminum V-8's.

Aluminum block helped bring weight down to '84 Vette's target, and Chevrolet engineers used Phoenix dragway to test the pre-prototypes' tires in impromptu match races.

Prototypes began to arrive at GM's Milford and Mesa proving grounds in the summer of 1981. One of the earliest carried subtle differences from final design, most obvious being roof, nose, spoiler, and mirrors.

Another early prototype shows aerodynamic fixes to improve cooling and help high-speed stability.

engine, the weight balance, the cross section of the exhaust system, the torque capacity of the drive line, suspension performance, etc., and it looked promising; more promising, in fact, than anything we were doing with a mid-engined V-8. It packaged a lot better, too, in terms of people and luggage.''

Experimental packaging of the various new Corvette proposals, including the new front-engined design, became the responsibility of Chevrolet's research-and-development group — a cadre best known for its work on the Chaparral race cars. The group included Al Bodnar, Jim Steele, and Bob Clemens.

McLellan continues: ''Chevrolet R&D started to do some serious full-sized layout work around the front-engined package; then we consulted with Jerry Palmer at Design Staff, and Jerry made a clay armature around the wheelbase, tread, height-of-engine, height-of-roof, and the very important seating package that we wanted.''

Dave McLellan's Background. David Ramsay McLellan was born in Michigan's upper peninsula in 1936 — in Munising, Mich. — but he grew up in the city of Detroit. He attended Detroit public schools, then enrolled in Wayne State University and graduated in 1959 with a degree in mechanical engineering. In 1965, he married Glenda Roberts of Pontiac, Mich. The McLellans have two sons: David Jr. and Philip Duncan.

After taking his mechanical engineering degree, Dave went to work for GM at its Milford, Mich., proving grounds in the noise-and-vibration laboratory. McLellan stayed at Milford for several years, at the same time attending night school, again at Wayne State. He was going for a master's degree in engineering mechanics.

In 1968, Dave became one of the first people in GM's engineering test department charged with running vehicle dynamics tests at ''Black Lake.'' Black Lake is a huge, unbroken, 59-acre expanse of asphalt in the heart of GM's Milford proving grounds. It's called Black Lake because, when the surface is wet, it looks so much like water that ducks often come in for pancake landings.

''We were consolidating a lot of our handling testing and developing instrumentation for vehicle dynamics at that time,'' recalls McLellan. ''I came to Chevrolet in early 1969 and worked for Chuck Hughes on the 1970 Camaro program. I was involved for several years on the F-Car.

''In 1971, I worked for a time at the Technical Center on a John DeLorean new-car program proposal. It was called the K-Car; it was to be a Nova/Camaro/Corvette combined basic vehicle. Duntov was very much against it. DeLorean wanted to explore it, but for a lot of reasons it never came to fruition. After that, I found myself working full time at the Tech Center, initially for Bob Dorn as the chassis engineer on the Camaro/Nova program.''

In 1973-74, McLellan gathered up his family and went off to Boston, to the Massachusetts Institute of Technology's Sloan School of Management as a Sloan fellow. This was with GM's encouragement, at company expense, and it gave Dave a chance to take a master's degree in management.

''That's a story in itself,'' he muses. ''The program put 50 of us mid-career managers together for a year. We had the unparalleled quality of education that MIT affords; also the unbelievable field resources. At MIT, our field trips took us to New York, Wall Street, to the financial community, to Washington, the federal government, and finally we got a trip around the world. This was basically to gain exposure to businessmen and financial and government leaders in the principal capitals. I think our class was the last to go all the way around the world. A tremendous year; one I'll never forget.''

He then came back to GM in the summer of 1974 and worked for about six months as a staff engineer under Duntov on the Corvette program. When Zora retired, McLellan took up Duntov's responsibilities, ''. . . and here we are.''

McLellan and Chevrolet's engineering director Lloyd Reuss opted for 1-piece liftout roof instead of a T-top. This caused some initial handling problems.

Chevrolet had to do some testing on public roads. Ace spy photographer Jim Dunne bagged several early Corvette protos, including this instrumented job.

By the winter of '81, Chevrolet was anticipating Jim Dunne and began masking most prototypes with fiberglass nose, door covers, and tail light lenses from a Ford product. All these bodies were handmade anyway, so it was no harder to disguise their lines than to follow Design Staff's still-evolving final shape.

One Arizona ride and drive saw two of the shortened '78 pre-prototypes stop for a snack with the then-current prototype design, which wore a bra and had a similar cover over tail lamps plus wings to hide liftgate glass. "Louvers" behind the wheelwells were nothing more than friction tape applied to the body.

"We had some short-term things to get out of the way: the 1978 and '80 programs, keeping the old girl healthy and legal. Those were basically maintenance programs. We also used that time to teach ourselves about some of the non-traditional automotive materials, like the use of structural aluminum in applications beyond wheels, the use of fiberglass in springs and bumpers and functional parts. I think that helped us a lot in preparing for the '84 car.''

Management Gives the Go-Ahead. Getting back to the engineering program, McLellan continues, "Briefly, then, that was the early housekeeping we went through, and next came the task of selling the front-engine/rear-drive program to management. Chevrolet Engineering had, by this time, started the experimental build of pre-prototype cars, and it was at this point that I went to top management with the formalized program. I told them how small the car could be, what kind of fuel economy it might get, how much it was expected to cost, and so forth. The market assessment and profitability analyses looked good, and that's where we got the go-ahead.''

Management, sitting as GM's powerful Product Policy Group, accepted McLellan's recommendations for the front-engine/rear-drive configuration with little serious doubt or argument. McLellan's presentation convinced everyone attending that the mid-engine configuration, while interesting, held no real advantage, especially if the Corvette were to continue using the V-8.

"At that time, too, we were developing the more fuel-efficient electronic control systems for the V-8, the 4-speed automatic transmission, the manual overdrive 7-speed, etc. And when we looked forward to 1986, the year the gas-guzzler tax threshold went to 22.5 mpg composite fuel economy, we felt we could meet it. We didn't want or need much margin. Our technology told us we could do it with a V-8. So with the V-8 being such an important part of the Corvette, why compromise it out of the program? In other words, the V-8 was in!

"There was a lot of emphasis by management," concludes McLellan, "to make sure that we were, in fact, taking maximum advantage of materials technology, electronics technology, powertrain technology, and so forth—that what we were doing was going to make the car an absolute technological *tour de force*. And that's how we proceeded.'' □

Chief Corvette designer Jerry Palmer (second from right) puts finishing touches on the 1984 car.

Shapes and Sizes

When a design group gets an assignment like the Corvette—a clean-sheet car—it's truly the chance of a lifetime. The task of designing a production Corvette doesn't come around very often, and when it does, everyone throws himself into it with total commitment.

"We're talking about a car that's very important to Design Staff," comments Jerry P. Palmer, head of the Chevrolet studio responsible for Corvette and Camaro design. "It's the flagship of the fleet for Chevrolet. It's the American sports car. The thing about the Corvette—regardless of the program status within the studio, we're always working on or thinking about Corvettes, not only because they're such an important part of our business but because they're such tremendous fun to work on."

Palmer's Chevy Three studio has been responsible for Corvette and Camaro design since 1974. He and his team styled the fascia, hood, bumpers, rear lip, and front airdam updates for all production Corvettes since that time. Chevy Three created the 1978 Silver Anniversary edition, the 1978 Indy Pace Car, the Mulsanne showcar, the PPG Pace Car, and the 1982 Collector Edition. "If they'd asked me to put one more dress on the old girl, though," Jerry told me with a smile, "I'm not sure I could have done it."

At the same time he was updating the then-current Corvette, Jerry's studio gave birth to the 1982 Camaro. And all that while, they were also creating the car destined to become the 1984 Corvette. The '84 Vette, as mentioned, was originally scheduled to be a 1982 model. In other words, Chevy Three was, at various times, working on special production Corvette models plus the 1982 Camaro plus the 1984 Corvette concurrently.

Nor was the job made easier by the mid-engine versus front-engine question. That point remained unresolved until fairly late in the game, which meant that two designs for the 1984 Corvette had to be brought along side by side for well over a year.

Meet Mr. Palmer. Jerry Palmer holds one of the great jobs in auto design—in the auto industry, in fact. Jerry grew up the son of a Pontiac salesman and worked his way through college at a Detroit tool-and-die shop, where he machined prototype parts for the Big Three automakers. He calls those years behind the lathe and drill press, ''. . . my true education.'' He's very good with his hands, and he can see things inside a billet of steel or a hunk of clay before the shape ever comes out.

Jerry Palmer now heads up the Chevy Three studio at General Motors Design Staff. The huge, contemporary Design Staff building connects via an underground passage to GM's new windtunnel next door. Together, they form the focal point of GM's 330-acre Technical Center in Warren, Mich., just north of Detroit.

In many ways, Palmer's still just a kid having a good time with cars. He's as ebullient today as he must have been in 1964, when he won a GM summer internship/scholarship from Detroit's Society for Arts and Crafts (now the Center for Creative Studies).

Jerry has always been crazy about cars. He sketched them endlessly in high school. He'd wanted to go on to Art Center College of Design in California, where most auto designers take their degrees, but he couldn't afford the tuition. So he lived at home and went to Detroit Arts and Crafts instead. There he was lucky enough to study under two excellent teachers: Alex Tremulis, who designed (among other cars) the 1948 Tucker — a man with a lifelong, contagious automotive love affair; and Homer LaGassey, Jr., the man whose professional credits include the Le Mans Ford GT-40 and Mark IV (again among many other cars).

''Actually,'' Jerry told me, ''I think I got as good an education, if not better, than I would have out in California, and I had General Motors only five miles away.''

Two years after his internship, when Jerry graduated from Arts and Crafts in 1966, he immediately applied to GM for a permanent job. The wait seemed interminable, but after two weeks, he got the phone call that changed his life.

The man who recognized Palmer's talent was Charles M. (Chuck) Jordan. Jordan is director of design, reporting directly to Irvin W. (Irv) Rybicki, vice president of GM Design Staff. Rybicki guides overall design for the entire corporation.

The two men's personalities are entirely different, but each is a strong, competent

Early sketches favored midship engine placement, mostly because it's easier to give a car a low cowl and rakish glass angles. These design studies from 1975 envisioned X-Car components, including crosswise V-6, probably turbocharged. Mid-engined Vette would have been smaller, lighter than it ended up.

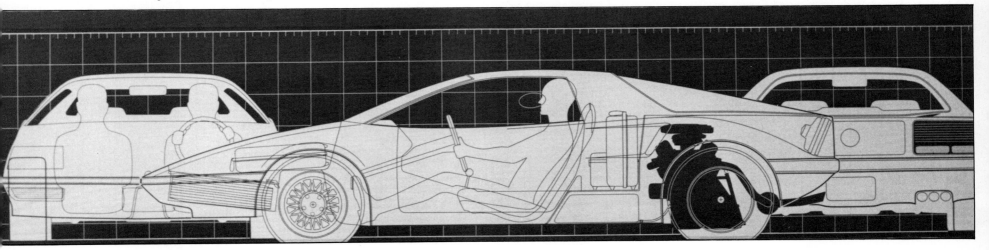

Irvin W. Rybicki

Charles M. Jordan

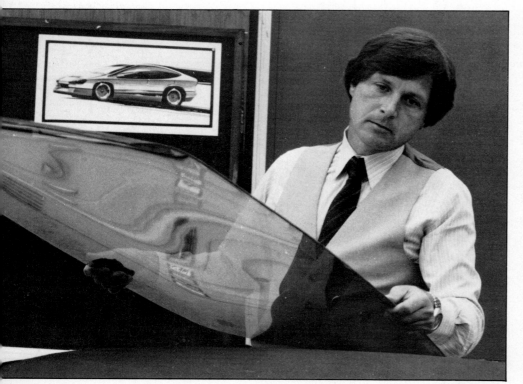

Jerry P. Palmer

designer in his own right. There's little doubt that they both agree on the importance of letting the studio designers have the freedom to explore individual, creative ideas, and that they want to give credit to those designers who contributed to the new Corvette.

Jerry Palmer runs his studio with a light touch, very relaxed; an air of informality. His sense of humor is as good as his sense of design, and he's the type who never seems to take life too seriously. Yet Jerry has all the right attributes: he's an excellent designer, imaginative, ingenious, reliable, thorough, and sociable.

Says Chuck Jordan of Palmer: "If I ever get tired of the normal routine—whatever I've got to do that day, whatever I'm looking at—when I want to relax I go in and talk to the guys in Chevy Three. It's exciting; they're all car nuts, and it's just a great atmosphere—the people, the enthusiasm."

Hello to the Mid-Engined Vettes. To understand the '84 Vette's antecedents, we have to go back as far as 1969. At that time, Zora Arkus-Duntov and William L. Mitchell, who preceded Rybicki as Design Staff vice president, began collaborating on a series of mid-engined prototypes and showcars. One of the first in that series was coded XP-882, and it used a small-block Chevy V-8 turned sideways behind the passenger compartment, driving the rear wheels through a modified fwd Olds Toronado transaxle. The original XP-882 was styled in Hank Haga's studio by Haga and his assistant, Alan Young.

Development stopped abruptly on the XP-882 when John DeLorean became Chevrolet's new general manager, but the program was reinstated some 12 months later by GM president Edward N. Cole after the first Panteras began arriving in Lincoln-Mercury showrooms. And the XP-882 got another boost soon afterward when Cole decided that the next generation of Corvettes should lead the switch to Wankel engines.

Thereupon, Duntov removed the V-8 and began substituting a series of Wankels—the 2- and 4-rotors being the best remembered. Under Mitchell's direction and Haga's studio guidance, Palmer helped design the 4-rotor Corvette in 1973.

The Wankel engine became a dead issue when Ed Cole retired and, in 1977, the 4-rotor gave way to a 400-inch Chevrolet V-8, again mated to the same reworked Toronado powertrain. At that point, the car took on the name Aerovette.

As we'll see, the Aerovette would have considerable influence not only on the 1984 Corvette but on GM's entire design philosophy. "You can't calculate how important the Aerovette was to our design development; how many ideas that one car generated," comments Jerry.

Two Camps. Palmer's group, working closely with Dave McLellan and his people at Chevrolet Engineering, got the assignment in early 1977 to begin developing an all-new Corvette for 1982 production.

But soon a difference of opinion arose on the Corvette's direction, similar to the one that split designers and engineers over the 1982 Camaro. In the Camaro's case, Design Staff originally favored a smaller front-wheel-drive car while Chevrolet Engineering wanted the Camaro to remain rear-drive.

On the Corvette, the same forces again formed two camps. Design Staff felt the new Corvette ought to be smaller and mid-engined, while Chevrolet Engineering favored front-engine/rear-drive.

Palmer explains it further: "At first we at Design Staff said there ought to be a new mid-engined Corvette, derived from X-Car components. While we were doing the design, Engineering built a running mid-engined component car off a Porsche 914. They used that car as a mule. They built up the suspension and installed an X-Car V-6 engine and driveline. Meanwhile, design studies for the X-derived Corvette were

Wide track gave full-sized clay a crouching stance.
Triple tail lamps lent the Corvette styling continuity.

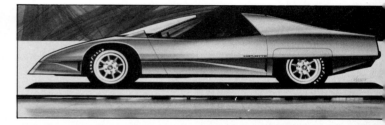

Obvious similarities exist between Aerovette and Corvette design proposals from late 70's. Prowed wind-shield, softer shapes, louvered B-pillars hark unmistakably back to Chevrolet's acclaimed Vette showcars.

The Ferrari 308 had recently come on the scene and also influenced Chevy Three designers. Chuck Jordan drove a red 308, which Palmer later bought.

Every once in a while, when they hit a snag, designers are allowed to go wild, as with this satchel-fendered model. Such tangents give rise to fresh ideas.

going on in my studio. But then early on, Chevrolet Engineering came back and said they were very unhappy with the performance and handling of that 914 mule as a Corvette. If you're talking about a 914 Porsche or a Fiat X1/9, that's one thing. But a Corvette needs a V-8 for strengths that these cars just didn't have.

"Then something happened that turned out to be very important. In the summer of 1977, Porsche came out with an all-new sports car: the 928, with a water-cooled V-8. The engine was in the front, with rear drive. The 928 had its impact, particularly after we drove the car. That's one helluva car to drive."

Dave McLellan, who'd owned several Porsches over the years, interjects, "I'm told that Porsche evaluated a 1976 Corvette in their development of the 928 for '78. The point certainly wasn't lost on us that Porsche had turned to a layout very similar to the Corvette's for their latest and most high-tech model!"

Jerry Knows the Way. Palmer continues, "So Chevrolet came back with a different proposal. They said they were very much interested in a front-engine/rear-drive configuration. And that's when the two camps divided — Design Staff and Chevy Engineering.

"Well, because of the nature of my studio, being a production studio, we tackled the front-engined car, even though the midship engine was the way we'd have liked to have gone initially. I knew full well that the conventional car would end up in production, not the mid-engined job.

"There were a lot of things going against the midship version. For instance, transmission torque loads. The midship Corvette wouldn't have used just a standard 60° V-6 engine. It would need a much more powerful version of that, either turbocharged or injected or a combination. Or punched out to 3.3 liters; whatever. It would be a lot more engine than the X-Car transaxle was ever designed for. Therefore, we would have had problems with the transaxle. And when you're talking about re-doing a transaxle, you're talking big dollars.

"So we established very quickly that the V-6 mid-engined Corvette wasn't potent enough, and Chevrolet Engineering had some pretty clear ideas of what the V-8 chassis ought to be. For instance, wheels and tires dictated the width of the new car, because Dave McLellan knew what kind of a footprint he wanted. The Corvette has traditionally had the largest tire offered by GM — the Goodyear Eagle GT P255/60R-15 for 1980-82. Dave wanted more footprint than that. And I wanted 16-inch wheels for aesthetic reasons. McLellan looked at 10-inch-wide wheels on the back for ultimate performance. And all that started our design parameters."

Setting Up the Package. Despite the early difference of opinion on positioning the engine, I can't over-emphasize the strong bond that linked Design Staff with Chevrolet Engineering. As colleagues and friends, McLellan and Palmer worked very, very closely in developing this car. Dave McLellan took a great personal interest in the '84 Corvette's styling, as did Palmer in its engineering. Palmer and his studio staff could understand and appreciate McLellan's engineering decisions, and vice versa.

Usually, a design team works to a pre-determined "package," that package being a simple set of dimensions: wheelbase, overall length, width, and height. The package normally also specifies engine and drivetrain placement, cowl and seating positions, hood and deck sight lines, plus any other specifications that can be pinned down with some accuracy.

The 1984 Corvette didn't begin, though, with a definitive package. The only initial dimension that Dave McLellan handed Jerry Palmer was ground clearance, which Dave set at 5.25 inches. Other than that, the package evolved around the seating space reserved for the driver and passenger.

"I wanted to get our full ride travel, with 3.5 inches of jounce front and rear, and we needed about 1.75 inches of additional wheel-well clearance to take care of the deflection of tires, the suspension system, etc.," says McLellan. The previous car had a minimum ground clearance of 5.0 inches, yet everyone recognized that the new Corvette would end up with a lower roofline. That meant tighter vertical packaging — a tough order to fill under the best of circumstances.

Design Breakthroughs. Tires became one of the critical determinants of the '84 Corvette's overall design. The 16's ended up with the same overall diameter as the previous model's 15's, so they didn't affect ground clearance. But they did become a crucial factor in establishing the car's overall width. Tire angle at full turn plus engine loading width set the basic cross-car dimension. The VR50 tires helped make the '84 Corvette two inches wider overall than the '82 had been, also helping give it 6.5 inches more shoulder room. Seating and the driveshaft tunnel further helped dictate total width.

"But the big thing that made this car practical," Palmer emphasizes, "was packaging the exhaust. Traditionally, the catalytic converter, being placed under the

Tucking converter up into tunnel created one breakthrough Palmer needed.

floor or the seat, establishes a car's H-point and cowl height. It dictates overall height as well. You can only do so much with seatback angle before the vehicle becomes uncomfortable to drive.

"We found that by widening the car instead of narrowing it as in so many downsizing programs, we could package the exhaust and converter underneath the driveshaft. That enabled us to lower the H-point one inch, because now we weren't concerned about the exhausts running under the seats. We also moved the H-point forward 8.75 inches and outboard 3.75 inches. Repositioning the catalytic converter

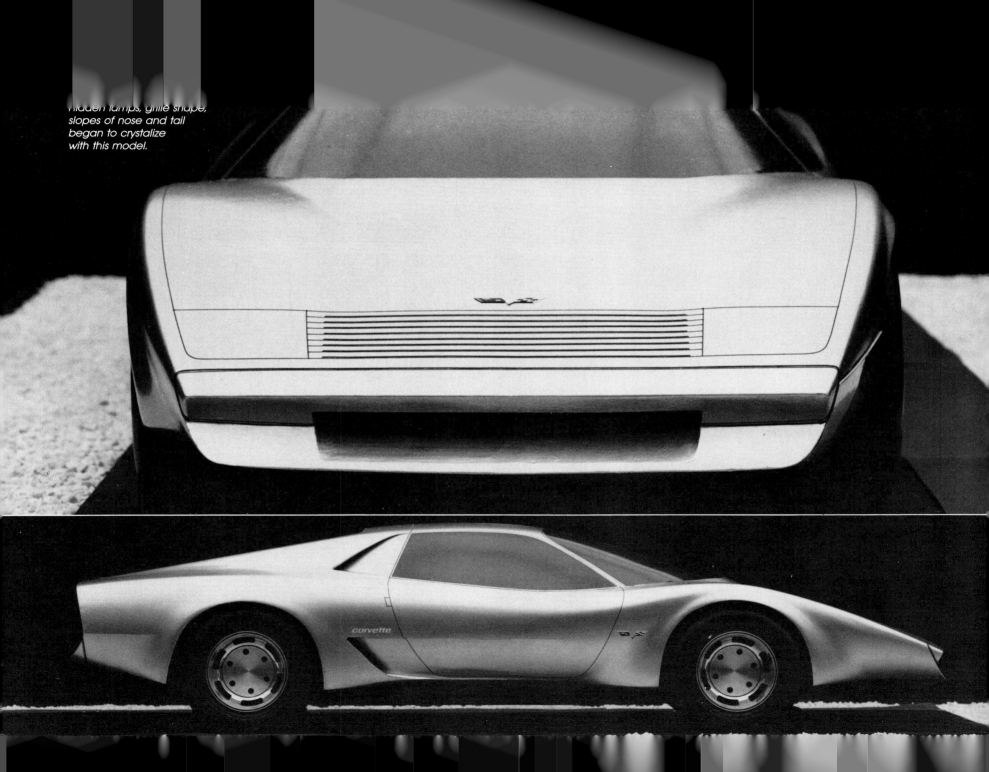

Hidden lamps, grille shape, slopes of nose and tail began to crystalize with this model.

By Sept. 1978, Palmer's group acknowledged that the new Corvette—then projected for 1982—would be front engined. The car's final form needed only refinement.

became *the* major breakthrough, and it helped sell us on the idea of the front-engined Corvette.''

The H-point Jerry's talking about is an imaginary spot inside the body of the seated driver and/or passenger. If you were to run a sword through the driver from side to side, just above his pelvic bone, and then another sword straight in from the small of his back, the intersection of those two sword blades would be his H-point.

''The other idea that helped us package this car was to straighten out the driveline; accept less angle between the transmission and the first U-joint,'' continues Jerry. ''By doing that, we were able drop the front of the engine down, which let us move the occupants forward.

''Another significant breakthrough had to do with eliminating crossmembers underneath the passenger compartment. With the new uniframe instead of a separate frame and birdcage, we didn't need crossmembers under the floor, so we could lower the floor itself to ground-clearance level. Finally, by moving the Corvette's steering gear ahead of the engine, we could lower the V-8 by tucking it behind the steering rack. That let us to drop the hoodline and package the whole car for minimum cowl height. We also made our commitment to the twin TBI intake system at that time, which gave us an inch lower hood than a carburetor would have.''

It's interesting to note that, because Jerry could lower the seating position relative to the previous Corvette—due to the absence of crossmembers and no exhaust system under the floor—and since the driver and passenger could be moved forward due to the farther-ahead engine placement, both occupants ended up with half an inch

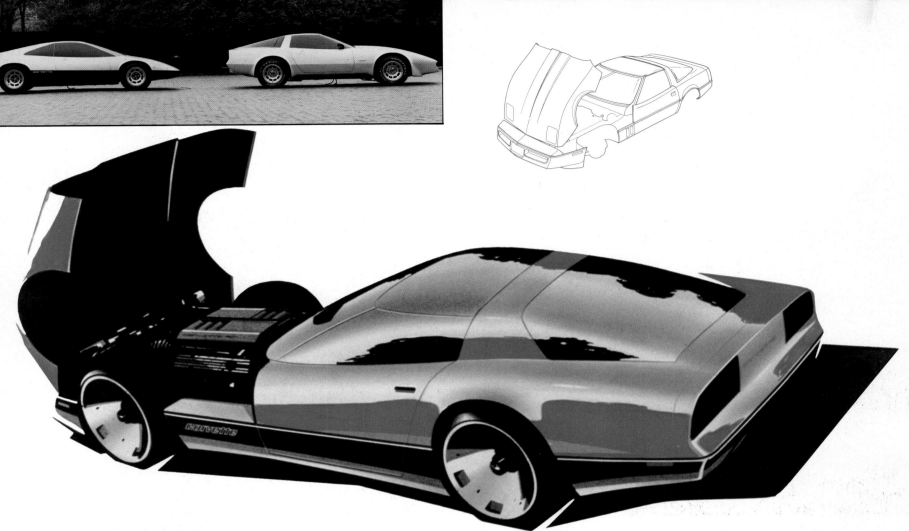

Designer John Cafaro's open-hood sketch introduced the circumferential body groove. Meanwhile, clays (inset) compared sizes of mid- versus front-engined cars.

more leg room, fractionally more head room, and that whopping 6.5 inches more shoulder space.

Wheelbase still hadn't been firmly established, but Jerry's group suggested 96 inches, based on the way the total package began shaping up. "Proportion, proportion, proportion," barks Jerry, hammering home the cardinal rule of any great design.

"We also arrived at the windshield angle at the same time as the wheelbase," recalls Palmer. "It started out at 67.5, which is essentially the same as the Ferrari Boxer or 308. We got knocked back to 64.5, but that's still the steepest windshield angle GM has ever released. So we had a pretty exciting front-engine/rear-drive package to begin with."

Battle of the Bulge. While these serious production preliminaries were going on, designer Ron Hill, chief of Advanced Three under David M. Holls, continued working on the V-6, mid-engined version. He took the X-Car-derived package and updated it. Both clays were shown together outside, and Palmer's — the conventional package — was thought to be too large. "Again a lot of people were sort of mesmerized by the feeling that the car should still be mid-engined," Jerry remarks.

At that time, several Design Staff members owned mid-engined Ferraris. Chuck Jordan drove a silver Boxer, and Jerry Palmer had just bought a red Ferrari 308-GTB. John Cafaro, junior member of Palmer's staff, had a Fiat X1/9. So there's no denying an acceptance of mid-engined sports cars at the highest levels of Design Staff and, as Jordan himself points out, "It's easier to do a mid-engined car, because the basic pro-

Cafaro's groove made a perfect parting seam and eliminated bond joints. Several grille themes made their appearance, but none was deemed appropriate.

portions are different. You can get a lower belt with a mid-engined car, because you can drop the cowl. When you get into the long-hooded look of the front-engined Corvette, it's more difficult.''

Not only does a midship car allow a lower cowl, but with no engine up front, the hood can slope downward more steeply—more in line with the windshield. Then, too, the passenger compartment shifts forward for tighter packaging.

On the minus side, though, mid-engined cars pay a penalty in luggage capacity and foot room. Comfort likewise tends to be compromised if overall vehicle height falls below about 46 inches. Finally, rear vision has always been a problem in midship designs.

Irv Rybicki adds, ''We fight tooth and nail to get the cowl down in every sports car program we do around here. That's one reason the mid-engined car appealed to us. It offered us a lot more possibilities for a new, fresh-looking vehicle. If you're looking for newness and real shock value, the mid-engined car is the easier way to get it. And although at that point our midship clays didn't retain a lot of Corvette flavor, we could have added that heritage and personality later if we'd gotten serious. In the first corporate show with both proposals, we were trying to prove how small we could get the machine if it were mid-engined.''

Size bothered Palmer, too. ''The '82 model seemed just too big for the times. Remember, we were downsizing everything. If you make a chart, the Corvette has tended to move up in total size scale .... Irv Rybicki was particularly worried, and rightly so.

''When we started the '84 program, we really wanted to get the smallest package possible. We tried to maintain the Corvette flavor, and we were able to reduce the car

Although the 1982 Vette had been a bottom breather, the '84 was assumed to need a grille until tunnel tests proved otherwise. Twin grilles smack of Oldsmobile.

The Corvette's designers enlisted computers wherever they could. Clay milling machine shown here can "read" a scale model from digitized data and reproduces it full size. It can also create mirror images, thus is able to sculpt a perfect other side. Modeling clay is heaped over lightweight styrofoam core.

in size. It's 8.4 inches shorter than the previous Vette. And despite more ground clearance, it's an inch lower in overall height.

"But you really don't see that much difference, because in sideview you're always reading the corners. Very rarely do you read centerline to centerline unless there's a tremendous amount of plan view. We tend to be concerned about numbers when we're talking lengths; more so than the apparent length of a car. The new Corvette as it came out for 1984 looks as long as the '82 car."

Inside Chevy Three. By Mar. 1979, Dave McLellan and his staff at Chevrolet Engineering had several front-engined component cars running, and the Corvette production studio continued exploring front-engined/rear-drive designs in earnest.

Palmer's 4-man studio worked as a close-knit team. Palmer himself, of course, acted as chief designer. His assistant, Roger Hughet, had come up from Advanced One, where he'd earlier created the theme car that led to the 1982 Firebird/Camaro. John Cafaro, youngest studio member, showed great promise and made a number of valuable contributions to the new Corvette, including the horizontal body molding and the basic wheel design. And Randy Wittine, a veteran of several productive years in Palmer's Chevy Three, had been one of the people directly involved in the 1982 Camaro.

Assistant chief designer Ted Schroeder also needs a tip of the hat, because he was in Palmer's studio until Aug. 1979, after which he joined a Buick studio. Ted worked

on the '82 Camaro, and his great 1984 Corvette contributions had to do with laying out an entirely new cockpit section plus the rear profile. The studio's other personnel included designer Tom Covert plus senior technical stylist Jim Miller.

George McLean and Ron Nowicki acted as Chevy Three's engineers at various times, with Robert Clancy as assistant chief. Al Tholl and Eugene J. Meso, the studio's chief clay modelers (also at different times), directed assistant chief modelers Don Brougham and Mike Costello plus modelers Richard Ziemann Jr., Dick Brosier, Brad Lloyd, Jerome McDonald, Thomas E. Reiss, and Gregory Stelmack. Tholl and McLean, who'd both been active in Corvette design since the days of the first Sting Ray, have since retired.

Too Often Overlooked. A lot of the credit for the '84 Corvette, of course, has to go to Design Staff management—men like Irv Rybicki, Chuck Jordan, Dave Holls, F.

Palmer and his Chevy Three studio staff spent considerable time cleaning up the engine compartment. They paid special attention to the magnesium aircleaner

and rocker covers, plus the routing of hoses and wires. Persistent rumors that port fuel injection would supersede TBI led Palmer to also work on that possibility.

Edward Taylor, and Jack Humbert. All these gentlemen spent considerable time in the studio, talking design direction and reviewing the clay model. Rybicki and Jordan offered innumerable suggestions for improving design quality as it progressed.

"We were in there every day," notes Rybicki, "discussing the car with Palmer and his gang, making changes almost hourly at times. Take the body side surface on this new Corvette. I think Chuck and I were in there every day for several weeks, because we couldn't get the lights to flow where we wanted them. Palmer had one idea, and we had another. We kept going back and forth until we got the problem solved."

"We were very concerned that we didn't have enough leap over the wheels in profile," amplifies Jerry Palmer as he looks back at the beginnings the front-engined version. "Now remember, we're coming off that mid-engined car, which was much flatter in section and flatter in sideview profile in terms of the execution of fender forms.

"Essentially, the theme stayed the same, but the surface development changed. We're coming away from the age of the Italian sheer look, and we're again convinced that form is really a very important part of design. If you look at the automobile as a piece of 3-dimensional sculpture, form is what's going to make it exciting, not flat planes.

"Now something very subtle began to happen. We did one clay model where the right side of the car still had a straighter, tauter fender profile. The left side had a little more of the bump or fender kickup that we felt the car needed. Irv Rybicki was very instrumental in making sure we didn't lose the amount of flow in those fender forms. He was very concerned that we were getting too linear with the car. 'Put some roundness back into it,' he kept telling us. Irv and Chuck, coming in cold, could see things that we in the studios didn't see immediately. We were too close to the car."

John Cafaro also talks about the new Corvette's side surfacing: "Right at the door is where the dying in, dying out of the fender highlight happens. We were looking at the highlight going all the way through at one time, and then we brought the Aerovette up, and management liked the way the Aerovette's fenders pulled out of the doors. Jerry successfully incorporated and adapted this theme into the final design."

Chuck Jordan adds: "You know the shoulder that comes up from the front fender and how it goes into the door? That's very subtle sculpturing. We kept looking back to the execution of the Aerovette, because that was essentially a rounded car, but lean; stretched-looking. We had a hard time capturing that in the 1984 Corvette, but by God, we did it."

Cafaro Enters the Groove. An early styling and body-engineering innovation came about when John Cafaro drew a simple sketch showing a car with its hood and hatch wide open. The hood amounted to the entire front end of the car, hinged at the grille like the old E-Type Jaguar. But the innovation had to do with Cafaro's use of a groove that encircled the car, marking the parting line that separated the bottom from the top of the body itself. This line, or groove, would prove of great importance to Corvette body engineers, because it would make the car much easier to manufacture.

"John Cafaro was responsible for getting the body groove started," remembers Jerry Palmer, "although the idea wasn't totally new. Ferraris have had similar grooves for some time. But in the case of the Corvette, it makes a natural break for the body engineers to use as a panel parting line. We wanted to stay away from the bonding seams that had plagued Corvette manufacture for 14 years on the previous cars. This one has no bond seams."

Adds John Cafaro: "It started when I taped a line on the car. There are no more bond seams in the fenders, and since the body engineers didn't want any more bond

seams, it turned out to be a logical thing to do for a fiberglass car.

"But I was thinking aesthetically at the time; you know, Ferrari 308. Maybe put a body side molding in the groove. One thing led to the next, and people liked it. The engineering guys came in and said it made a lot of sense to do it that way. And from then on it stayed."

Palmer and McLellan took a long look under that big, wide-open hood and decided to do some housekeeping. "We've been concerned for years," remarks Jerry, "about underhood appearance. We did new magnesium rocker covers for the 1984 Corvette." Roger Hughet adds, "We spent months and months doing that mag aircleaner. There was only so much clearance between the TBI and the hood, so it became a big challenge."

The Engine Compartment as Art. For '84, no part of the underhood environment escaped the designer's touch. Jerry and his team concentrated not only on the rocker covers and the large magnesium aircleaner but on routing the wires, selecting colors for the wires, for the engine, and even for the battery itself. The Delco Freedom battery no longer came in red, white, and blue; the Corvette started the trend to black and silver.

The engine block also became black, with silver ignition wires neatly routed under the painted air cleaner. Mentions Corvette assistant staff engineer Paul Huzzard, "It presented quite an unusual and amusing picture to see Jerry Palmer telling the chassis guys where to put what. He told them what color the plug wires ought to be, the engine block. At first the engineers figured, Is this guy for real? But again, Dave McLellan was very much the driving force, and he wanted this car to be a showcase. If you compare the 1982 engine compartment with the new one, you don't realize that they both have the same number of wires, tubes, pipes, and plumbing fixtures, because the new car is so much neater."

And Chevrolet general manager Robert C. (Bob) Stempel observes, "We think a lot of our dealers are going to display this car in the showroom with the hood open, because it gives customers a chance to see the tire tread, the aluminum forgings in the front suspension, the designer engine dressup, and all the silver and black. In fact, the Goodyear people, when they realized that their tire was going to be on display— not just the face where you read their name, but the tread, too—they cleaned up their tire design. It's a very neat-appearing tire along with a neat engine compartment."

Bottom-Breathing Breakthrough. Roger Hughet explains another significant design discovery: "We found we could cool the engine adequately by taking in air just underneath the bumper and not through the grille or the face of the car, as we normally do. That was a real boon, because it helped us keep the aero numbers low. Jerry and I worked very closely with Corvette cooling engineer Frank Reukel—test after test after test in the Harrison windtunnel. Not only just with the clay, but they also set up radiators and engines in bucks at Harrison Div. The radiator tilts opposite from previous models, but that's how we maximized airflow."

Jerry Palmer adds, "On the front end, we were looking for a new way to do the theme. For a long time, we just weren't happy with the way the front was going. We tried various openings and shapes, but nothing looked right. Then suddenly . . . after our wind tunnel testing, we found that the new Corvette could be a bottom breather. We could take in all the cooling air we needed from underneath. That plus having an electric fan under the hood gave us greater leeway in positioning the cooling system which, in turn, allowed us to do something functional with lighting that we hadn't done before, namely block off the 'grille' air intake and install the turn signals. We even got quartz halogen fog lamps in those spaces."

In addition, Chevy Engineering insisted on skegs underneath the new Corvette's

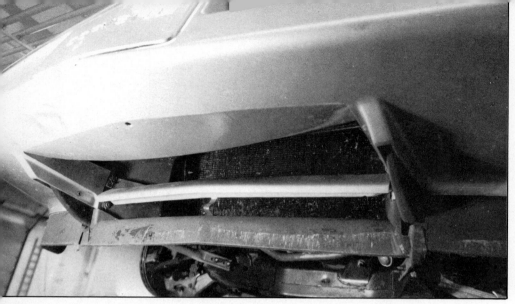

To fill the void underneath the Corvette's chin, and also to help direct cooling air into the radiator, Jerry Palmer added what he calls his anti-Spinks bar.

Aero lab engineer Max Schenkel, along with Palmer's people, trimmed up the final design in GM's windtunnel. They refined the racing version at the same time.

chin. There are two of them, and their purpose is to ride up over curbs to protect the car's front airdam. "If you look at the 1980-82 Corvettes," notes Palmer, "you'll sometimes see the valances broken where guys have hit curbs. We wanted to make darn sure that didn't happen for '84. If a person hits a curb or bump stop, the car will ride up over it, but it won't distort the fascia."

And he continues: "When I looked at the first prototype out at the Proving Ground, particularly underneath in the lamp area, the thing that bothered me was that it looked like Leon Spinks without his teeth. That's important, because we'd been playing with this air inlet for a long time by then. Roger Hughet and I felt we had to make a change, and we decided to install what we call the *anti-Spinks* bar. That's the bar across the main air inlet; it's a continuation of body color across the opening."

Dave McLellan adds, "We in Engineering rejected Jerry's anti-Spinks bar until we found that it also served a useful purpose. It now protects the radiator condenser from stone damage."

Making it Slippery. Aerodynamics played an important role in determining the shape of the new Corvette. The proposed Corvette body, while still in clay, was tested at simulated airspeeds up to 140 mph. The Corvette's aero clay armature had the most detailed undercarriage that General Motors had ever run. That accounts for the clay and the prototype model coming within 1% of each other in Cd (coefficient of drag). There can ordinarily be as much as a 10% difference in drag coefficient between the clay and an actual sheetmetal car or fiberglass mockup. Design Staff aerodynamics engineers, under Charles (Chuck) Torner, had installed 1980 production front- and rear-suspension components, plus working headlamps from GM's Guide Lamp Div., under the aero-test clay.

Roger Hughet comments: "All the aero work we did played a big part in shaping the car. We tested it a lot, and in different windtunnels. I took it up to the National Research Council tunnel, owned by the Canadian government, in the fall of 1978. We also went to the Lockheed-Marietta tunnel in Georgia. Finally, when the GM tunnel opened here at the Technical Center in 1980, we finished some of the late work on the premises. That's when we settled on what the front was going to be. And the shape of the rear quarter, height of the rear deck — everything's that's been optimized on this car.

"We hope not to change the Corvette in the future," Roger continues, "unless there's a good reason, and that reason would most likely be aerodynamics. If we can find a way to improve the front or rear aero, we'll change it, maybe by '85 or '86. If we can't make it better, we'll just leave it alone."

The new Corvette can't claim the industry's lowest Cd, but its 6.57 CdA (coefficient of drag times frontal area) makes it one of the most genuinely aerodynamic designs in the world. This comes from the body's relatively small frontal area. Considering the Corvette's massive tires and its large, 140-mph cooling-intake capacity, it's a wonder that the designers managed to keep CdA as low as they did. To illustrate how slippery the Corvette really is, it takes only 97 bhp to power the car at 130 mph on level ground and in still air. The Porsche 928 absorbs 138 bhp at that speed, and the 1979 Corvette needs 143 bhp to sustain 130 mph.

General Motors' Windtunnel. GM's windtunnel opened for business in 1980, and the 1984 Corvette was the first car ever developed in it. The tunnel itself is roughly square in plan view. It covers half a city block, with the interior loop measuring 425 feet long by 166 feet wide by 50 feet high. A huge 43-foot-diameter fan is turned by a 3000-bhp electric motor and is capable of creating constant wind velocities of 140 mph, with bursts up to 158 mph.

Inside the windtunnel, airflow can be made visible by using either tufts of yarn, ink droplets, or a wand that shoots out nitrogen vapor or smoke. The most important measurements, however, are aerodynamic drag, lift, and side force. These are measured by a very precise balance that's mounted beneath a circular platform that fits flush with the floor at the center of the tunnel's test section.

In addition to aerodynamic forces, the wind's twisting effects, which engineers call moment, yaw, pitch, and roll, are also accurately measured by this same balance. Yaw refers to rotation about an up-and-down axis. Roll means rotation around a fore-to-aft axis. And pitch takes into account movement around a side-to-side axis.

Aero engineers can simulate sidewinds if they rotate the test platform in the tunnel, complete with the entire balance mechanism. This cocks the car or model at an angle to the airstream. The tunnel test section is designed to simulate and measure actual highway wind forces very precisely. The test section's dimensions are 70.0 x 31.1 x 17.7 feet (length, width, and height).

An interesting side note to the Corvette's aerodynamic story involves the "gills" behind the front wheel cutouts. Roger Hughet told me, "There was a lot of talk in the studio about not having them. We showed the car many times without any gills at all. In our tunnel testing, though, we found that having them there helps reduce front-end lift. They help reduce pressure inside the engine compartment. So that's one of the reasons they're there."

Another reason, of course, had to do with aesthetics and a bit of nostalgia. Jerry Palmer feels that, "...the gills amount to a little heritage. They go back to the Mako Shark and the production 1965-69 Corvette, both of which got part of their mean look from these vents. But the gills also help shorten that visual dash-to-axle distance in the new car. If we took out the gills, the '84 car would have looked even longer."

Mortarboards and Birdhouses. Considerable perspiration went in to the design of the new car's disappearing headlamps. Design Staff went through dozens of variations and countless ways to make the eyelids open and shut. One version, called the birdhouse, looked like one and had a theoretical pivot point near the centerline of the wheel. No way that version would work. Another discarded design wore a little graduation cap — the so-called mortarboard.

"It was a heckuva trauma," mentions Palmer. "Then just for the devil of it, we shot the lights all the way back up on the hood, and they looked like twin waterski jumps. We were never too happy with the vacuum actuators on previous cars, mostly because they never opened or shut the lights simultaneously. At any rate, Jack Humbert, who's our executive chief designer, was the guy who came up with the 167° rotational flip of the lamp bodies and electric motors that finally ended up in the 1984 car."

The quartz halogen lamps themselves rest in aerodynamic housings that were again designed in the windtunnel. Recalls Roger Hughet, "I think we spent as much time developing the headlight system as we did the whole rest of the car. With the help of Tom Delano [body engineer for front-end "sheetmetal"], we went through about seven totally different systems. We always knew the lamps were going to be retractable, but we started with what you'd call normal flip-up lamps, where you take a piece of the hood surface and just rotate it up. Then we went through that birdhouse idea that lifted straight up in the air. It had a little canted roof. That was horrible. We also looked at the old Opel GT, whose lamps rotated around a longitudinal axis, but that type wouldn't work at all in the Corvette.

"Finally we wound up with the neatest possible deal. The lamps in the new Corvette tumble. The headlights rotate through 167°. When they do that, what started out as the normal surface is now rotated back down and under. When the headlights come up, they show a special aerodynamic housing. With the '84 Corvette headlight in the

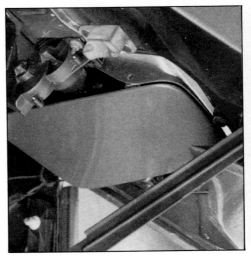

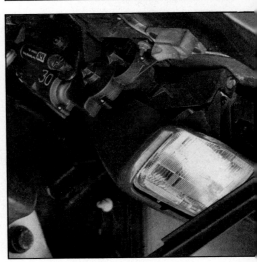

Headlamps and retractors went through seven different systems, including mortarboard and birdhouse. Aerodynamic production pods rotate through 167°.

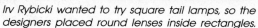

Irv Rybicki wanted to try square tail lamps, so the designers placed round lenses inside rectangles.

Early 16-inch wheels put smoked Lexan insets in machined grooves, but Palmer thought they

looked too much like wheelcovers. Besides, sharp grooves cut fingers when anyone changed tires.

up position, you pick up something like 17 counts in the windtunnel as compared with the Firebird, whose headlights increase the similar aerodynamic measurement by about 60 counts.''

Roger Hughet worked on the headlamps along with body designer Jerry Lattimer and engineer Tom Delano. Palmer takes up the narrative again: ''Lattimer came on board early and kept us honest regarding engineering requirements, and he put that front end together in the studio. Every time we'd change the hood cut line, the pivoting axis of these lamps would change. We didn't have the space under the hood to do just anything we wanted. It was very tight, and Lattimer made sure the lamps worked after we would come up with another variation.''

Rectangles and Rounds. Rear-end graphics likewise went through a number of changes. Irv Rybicki recalls: ''I remember that little battle all too well. I was the one who didn't want to do the round tail lamps again. I had the studio doing rectangular shapes and shutters and louvers. Charley [Jordan] and his gang got after me, because they wanted the round ones. I finally capitulated. The fellows felt we should strongly identify the car from the rear view, so I backed off.''

And the 16-inch wheels also underwent considerable change. According to Jerry Palmer, ''We were pretty far along with a preliminary design; had a lot of time invested in a 5-spoke wheel similar to the Citation X-11's, but much larger. Chuck [Jordan], though, wanted to break away from the spoke idea and told us to look for a more contemporary wheel.

''We needed a sophisticated design device, which turned out to be a flush-fitting

aero casting intersected by turbine-shaped blades. That wheel came from another John Cafaro mockup.'' And when I asked Jerry whether he was aware of the Lamborghini Jalpa wheel — a wheel very similar to the Corvette 16-incher — he replied, ''We'd already done our wheel, and then someone brought back pictures of the Jalpa from a European auto show, so it was a coincidental design. The Jalpa wheel did influence me later, though.'' We'll come to that in a moment.

In the beginning, Chevrolet resisted the 16-inch wheel with twisting turbine blades because of a casting problem. Jerry kept insisting and eventually got the wheel he wanted, but not in its original form.

''If you look at the turbine blades in a turbocharger, you'll see the complex, compound shape of the vanes we had on the original wheel. We started out with that kind of a spoke. As the vanes returned in, not only did they have an ever-tightening radius, but they were twisting at the same time. It was a beautiful shape.''

Unfortunately, though, Chevrolet couldn't core the twisted-vane wheel to pull it out of the mold. The foundry would have had to go to rotational molds, and that would have been too expensive even for the Corvette.

''So we took the warp out of the spokes, but we still had a chute running back, and we got into a solid spoke,'' continues Jerry. ''Then, through trial and error, we came up with the curving spokes on the wheel now. You'll note that they don't radiate from the wheel center, they radiate off a tangent around the bolt circle. That's what gives them that grabbing look. It's not a straight line; it's a sweeping curve off the tangent.''

The preliminary design for this wheel had a smoked Lexan cover fitted flush to the front of the aluminum dish. This cover snapped into a groove machined into the central cavity. In the studio and on the fiberglass model, Palmer and his staff thought the wheel looked great. But when Palmer saw it in the real world, out at GM's Milford Proving Ground on the first real prototype car, something bothered him. He felt the wheel took on the 2-dimensional quality of a wheelcover.

"Here we had a set of wheels that no other car would offer," Palmer told me, "and we were disguising it. The wheel didn't grab me." Here the Jalpa wheel exerted its influence. It had no cover and it "had more brutality," according to Jerry, so he removed the 2-dimensionality by taking off the Lexan cover and machining a large radius that rolled into the wheel center. "After we'd done this on the prototype wheel," says Palmer, "we looked at it again on the fiberglass car out in the Design courtyard, and the results were spectacular. The wheel now had visual depth. The center looked like a high-tech turbo inlet. We got rid of those sharp machined edges, too, which nipped at your fingers whenever you took off the Lexan cover to change a flat tire."

Finally, the 16-inch wheels were designed so there'd be one for each corner of the car—right and left because of turbine direction; fore and aft because the Z-51's rears are wider. However, the left wheel ended up on the right side, and vice versa, because the vanes looked more aggressive digging down than rotating upward, and they also help cool the brake rotors that way.

A Roadster and a Buy-Off. One of the last minute changes in the '84 Corvette's development program had to do with the targa roof. The car was originally slated to have a T-top, with a central T-bar between the windshield header and the roof basket handle. But then Chevrolet Engineering decided to go to a full targa roof by eliminating the center bar.

This decision didn't greatly affect Jerry Palmer's Chevy Three studio , because the structural changes had to be taken care of by Chevrolet Engineering. We'll talk more about this in Chapters 4 and 5. However, the targa roof did have an impact on the Corvette's interior designers, as we'll see in a moment.

To the exterior design team, the targa roof meant the possibility of a full convertible top. It's not a big step from one to the other. And a convertible or roadster had often been talked about. Palmer told me that at one time, he and his staff considered a Corvette convertible "very seriously, and there's a chance that we still might build one." John Cafaro sketched a red roadster, and at that time the early Eighties ragtop revival was just gaining momentum. Says Cafaro, "There's been a lot of talk about doing a convertible. To do it, they'd have to add some weight. But maybe there's still a chance."

Then toward the end of Jan. 1980, with the '84 fiberglass mockup finished, the engine detailing done, and the interior studios down to two likely candidates for the new car's interior, Design Staff held a show for GM's influential Product Policy Group. Soon afterward, they put on a second and even more spectacular show in the Design Staff dome for corporate brass, Chevrolet management, and the Campbell-Ewald ad agency personnel. This major show lasted three days and, in addition to the groups just mentioned, Dave McLellan invited 10 of Chevy's top Corvette-selling dealers.

The designers, McLellan and some of his engineers, plus the Corvette marketing people were anxious to talk to these dealers and get their reactions to the car and its features. To a man, the dealers expressed great enthusiasm and admiration for the vehicle, and all felt the new Corvette was absolutely right for the time and market. No one considered it too large or in any way out of keeping with the tradition established by Corvettes of the past. In all, it was very gratifying to the many exterior designers involved. □

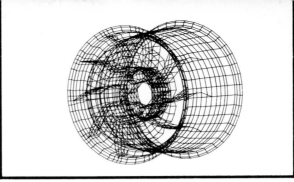

Turbine blades radiate off outer hub, not wheel center. Twisted blades in the original design presented casting problems, so radical twist was removed. The 15-inch wheels, while catalogued, haven't been installed on any new Vette.

John Cafaro proposed a roadster, and it's been given serious consideration. It seems a natural. Several customizers are currently planning to offer roadsters.

GM's Product Policy Group, along with influential Corvette dealers from all over America, viewed the '84 Corvette and its major rivals in Jan. 1980 buy-off.

Meanwhile, as the new Corvette's exterior took shape in Chevy Three, other teams went to work designing the car's interior. And although the interior designers couldn't know it at first, they'd soon be facing considerably tougher challenges than Palmer's people.

The Corvette's interior designers, under George E. Moon and his assistant, George Angersbach, were about to come face to face with two major problems. First, they would be asked to lay out a liquid-crystal instrument cluster. Large liquid crystal displays (LCD) had never been done at GM before and represented a totally new and untested technology when the Corvette program began.

Second, Design Staff's interior studios would soon have to look for new ways to meet the on-again, off-again federal safety standard referred to as *MVSS 208*. Chevrolet's then-director of engineering, Lloyd Reuss, and Corvette chief engineer Dave McLellan were determined to meet the government's 208 standard without airbags and preferably without self-fastening (passive) seatbelts.

Those two bits of business loomed as the interior designers' major challenges, but there was one more. They were asked to develop two sets of new Corvette seats: a standard seat and an optional competition-type Sport seat. I've been told that designing the Corvette's seats seemed like a piece of cake after the other two jobs.

Cathy Wagner, the only woman who worked on the Corvette's interior, remembers how hectic the program grew as more and more demands piled up on the designers. "All of a sudden, cardboard and knives and papers and mockups were flying in the air, and we were working Saturdays and Sundays. Every day was a time pressure. They'd change design direction, then new test information would come in, then somebody else had a better idea on how to build this or that. We were running around like chickens without heads. It was crazy."

Two Separate Studios Involved. The first challenge, of course, concerned development of the LCD instrument panel. I'll discuss in Chapter 6 how liquid-crystal

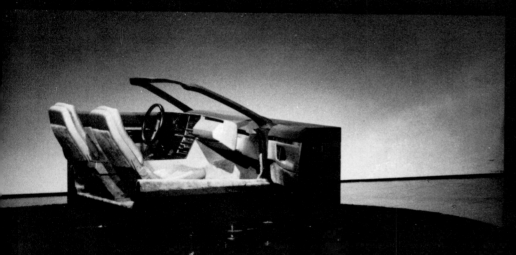

Chapter 3
Inside Story

Two seating bucks by Art Pryde await judgement of Product Policy Committee during GM buy-off.

displays work and what the production panel can do, but in its initial forms, the proposed instrument panels weren't liquid crystal at all. Early versions were mechanical and, as it turned out, a backup mechanical system remained under development alongside the LCD right up to release. Until the very last minute, no one felt totally confident that the LCD instruments could pass muster and be produced to Chevrolet Engineering's standards. As we'll see later, GM's AC Spark Plug Div., which had responsibility for developing the LCD panel and its manufacturing techniques, found a number of problems—mostly having to do with LCD performance in extreme climates—that left the program cliffhanging from week to week.

In the beginning, two different studios labored to develop a theme for the 1984 interior. There was the Interior Concepts studio, under John Shettler, with designers Gordon Severson, Marvin Fisher, and Julian Carter. The function of Interior Concepts was (and is) to think several years ahead and develop panel themes that might eventually be put into production in cars to come. During the period from early 1977 through late 1978, however, Shettler and his Interior Concepts people were very much involved in the here and now. They were specifically assigned to come up with an acceptable theme for the projected "all-new 1982" Corvette.

Then, in addition to Concepts, the other studio involved in the same search was known at that time simply as *Chevrolet Interiors Two.* This was a production studio, as opposed to a concepts or advanced studio, and it was unusual for a production studio to "compete" with a concepts studio in the search for a theme. William D. (Bill) Scott acted as Chevrolet Interiors chief designer, under George Angersbach. Angersbach was the man who'd come up with the double-bent instrument panel for the 1970-78 Camaro, and Scott had done both the Camaro's 1979-81 and third-generation panels. Assisting Scott as staff designers were Art Pryde, Cathy Wagner, Chao-Hsi Wu, and Karel Moravek.

To confuse the issue a bit more, in 1976-77 Bill Scott became chief of both Chevrolet Interiors studios: One and Two. Then about halfway through the Corvette program, Scott left to become head of Pontiac Interiors, and Pat Furey took over Chevrolet Interiors Two. So it was under Furey's direction that the finishing touches were put on the new Corvette's instrument panel, seats, doors, rockers, roof, sound system, hatch area, interior colors, fabrics, and so forth.

The Ever-Elusive Theme. Those earliest searches still hadn't pinned down an interior theme, and Bill Scott told me later, "I counted no fewer than 13 serious proposals for interior themes at one point—far more than the two or three we normally do."

One of the earliest serious themes was by Chevrolet Interiors designer Chao-Hsi Wu—a buck carefully detailed and made up mostly from foamcore and cardboard. (Foamcore is a tri-laminate, with a thin sheet of styrofoam sandwiched between two outer layers of brown bag paper. By scoring the back, a designer can bend foamcore into various shapes. Lightweight, versatile foamcore can be textured, painted, or covered with Di Noc.)

Chao-Hsi Wu's theme was rejected initially but came back later to serve as the model for the production instrument panel. Wu, who was born in Nanking, China, is thus credited with fathering the LCD theme that you see in the car today.

Chao-Hsi Wu has an unusual background, as do several people associated with the Corvette program. He moved with his family from mainland China to Taiwan in 1948. Wu wanted to study product design in America, an extraordinary ambition in itself and, in 1964, he was accepted to the Pratt Institute in Brooklyn, N.Y. He graduated four years later in industrial design and came directly to General Motors Design Staff, where he's been ever since.

"I wasn't a car nut at the time," Wu told me, "but I loved cars. Even so, I didn't know much about the mechanical workings of automobiles. My father had owned a

Beginning in 1978, Corvette interior designers searched seriously for a theme. Chao-Hsi Wu's Camaro-like treatment contrasts with Marv Fisher's aircraft-type panel. Two Pryde renditions (bottom) have ride-down and breadloaf.

1939 Dodge in China. Cars were symbols of the West, one of the luxuries." At GM, Wu became one of the principal designers of GM's contemporary G-Vans. He's also worked on passenger cars and has done interior-concepts research.

Enter the Dreaded 208. Two other very competitive Corvette instrument-panel themes came from Karel Moravek and Art Pryde. Pryde's panel, in fact, had been favored by management from the beginning and probably would have been chosen, but MVSS 208 intervened, and Chao-Hsi Wu's theme adapted more readily to the controversial safety criteria.

Meeting MVSS (Motor Vehicle Safety Standard) 208 called for development of a *ride-down* system ahead of the passenger. In other words, just as the driver can "ride down" on the collapsible, telescoping steering column during a head-on crash, Reuss and McLellan wanted to fashion a T-shaped member, integrated into the dashboard ahead of the passenger, that incorporated a heavily padded "breadloaf" atop a shock-absorbing, telescoping piston. This, they reasoned, in combination with a padded knee restraint along the bottom edge of the dashboard, would do for the passenger what the steering column was doing for the driver.

The MVSS 208 standard came into effect in 1977, during the Carter administration. At that time, it carried a 1982 deadline. The deadline was subsequently extended to 1983, '84, and finally '85. In Oct. 1981, though, President Reagan's NHTSA head, Raymond Peck, rescinded the standard altogether. Whereupon the Center for Auto Safety immediately sued NHTSA to reinstate MVSS 208. And there, at this writing, the case rests. It hasn't yet come to trial.

The new Corvette, as it's produced, does not have the "stroker"—the energy-absorbing device on the passenger's side. The breadloaf, however, remains.

Ironically, one thing that concerned GM about meeting the 208 standard was doing the job too well. "The public might have felt they didn't need to wear seatbelts," mentions Paul Huzzard wryly. "They do have to wear belts for all-around safety. If someone chooses to run his Corvette head-on into the side of a building at exactly 30 mph, he might survive. But if he decides to take on a tractor/trailer at an angle, that's a different story. I feel this car has the capability of meeting the law, but it isn't utopia. When you get into the car and fire it up, you should have your belts on."

I asked Paul Huzzard whether Corvettes aren't the kinds of cars that people like to buckle up in anyway. He answered bluntly: "I don't have any scientific data, but every so often, since I'm very interested and have long been involved in Corvettes [Paul was one of the 1968 Corvette's development engineers], I do my own surveys on the road. I cruise down the expressway about 50 mph, forcing most cars to pass me, and from my observations, I've found that Corvette drivers don't wear their seatbelts and shoulder harnesses any more often than anyone else. That's an extremely small and unscientific sample, as I say, but this country has a long way to go in educating people to wear belts."

As an aside, he points out that, "... ironically, there's no question about buckling up in an airplane, which is one of the safest forms of transportation known. There's a perceived danger riding on an airplane that barely exists. Yet when you get into your car, there's a very real danger that most people won't let themselves admit."

Proving Out the Breadloaf. Chao-Hsi Wu's instrument panel then, as mentioned, lent itself better to incorporating the 208 criteria than did Art Pryde's, Karel Moravek's, or Cathy Wagner's, although all four were in contention.

The mechanics of proving out the breadloaf required, as Bill Scott explains, a long series of trials. "We ran into philosophical problems, plus testing problems. We were breaking new ground. The engineers had to mock up the breadloaf, test it, and

see if it really worked with dummies. That's difficult. Also, they were using fairly crude prototype parts at that time, so the tendency for the engineers was to over-do everything. If the engineers thought they needed a 6-inch frontal width, they'd tell us to go to a 9-inch width. Or if it should deflect six inches back into the car, they'd tell us 10."

Pat Furey continues, "We ran into some reluctance about incorporating the breadloaf because of its intrusion into the passenger compartment. It psychologically tended to make some passengers feel squeezed in. It also made it a little harder to get into and out of the vehicle, especially with the tall rocker sill and the high seat wings."

During this time, design engineer Steve Schwab was running the sled-test program at GM's Inland Div. He recalls that, "Our initial testing started with the breadloaf in the same fore-and-aft plane as the steering wheel. We felt we could make that work based on previous experience with [unbelted] drivers. As we went along, we were able to push the breadloaf farther and farther away from the passenger.

"Each 1-inch move forward involved 5-10 sled tests using handmade parts. Under normal circumstances, a sled test of this type would take 4-5 days to prepare, but we were running 1-2 shots a day. With each new success, Design Staff would carve a little more clay away from their buck." After he finished the preliminary testing, Steve was transferred to Chevrolet and became responsible for the production design of the instrument panel and console.

Bill Scott adds, "The program peaked and lulled, peaked and lulled. There are so many things about this car, inside and out, that have always been controversial. The 208 criteria caused some pretty emotional discussions between Design Staff and Chevrolet Div. Chuck Jordan, for instance, never cared for the 208. He had several serious talks about it with Dave McLellan and his engineers."

Buying Off the Interior. Near the end, late in 1980, the three leading instrument-panel candidates "competed" in a buy-off—a competitive show in the Design Staff auditorium.

This showed Art Pryde's panel in its final form; the very podular Moravek panel, slightly detuned; and Chao-Hsi Wu's theme that was easiest to modify to meet the MVSS 208 criteria. So the showdown had Art Pryde's panel in its best form as a final statement to circumvent the 208 standard. Chuck Jordan and other members of Design Staff were, in effect, lobbying to satisfy the 208 by going with passive belts and Pryde's more traditional panel.

In the final analysis, of course, Wu's panel won out, and a good deal of the 208 standard can still be seen on the passenger's side. If you've wondered why there's no glovebox and a big breadloaf instead, now you know the reasons.

The LCD instrumentation, however, did grow out of Art Pryde's design, particularly the tach and speedometer graphics. "The concept," amplifies Pryde, "came to me as I was staring at a power-curve graph for a racing engine. I asked Dave McLellan if his people had established a power curve for the new Corvette V-8. He said they had, and he sent the graph right over.

"The bargraph display for the Corvette's tachometer represents that power curve. It not only tells the driver the engine's rpm limit but, more importantly, when the engine is producing peak power. The speedometer reflects the tach but doesn't mimic it. This makes it easier to tell one from the other."

Pryde's original design included four additional bargraph gauges similar to the fuel gauge. The production version, though, was simplified to provide more information by using the idea of time-sharing. I'll talk more about that in Chapter 6.

Several weeks after that first buy-off, another high level show was held, this one demonstrating both interior and exterior styling. Here, Design Staff and Chevrolet

Clearly visible in this buck, Pryde's passenger-side ride-down repeated the collapsible steering column, which here mounted instrument pod near driver.

Cathy Wagner sculpted the Sport seat first in clay, an unusual step, and then made up several prototypes from different densities of foam rubber.

Engineering invited not only the divisional and corporate heads but those same 10 leading Corvette dealers. The idea was to get reaction and approval for the new car *in toto,* and that approval was enthusiastically given.

Sitting Pretty. The next challenge for the Corvette's interior designers was to come up with two good levels of seats. The base seat had to have better articulation and improvements over the previous generation. And the up-market Sport option (RPO AQ-9) had to be absolutely superior in every way. As with the all-new exterior, it was one of those jobs that designers don't get a chance to do very often.

On the engineering side, the people primarily responsible were Paul Huzzard and his engineer, Phillip Rezanka. Huzzard had never been totally pleased with the way any of the 1968-82 seats had come out. "The 1982 seat, like those before it, suffered from that car's coke-bottle shape," observes Huzzard, "which made for a very tight compartment. I wasn't happy with the '82 Corvette seats, but then I've got a big can and don't fit very well into those seats. I determined the 1984 seats would be a little wider, and I told my guys to make me a *Paul Huzzard* seat, so after I've driven the car for 2-3 hours I wouldn't feel my wallet pushing through my rear like a burning brick. I think anyone who's compared this new seat with the '82 version will find the '84 much more comfortable."

Corvette seating engineers began by working with Fisher Body Div. on human accommodations. They later did a complete seat design with Recaro, then another with specialists at GM Research Labs, and a third at the University of Michigan. Design Staff, though, oversaw development of the final seats used in the new car.

According to GM interior design director George Moon, "Chevrolet started a program, unbeknownst to us, with Recaro to develop a new seat for the Corvette. We went on our way to do the same. As it turned out, we finally got to work with the

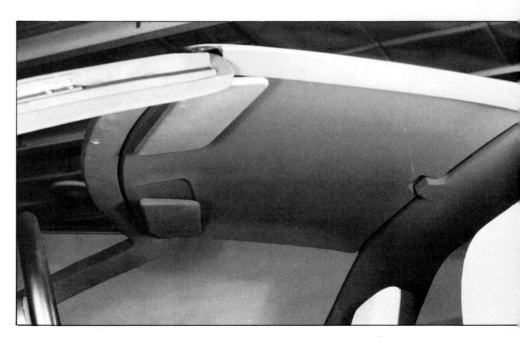

When decision came down to switch from T-top to targa roof, Chevy's interior designers, under George Moon, researched manageability, stowage.

Recaro people ourselves for a while. The seat that eventually evolved is extremely comfortable and highly supportive. It's a good seat anthropometrically."

Design Staff pretty much adopted the Recaro philosophy of the segmented seat, with high side and thigh support. "We didn't get all the adjustabilities into our standard seat that Recaro offers," says Moon, "but then the full-feature Recaros cost about $1000 each. We certainly were influenced by how they derive comfort, though; the pressure areas."

Riding the Range. Chevrolet Engineering undertook an extensive ride program before settling on the best seat to emulate. Alfred R. (Bob) Carr, assistant executive in charge of Chevrolet interiors, conducted a 2-day ride, on which Corvette engineers, designers, and some members of Chevrolet management drove all the competitive performance seats: Recaros, Scheel, Porsche, Ferrari, Supra; any car that had a different kind of seat. These people — men and women — drove across the state of Michigan and back, comparing. They came up with a score sheet that competitively rated the qualities and features of each seat and thus outlined to Design Staff what would ultimately be required for the Corvette.

"We all took that long road trip," recalls Scott. "Out of that, we came up with the voting sheet to determine which seats placed first, second, and third overall. I think the Porsche 928 seat — made by Recaro to Porsche specs — came off best. It became our target."

Cathy Wagner was given responsibility for designing the new Corvette seats. This was an unusual process, as George Moon explains.

"We went straight from Cathy's sketches and full-scale drawings to a clay model. Cathy modeled the seat, and that was quite a job in itself, because we don't often model a seat. Working with sculptors Joe Di Liberto and Alex Buchan, she did the clay model, painted and detailed it, and then an approved version was cast in plaster and finally mocked up as a fiberglass seat form. This was a hard model that we sat in, without deflections. Next, we started building up foam bolsters of varying densities to the shapes Cathy had modeled in clay. We paid great attention to designing both comfort and support into this seat.

"It also had to be a seat that allowed you to contort yourself over the relatively high rocker sill, under the steering wheel, and not hit your head on the roof as you got in. We had to have enough lateral support in the seat itself, but we couldn't block people from getting in and out. All those requirements together made it a very tricky job."

Here Comes the Sport Seat. After modeling the base seat and bringing it nearly to production, Cathy Wagner, being in Bill Scott's Chevrolet Interiors studio, was transferred out of doing Corvette work, and Pat Furey took up the project. He explains what happened next.

"When I came in, one of my first tasks was to review the Sport seat option. We had what then amounted to the full production base Corvette seat — production buns and all the refinements. For the Sport seat, though, the only real comparison was the Recaro.

"At that point, shortly after I took over, Chevrolet gave me a premium of $60 over the base seat for the Sport option. That's an awful lot of money. Initially that $60 was earmarked just for trim material. Well, I could do a seat in gold lame and not spend $60. I ended up with $25 for material, and we decided to take the extra money and put it into a lumbar bladder system."

To keep the driver upright and in place in hard turns, Chevrolet specified adjustable wings for the Sport seat. This up-option seat is available only in cloth, again to keep the driver and passenger from sliding around. Chevrolet eliminated a thigh support adjustment because the 6-way power option makes the Sport seat fully adjusta-

Sport seat shares center contour with base bucket. Cathy Wagner had to make car enterable. This buck looked at rockers, seat wings, adjustments.

ble for pitch. And the Sport seat's settings are all electric, which lets the driver and passenger sit in a normal position while they set the wings, seatback angle, and lumbar support.

"If you compare the two seats — base and Sport — the centerline contours are essentially identical," continues Furey. "When you get a good base seat, you don't arbitrarily start putting buttons and bows on it. That's what hurts seating in many family cars: styling tricks. The more you get off a sound overall contour, the less comfort you're likely to have.

"For the Sport seat, we decided on a system of three air bladders for lumbar support. Rather than using a hand pump, we went with an electric pump, feeding air to those three bladders, so the driver can tune it in. We're getting into the world class. It's a sore point with me that we have a slightly tainted reputation for Corvette seating, and these new base and Sport seats will go a long way toward turning that around. Actually, I hope the seating level of this car will rub off on our other vehicles."

Traditionally, seats for General Motors vehicles are provided by Fisher Body. For the Corvette Sport seat option, however, Lear-Siegler supplies finished seats, each one crafted and ready to install.

The base seats are made by GMAD in Bowling Green, with help from Findlay Industries in Ohio. Findlay does the cut-and-sew for the cloth and optional leather versions and ships the trim-cover assemblies, including the buns, to Bowling Green.

Chao-Hsi Wu's panel with Art Pryde's LCD instruments were finally chosen. This is an early Wu.

Another Arthur E. Pryde interior incorporates modified breadloaf, digital LCD instrumentation, and full console. Steering wheel, too, took many forms, including a single-spoke design judged too buzzy to use.

Prototypes came through with script on rockers, but since it printed in carpet, it was dropped.

GMAD, in turn, using additional subcontracted pieces (the seat pans, for example, are made by Butler Plastics), adds the Findlay components to get the seats ready for installation.

All trim levels include a wool fleece interliner between the trim cover and the molded bun. No matter how tightly you compress the wool layer, a degree of air can always circulate through it, so the subdural wool assures adequate temperature and moisture control regardless of how hot or cold it gets.

Those Important Finer Points. In finishing up the 1001 smaller interior details, Bill Scott's team had come up with some good ideas about storing the targa roof panel inside the car. Working to a concept generated by Chevrolet Engineering, he fastened the top panel firmly to two special, slotted attachments above the rear wheel arches. The top thus became a second security screen in addition to the movable shade provided for that purpose. If properly lashed down, the top is so solidly in place that it stays put even during a 30-mph barrier crash test.

The new steering wheel also went through a number of iterations. Its rim section was always agreed upon: fairly bulky, giving a solid grip, with either a vinyl or leather covering. But the designers had a hard time deciding on a center section. For a long time, they wanted to use a one-spoke wheel, but that turned out to be impractical.

Finally, Pat Furey points out what his studio did in terms of interior color selec-

tion. "I think we've got some particularly good color availabilities for the new car," he affirms, "... some very subtle 2-tones that tie the inside color in far more with the exterior than we normally do. We're still offering some of the more traditional colors, like bright red, white, and black. But all the rest are very subtle, contemporary, metallic colors that really highlight the vehicle.

"We even have a slight touch of metallic in the trim, which sounds like something out of the Fifties, but people are surprised how good it looks. Strong and undiluted. We were left alone to really tune in the color range. Dave McLellan and everyone else did very little haggling about color. It's a very pure color range. The metaltone combinations are really outstanding, I think."

George Angersbach amplifies, "We looked at several different no-gloss black finishes for the top of the instrument panel. This was to keep down veiling glare and reflections in the Corvette's 64.5° windshield. We finally ended up using Dulzo, which is a zero-gloss black paint. That's what determined the black above the beltline."

As it turned out, and impossible as it seemed at first, the new Corvette's interior managed to incorporate everything the designers and engineers had asked for: more space for the driver and passenger, the LCD instrument panel, advanced sound systems, compliance with MVSS 208, far better seats, a very usable hatch and top-storage area, harmonizing and pleasing colors; in short, all the elements of a practical, harmonious, cooperative sports car interior. □

Chapter 4

Engineering the Vette

Corvette engineer William J. Wartinbee examines an unskinned prototype.

The Corvette remains one of GM's few cars that still gets engineered all in one division. You're probably aware that, up through the Sixties, each General Motors car division engineered all of its own automobiles. Chevrolet engineered Chevrolets; Cadillac motorcars were done by Cadillac; Oldsmobiles were engineered by Oldsmobile; and so forth.

That's no longer how it is. During the Sixties, the General Motors engineering process began to change and, by 1972, no single GM car division had anything like full responsibility for most of its own products. Since that time, in what's called the *lead division concept,* each division has had overall engineering responsibility for a given system or set of components. All other GM auto divisions then share those components — or at least share the expertise that brought them about.

For example, for several years now, Chevrolet has been assigned engineering responsibility for most of the corporation's auto engines and front suspension systems. Pontiac's contributions have centered on rear axles and fuel tanks. Buick traditionally designs the braking systems for all GM cars. Oldsmobile handles diesel development, and Cadillac does the corporation's automatic temperature control systems.

Then, going a step further, in 1977 GM introduced the *project center* concept. GM's project centers began bringing together engineers from different divisions and disciplines to work on one specific car. Groups of engineers, including those from Fisher Body and GM Design Staff, now sit side by side in rooms the size of football fields to develop each of GM's new cars. These are all cars that several GM auto divisions ultimately share. The X-Car, J-Car, F-Car, A-Car, and others were born in GM project centers.

But the Vette's Different. Now that I've explained how General Motors normally engineers its new cars, I hasten to add that there are two that don't fit the mold. Chevrolet's Corvette and Pontiac's Fiero stand alone as throwbacks to that bygone era when one division engineered one car (although Fisher Div. helped engineer and now manufactures the P-Car body). The Corvette is not the product of a project center, nor did any other GM auto division have a hand in its creation. Fisher Body Div., which develops and builds bodies for all other GM cars, enters the Corvette's manufacturing picture only as the supplier of door locks. Corvette is like a division within a division; an old-fashioned division inside a new one.

From Day One and the ground up, Chevrolet had full responsibility for every facet of the Corvette's engineering. That alone gives the Corvette a distinction and a developmental history very unlike most General Motors automobiles. Nor does any other division share the Corvette. Unlike the F-Car, which Chevrolet and Pontiac sell as the Camaro and Firebird, only Chevrolet sells the Corvette. That, too, makes the Corvette unique.

As does the fact that it's built in only one plant. Most GM cars are built in several, along with other nameplates. And except for the engine block and automatic transmission, no other GM automobile shares any of the Corvette's major powertrain, chassis, or body components. So it's different in nearly all ways.

A Little Craziness Helps. Consider the typical Corvette engineer. If you think of him as bright, progressive, aspiring, performance-oriented, enthusiastic, and a little apart from his brethren, you're right. The average Corvette engineer was in his mid-30's when he worked on the new car. And as Paul Huzzard puts it, "We've always been a young group and a slightly odd one. A person doesn't have to be crazy to work on the Corvette, but sometimes it helps."

The new Corvette was engineered by a relatively small group of people. Dave McLellan's staff averaged about 35 Chevrolet engineers during the most active period of the program. Also assigned to McLellan were nine engineers from GM's central engineering staff, including several in computers. Additional engineering support came from GM's supplier divisions — from all four Delcos, Harrison Radiator, Guide, Fisher Body, AC Spark Plug, Inland, and Saginaw.

Finally, another 41 engineers from a private design contractor called Detroit Industrial Engineering (DIE) were put on the 1984 Corvette payroll. DIE played an important role in following through with some of the routine but necessary design functions, such as drafting, making blueprints, and checking myriad details. DIE had worked with Chevrolet before on several projects besides the Corvette.

Dozens of outside suppliers also helped engineer the new Corvette, including but not limited to those listed in the chart on p. 124. The Corvette probably gets more parts and expertise from non-GM sources than any other car built by the corporation.

Why the Front Engine? Dave McLellan, along with then-Chevrolet director of engineering Lloyd Reuss, decided early in the program that the next-generation Corvette would stick with the front-engine, rear-drive configuration. We touched on this in Chapters 1 and 2. But when I asked him to go into more detail on this important point, McLellan replied:

"You have to remember that even the aluminum-bodied, midship Corvette [prototype] weighed almost 3300 pounds. So there was no real advantage to it in terms of weight. But the midship Corvette really had its coffin nailed shut when we decided to stick with the V-8 and not go to the V-6."

Lloyd Reuss amplifies, "During my tenure as Chevrolet engineering director, we invited Keith Duckworth over from Cosworth in England. He and Paul King and McLellan and I discussed working up some new cylinder heads for the V-6 so that if we had to phase out the V-8, we might have a V-6 with four valves per cylinder. That was still in the discussion stage when I left."

The determining factor, then, was wanting to stay with Chevrolet's V-8 engine, a decision supported by the 1982 Camaro offering a V-8 and backstopped by the Porsche 928 V-8. It hardly seemed logical to give the public a V-8 Camaro alongside a V-6 Corvette that had to compete with a V-8 Porsche.

As he continued explaining his reasons to me, McLellan quickly added that the V-8 engine alone didn't rule out the midship configuration. I again asked him to expand on his thinking.

"My feeling going in was that if we just put the Aerovette into production, we'd have a terribly exciting automobile — no question about that. Frankly, though, when you look at the Aerovette in detail, it's got some pretty heavy flaws.

"First, it's about a ⅞th-scale car. By the time you make an honest production vehicle out of it, there's not enough room for all of the mechanical and functional things you need. Even though the plan view looks fairly large — the wheelbase, tread, and length dimensions seem about as big as a Citation — the car is so darn low that there's just not enough cubic volume inside to fit everything.

"You quickly consume the packaging space with people and big tires and a big engine. There's nothing left to cram all the other stuff into. The car you see out there now [the new-generation Corvette] is an absolutely jam-packed automobile built around those big tires, the 205-bhp, 290-foot-pound engine/drivetrain, and all the convenience accessories and auxiliaries you have to have — plus a little space for some personal belongings in the rear."

Reuss mentions another handicap of mid-engined cars. "There's the inherent complication of providing a good heating and air-conditioning system; climate control. You can do it so much more easily and better in a conventional front-engined, rear-drive design.''

Checking Out Production Midship Cars. Early in the program, Chevrolet Engineering organized ride-and-drives of all the serious sports and exoticars then available. These took place on Michigan highways and also at GM's Milford proving grounds. Among the cars they evaluated totally were the Ferrari 308, Lotus Esprit, Porsche 928, and Porsche 911 Turbo.

Continues McLellan, ''If you look at the mid-engined cars now in the marketplace —those with big engines—they all tend to be pretty hard to live with. The Pantera, the various Ferraris, the Maserati Bora and Merak . . . these are very exciting cars, but they aren't easy to live with, and they're extremely special-purpose. The Countach and the Boxer are special-purpose even beyond the rest.

''Nobody has figured out how to make the mid-engine design a good arrangement for carrying two people plus luggage. Even the Porsche 914, with its much smaller engine, wasn't all that successful. DeLorean had the same problem. The Fiat X1/9, too. You had no contiguous luggage space as you do in a Corvette. If you want to put your coat someplace, you barely find enough room.

''So by the time you go from something as exciting as an Aerovette or a Countach or a Boxer to putting that ounce of practicality into it so it's acceptable as a road car— not as an absolutely no-compromise, take-it-or-leave-it vehicle—it drives you back into the position of a conventional layout.''

More Midship Problems. McLellan pauses and then goes on. ''The Aerovette had another problem: a difficult manual transmission layout. The entire drivetrain became complicated by having to circulate the torque flow around the engine compartment a couple of times.

''The mid-engined car is certainly do-able. I wouldn't say we couldn't have done it from the powertrain standpoint, either as a manual or an automatic. The last go-around that Zora made produced a very complicated drivetrain, trying to use existing transmissions. The engine was transverse, and trying to tie it into an existing, available, basic drivetrain was difficult, to say the least.

''If you do what we've done on the Olds Toronado, where you run one of the driveshafts underneath the engine, you end up raising the whole engine package. It forces the height of your powertrain up 3-4 inches. For a large car like the Toronado, this isn't a huge problem, but where you're trying to do a very low car, you wind up as we did in our packaging studies — with a car that had a higher engine center of gravity and very poor rear visibility. The top of the engine dress was so high that by the time we put the hood or cover over it, the deck stood at eye level.

''Nor does the Toronado/Eldorado transaxle adapt itself well to a manual transmission. As you know, we also looked at X-Car components, but they limited us in engine size and torque capacity. Those were a few of the things we had to deal with.''

No Handling Benefit. Another drawback inherent in the midship concept was that it showed no advantages in handling. As it now stands, the new Corvette's weight distribution is very nearly 50/50. Without occupants, distribution comes to 51/49. With two average adults aboard, it changes to 48/52. One of the main virtues of mid-engined cars has traditionally been to equalize weight distribution, but that's something the 1984 Corvette doesn't need.

''From all indications,'' notes McLellan, ''the job of optimizing handling becomes much tougher as you bias a car's weight to the extreme rear. It gets tough because, whereas in a race car you're able to take driver expertise as a given, in a road

Tire Speed Ratings	
Letter code	**Max. speed**
"S" cross ply	95-110* mph
"H" cross ply	110 + mph
"R" radial ply	100 mph
"SR" radial ply	113 mph
"HR" radial ply	130 mph
"VR" radial ply	130 + mph

* depending on size

Goodyear tire engineer Tim Miller (right) worked closely with Corvette handling staff to maximize wet and dry traction and tread longevity.

car the price of admission has nothing to do with driving skill. We had to make the Corvette very stable at its limits.

''Our objective was obviously to give the car very high limits from a handling standpoint; to make those limits stable in the sense that the driver doesn't have to interact with the car in trained ways. In other words, the car isn't going to spin out on him when he closes the throttle. That's really what it comes down to. Drop-throttle steer can be very difficult to deal with when you get your configuration skewed way out.

''I think that's part of what frustrated Zora back in the early Seventies,'' Dave points out. ''None of the mid-engined proposals, when they went through the marketing department, showed any advantage over what we were building at the time . . . which was paid for! So, you know, it was one big yank of the rug.''

McLellan then takes another tack. ''Finally, there's the crash-integrity issue: having that very large engine behind you when you have to deal with real-world collisions. Those are mostly frontal collisions. To contain the engine behind the occupants becomes not an impossible job but an additional job. That task, of course, gets easier when you have a small, lightweight engine, like the X1/9 or the P-Car.

''In thinking about safety, we asked ourselves whether we could utilize the long-

Unidirectional VR50 forces water out to sides. Contact patch at 60 mph (left) is nearly as big as at 20 mph, indicating good siping.

Backside of 16-inch wheel shows deep offset, turbine-blade contours, taped-on balancing weights. Spare 16x4 wheel is also alloy.

Goodyear has capability to build custom tire of any compounding in a few days. Here a technician checks interior of halved VR50 via holographic photography.

nose characteristic of the Corvette to make it meet the MVSS 208 standards [see Chapter 3]. We haven't yet generated all the data that says we're successful, but I expect we'll be close by the start of production. We hope to demonstrate that the relatively long hood, the engine up front where you don't have to deal with it as a mass that has to be totally contained by the rest of the structure, and the design of the interior . . . all those have been developed toward meeting the 208 criteria.

"So to make a long story short, yes, the mid engine would have given us a more extreme appearance change. But that's about the only real advantage. The Corvette buyer, according to our surveys, didn't much care where we put the engine. And there were just too many reasons why we felt better off going front engine."

Starting Over From the Ground Up. With that question out of the way, the real job of engineering the new Corvette could begin. I talked in Chapters 1 and 2 about some of the breakthroughs that brought about the general configuration of this car: tucking the exhaust system up inside the driveshaft tunnel, eliminating crossmembers under the floor, moving the engine down and rearward by mounting the steering rack ahead of the block, and packaging the occupants farther forward. Those were some of the basic, initial ideas that set the new Corvette's major elements in place early in the

program. From there, the car evolved, literally and figuratively, from the ground up.

Design Staff worked closely with McLellan's group in deciding where the car stood in relation to the road: wheelbase, ground clearance, tread width, projected overall length, width, height, etc. The next thing that proved pivotal was the road interface — the connection between the car and the pavement: the tires.

Developing the right tires marked a critical point in the program and one that Chevy Engineering went to work on very early. Jim Ingle, who'd long enjoyed responsibility for the Corvette's tire development, had worked for several years with engineers at Goodyear. Together, Ingle and Goodyear's Bob Stella had provided the 1977-82 Corvettes with some of the best all-around performance tires then available. During those years, Corvettes used Goodyear's Custom Polysteel P225/70R-15 as the base tire. Then for 1978-79, the P255/60R-15 Customgard GT radial was added as an option, and the P255/60R-15 Eagle GT became optional for 1980-82 Corvettes. So the Goodyear/Corvette connection was nothing new, and progress had been continuous.

Tire Development. Goodyear tire engineer Bob Stella told me that the Corvette's ride-and-handling team came to him with a fistful of goals, but it all boiled down to one thing. "Jim Ingle, Dave McLellan, and the entire Corvette engineering staff were after the best-handling car in the world," says Stella, "and they wanted the world's all-around best handling tire to get it there. That became our objective; that's where we started."

Stella points out, however, that a tire designed totally for handling sacrifices everything else: longevity, ride, rolling resistance, silence, and sometimes even high-speed durability. Chevrolet wouldn't accept a compromise in any of those areas.

The first objective was a very high ultimate cornering coefficient, which Ingle targeted at "over .300." Cornering coefficient is an indicator of maximum lateral acceleration (see Chapter 5). You calculate cornering coefficients by measuring the amount of lateral force generated at 1° of tire slip angle. "You divide the lateral force by the vertical load," explains Bob Stella. "For example, if you have 300 pounds of side force at 1° of slip, plus a 1000-pound vertical load, you'd have a cornering coefficient of .300. Jim Ingle wanted better than that, though." Today's original equipment baseline passenger-car tires usually run a cornering coefficient of .150 to .190.

Chevrolet's second criterion had to do with high-speed capabilities. The new tire had to be *V-rated*, which meant it had to be good for sustained speeds over 130 mph. Actually, to earn the European V rating, a tire has to be tailored to the car's top speed which, in the Corvette's case, came to 142 mph, not 130.

The trouble with most high-speed, ultimate-handling tires is lack of longevity. They tend to wear down to the cords quickly, because many manufacturers lighten the gauge of the tread. They do this for two reasons: 1) to minimize centrifugal expansion at high speeds, and 2) to give less tread compliance at peak cornering loads. But Chevrolet insisted on full tread depth for durability. Full tread depth meant ⅜ inch (9.2mm) for a projected tread life of 30,000 to 40,000 miles. Many rival performance tires, especially when driven over Europe's twistier, bumpier roads, tend to go bald at 8000-15,000 miles.

Third, Goodyear had to come up with an acceptably smooth-riding tire. To get that, they used a trick they call *graduated sidewall stiffness,* which means they taper the sidewall's stiffness from the bead bundle to the top of the apex — the point at which the sidewall plies meet after wrapping around the bead. The sidewall is actually much stiffer at the bead than at the tread. Goodyear had used tapered stiffness in its NCT's, Wingfoots, and Eagle GT's.

Fourth, Chevrolet wanted a very quiet tire. Wide, stiff-walled tires have a tendency to get annoyingly raucous at highway speeds. "The objective for this new 50-series Corvette tire," affirms Bob Stella, "was to duplicate the sound level of our P225/70R-15 Custom Polysteel — the old Corvette's base tire. As you know, the Polysteel has a 5-rib tread design, with a solid shoulder, solid centerline rib, and it's quieter than the Eagle GT. Keeping the 9-inch-tread, 10-inch-wide, flat 50-series tire at that sound level became a tall order, but we did it with a combination of tread pattern, ply selection, and compounding. We worked out the details in our own sound chamber in Akron."

Establishing the Tread Pattern.

Most people don't realize that Goodyear (and other major tire companies) can whip out a totally new prototype tire in a matter of days. It's easy and even fairly routine. Goodyear has shop facilities inside its Akron plant where technicians custom tailor prototype tires. They can vary ply and bead structures, tread patterns, and rubber-compound formulations. To the outsider, creating a prototype tire seems an inordinately complicated task, but it's really not.

"We went through a lot of tread-pattern variations," continues Stella. "One came out of a discussion I had with Tim Miller in Goodyear's racing group. Following some tread work we'd done on Formula One rain tires, he'd worked on what we called a *natural path* design. We carved up a couple of variations and ran them in our anechoic chamber. It turned out that we had a very quiet tire."

Tim Miller had designed the Goodyear Gatorback rain tire that not only did so well in Formula One auto racing but which 500cc motorcyclist Kenny Roberts drove to three world road-racing championships in 1978-79-80.

"This particular tread pattern," continues Bob Stella, "has a very tightly controlled group of materials. Our tire compounders can reformulate the tread compound for different characteristics. If you want low rolling resistance, we can give you a tire that'll roll forever, but it won't have good traction. Or vice versa.

"We tested different versions all along. Chevrolet ran them on a pre-prototype mule that was all cobbled up. We'd given Jim Ingle and his crew versions of our original 50-series tires. You know, we can build this tire in virtually any shape real quick. We saw what they needed, gave them a tire, but they kept changing their car, too. So it was like shooting at a moving target. They'd change a suspension link or a spring, and then they'd arrive at another bogie. So we had to do the same thing they'd do. We'd submit two or three prototype tires. They'd pick one and use it as the bogie. Then they'd evaluate their suspension settings to that bogie tire. But while that was going on, we'd give them a new, better set of tires, and they'd pick another from that batch. So it was sort of a stairstepping process."

The Eagle VR50 Arrives.

Finally, Chevrolet's and Goodyear's combined forces settled on the ideal rendition — the Corvette's Eagle VR50. The tread pattern has five circumferential ribs (the F-1 auto-racing rain tire uses seven ribs). It's a unidirectional tire, which means it's designed to have a preferred rolling direction. An arrow tells which way it mounts. But Goodyear quickly points out that if the tires get mounted backwards, it's no big thing. Most drivers probably wouldn't notice a difference in ride or handling. Observes Stella: "We made sure that this VR50 was better in the reverse direction than the Custom Polysteel. It's about 10% better backwards and 20% better forward at 60 mph.

"And if you look at the VR50 tread pattern," Stella adds, "you'll see that no matter which way you turn the tire, the side forces will always be generated in the same direction against the tread blocks." When mounted on the Z-51, 16x9.5JK alloy wheel, the VR50 has a tread span of nine inches and, at the recommended 35 psi, a total contact patch of nearly 50 square inches.

As for ply construction, "We wanted a polyester carcass for ride," says Bob. "We use polyester exclusively here in the States. And GM wanted steel belts. Actually we felt steel belts would give us maximum steering response because of the tread stiffness. We have two plies of polyester, then two steel belts, and we have two nylon overlays. The nylon overlays run at zero degrees. What they do is restrict the growth of the tires' shoulders and also the centerline at high speeds. They maintain the tread radius of the tire."

Bob Stella goes on to explain: "In a normal tire, centrifugal force causes the shoulders to rise as speed increases. Then, as they're forced back down by contact with the road, they generate a lot of heat and, as you know, heat is the principal destroyer of tires. By putting the nylon overlays in this VR50, we hold in the shoulders to decrease the heat buildup and thus increase the high-speed capability of the tire.

"As a rain tire, the VR50 turned out superior to the Custom Polysteel, which is a very good tire in its own right. But the Custom Polysteel would get rid of water only one way — front to rear, through the straight circumferential grooves. What we wanted was to channel water not only forward and backward but also from the centerline out to the edges of the tire.

"In racing, we found that the best way to do that was to create a natural path that would start the water moving from the centerline out at about a 45° angle. It pushes

350-CID V-8 delivered 205 bhp with twin TBI for 1984, but port fuel injection, rumored for later models, raised this figure. Corvette uses aluminum extensively in brakes and suspension.

Catalytic converter tucks up under driveshaft channel beam, with 5-link rear suspension again making extensive use of lightweight aluminum.

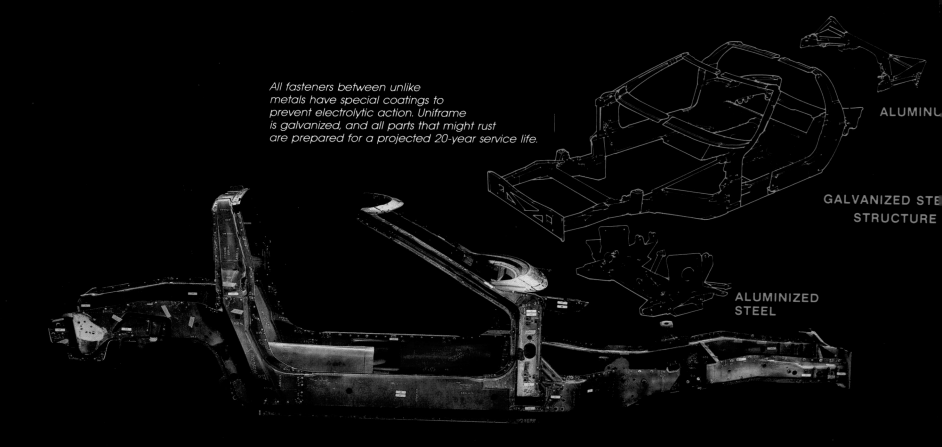

All fasteners between unlike metals have special coatings to prevent electrolytic action. Uniframe is galvanized, and all parts that might rust are prepared for a projected 20-year service life.

ALUMINU

GALVANIZED STE
STRUCTURE

ALUMINIZED
STEEL

the water out through that groove and then back out through the sidewall. If you look at the photos, you'll see the squirts coming out those grooves at the sides.

"In this particular tire, the groove angle in the outside ribs lie in the same direction for both shoulders. In an Eagle GT, they're the reverse of each other. So in an Eagle GT type of tire, it's a little harder to get water to squeegee out from the center to the sides, because the water has to reverse its path. So we straightened out the VR50's flow to get a hair better action. It works quite effectively."

Designing the Uniframe. In order to suspend the wheels and tires, to contain the seating package, and to cradle the engine and driveline, the car needed a skeleton. That meant creating a frame, in this instance a uniframe. And the Corvette's uniframe is unlike anything before it because: a) it's made up of relatively thin sections of sheet steel spot-welded together and, b) the fiberglass skins, unlike a monocoque or even a conventional unitized body, are virtually unstressed.

Ronald N. (Ron) Burns, working under staff engineer Robert A. (Bob) Vogelei, explains the uniframe structure this way. "I think the basic concept really came out of marrying the frame with what we called the birdcage or upper structure of the previous car. In all past Corvettes from 1963 through the 1982 model, the birdcage surrounded just the passenger compartment. The birdcage perched atop the old frame rails on rubber body mounts."

"The '84 vehicle," Burns continues, "married those two elements together into an integrated body/frame structure. There's no more separation of frame rails and birdcage. Everything's welded up as one unit. What results is a stiffer, better structure from the mass- and cost-efficiency standpoints."

One thing that made the new uniframe very unlike Corvette frames of the past was its total lack of central crossmembers. Except for the bolt-in crossmember up front, which serves triple duty to anchor the suspension, engine, and steering rack, there are no crossmembers underneath the passenger floor. That again helped lower the car by putting the floorboards as near the road as possible.

"Another important element in the uniframe," adds Ron Burns, "is the extensive use of the high-strength, low-alloy [HSLA] steel. We worked very closely with our GMMD [GM Manufacturing Development] group, the GMAD tooling people, the Bowling Green tooling people, and our suppliers in perfecting techniques for welding the high-strength, low-alloy material to itself. This became a big part of the program. GMMD and GMAD also developed new techniques for non-destructive testing of welding in production. I should add, too, that design engineer Walter D. Jaeger and structural analysis engineer Adolph K. (Dolph) Lohwasser were instrumental in the design, build, and testing of the uniframe structure." Walt Jaeger was the Corvette engineer under Ron Burns who had hands-on responsibility for designing the uniframe.

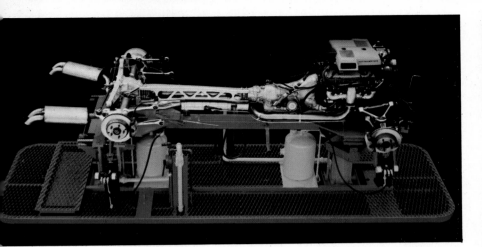

Corvette's powertrain and suspension form a single unit that's assembled separately from rest of car, making access and alignments easier to control.

The New Welding Techniques. In toto, the entire uniframe weighs 351 pounds, thanks in large measure to the liberal use of HSLA steel. The front and rear frame rails plus the entire roof bow are all HSLA steel. The rest of the uniframe, though, is made of conventional mild sheet steel.

General Motors had used HSLA steel in other vehicles before: in the X-, J-, and A-Cars as well as in pickup tailgates. What makes the Corvette application of HSLA different, though, are four factors: 1) the gauges specified, 2) the fact that the Corvette's uniframe is galvanized on all inner and outer surfaces, 3) the complexity of the individual pieces, and 4) the new welding technology that had to be developed for joining HSLA to mild steel.

The HSLA sheet material is first galvanized on all surfaces and then welded. Before the Corvette came along, GM had welded HSLA to only mild steel. "But today we're welding HSLA to itself," explains Ron Burns, "in two and sometimes three metal thickness layers. That's part of the new territory we've managed to open up."

Uniframe design engineer Walt Jaeger elaborates. "We discovered that welding HSLA to itself takes much higher welding currents plus higher cycle times than normal mild-steel welds. We found we had to go with what we call a dual-pulse weld, with up-slope and down-slope controls [see drawing]. Normal arc-welding temperatures would spatter the galvanized coatings, so we first hit the metal with a much hotter, controlled, increasing-energy pulse — the up-slope. Then we drop the current, then cut it off completely, and finally we give it one more jolt. All these pulses are controlled by computer. It took a lot of time to figure out the best current profiles. We ended up with a computerized, automated welding technique that uses 4-5 times more energy than a typical weld, but it certainly does the trick."

Computers Again Indispensable. Chevrolet used computers quite a lot in designing the Corvette's uniframe structure and suspension system. Ron Burns points out that, "... we worked very closely with the structural engineers under Harry Lange and, later, Dolph Lohwasser; also the engineering analysis group under Joe Majcher. Joe's people operate as a service organization within Chevrolet Engineering. They assigned three (and at one time four) analytical engineers to support our activity. Then they, in turn, hired some outside consulting firms to do the digitizing and run

"Speedy" computerized robot welder, one of four, is part of 6-stage weld area with 133 guns. These build up Corvette's uniframe. Due to the extensive use of HSLA steel, galvanized surfaces, engineers developed new welding techniques.

the various programs that were generated: finite element analysis, etc. We worked hand in glove with all of them right through the entire program."

It sounds good to say that a car "gets designed by computer," but those four words don't really tell the story. There's a lot more to it. First of all, computer modeling cut development time in half in most instances and up to ⅔ in others, such as in handling development, which we'll come to in Chapter 5.

Before Chevrolet put actual pre-prototypes and prototypes on the road, they needed to "build" models of these cars inside the computer. These models came off the drawings that the design engineers "concepted out." This means the engineers initially put down soft lines showing what the structural members might be and what Design Staff's layout and packaging schematics made the car look like.

Then the engineers built as fine a model inside the computer as time and computer space allowed. They used a process called *finite element modeling* which, oversimplified, spells out each element of a design in such a way that it behaves like the real thing. In other words, the computer engineer can define, say, a metal brace. That brace, in computer language, happens to be a series of numbers, but the numbers make it react like a real metal brace of a certain size, weight, and strength. In some computers, the brace can even be conjured up in 3-dimensional perspective on a video screen, so an engineer can "look" at it and see how it fits together with other parts.

If the computer operator "bolts" this brace between two sections of the computer-

Before actual prototypes and finished cars were barrier-tested, Walt Jaeger's staff built half-scale models to computer-recommended forms.

Jaeger's half-scale crash program refined uses of high-strength steel in forward rails. Final rail design manages crush so the cockpit area remains isolated.

defined "uniframe," it acts just as it would in real life. Additionally, the computer can then "twist" or "shake" that brace to see what happens to the overall structure. In fact, the engineer can print out a drawing or "cartoon" of the brace and the frame. He can "watch" the entire uniframe structure move on a display screen, so that during the twisting or beaming "trial," the brace and uniframe react in an exaggerated way just like the real thing. We'll talk more about that in our chapter on handling.

Computer Modeling. To explain more accurately what happens in finite element modeling: It theoretically breaks complicated forms and structures into lots of small, flat pieces that touch each other edge to edge. Imagine the slightly domed roof of a car squashed flat and then scribed with a grid pattern. The computer, in essence, does that.

The computer then goes on to use standard stress-analysis procedures to evaluate the 3-dimensional curves that make up that roof. It uses the same ways to analyze stress that engineers have been using for years, the big difference being speed. The modern computer has made it possible to quickly trace loads, deflections, and stress in thousands of small, finite segments at one time. Each little element in the grid has a number, and as the engineer twists the total shape, every one of those numbers changes. The computer's math model, then, tells the engineer what will happen for any given change in shape or material.

Initially, three major computer teams and several peripheral ones cooperated on the Corvette's computer modeling. Chevrolet's engineering analysis group, mentioned earlier, was under Joe Majcher and included Harry Lange. The second computer group worked at GM Engineering Staff, under Mitchel C. (Mick) Scherba, who'd previously done structures work on the 1982 F-Car. Scherba's principal assistant was Curt Vale.

Toward Strength and Lightness. In addition, Chevrolet hired several outside computer consultant firms, the main one being Structural Dynamics Research Corp. SDRC maintains an office in Detroit but has its headquarters in Cincinnati. Basically, what SDRC did was to take Chevrolet's initial drawings and digitize them into the computer. SDRC used computer programs that they and Chevrolet had come up with from previous jobs. They projected estimates of such things as uniframe structural stiffnesses, how rigid various structural joints had to be, stiffnesses of bushings and other rubber rates, suspension system geometry and reactions, and how to model the removable hatch roof. Finally, Grumman also lent computer support, especially in the areas of structure and barrier-performance testing.

A lot of computer modeling takes human judgement, though, because it's impossible — or at least impractical — to model some systems with an infinite number of variables or stiffnesses. Engineers have to use a finite amount of variables.

But once a car gets fairly well modeled inside the computer, the technician can test it under synthesized road conditions—loads that the car might encounter during cornering or running over potholes. The computer engineer can put loads right on that structure and find out where the high-stress areas are and how they respond.

Then, if the stresses are too high, he can add more metal to a given area—increase the size, say, of a rail section. That's what happened to make the Corvette's rockers so tall. Or if the stresses seem relatively low, he might take out weight by reducing the massiveness of a structural member or going to a lighter material. So the computer turns out to be an extremely valuable tool in setting up the initial structure—and thereby the size and weight of the car.

It's at this point that the manufacturer can take out a great deal of dead weight, because he doesn't yet have anything in metal. In the early computer-modeling stages, Chevrolet could change lines on paper, and that didn't cost much compared with changing prototype parts or components after tooling. The computer modeling process took about two years—late 1978 to early 1981. That was some of the work, then, that went into designing the first pre-prototypes, which were ready for the road in June 1980.

Crashing by Computer and Scale Model. Walt Jaeger points out another important area where computers helped design the uniframe. "Most of the impact energy of a front barrier crash has to be taken by the front frame rails. We ended up making these of HSLA, but very early in the program we started with a special state-of-the-art computer analysis which, unlike finite element modeling, can deal with large-scale, non-linear deflections of the metal and can predict the crush modes of complicated shapes, like the front rails. In essence, the analysis told us where these rails would

Another way to analyze uniframe's structural strengths and weaknesses uses exact plexiglas replicas. Each section conforms to spec, but in ½ scale.

bend in a crash, how they'd crush, and at what load levels the crushes would take place. Furthermore, the computer was telling us how much energy was being absorbed along the way as the crush progressed.

"We followed up this work with a program using half-scale models. We'd barrier-crash them to confirm what the computer was telling us. We ran these tests with actual half-sized Corvettes. They were accurate in every significant structural detail. We crashed these models into a wall at 30 mph. So by testing various designs this

By applying a special paint and then twisting plexiglas uniframe, cracks in the finish will pinpoint areas of greatest stress, which can then be reinforced.

way, we could get the basic barrier performance where we wanted it before we ran our first test with a full-sized prototype.

"What resulted," concludes Jaeger, "was an efficient rail design that manages the barrier-test energy in a very precise way. The front rails absorb nearly all the energy of a 30-mph crash, leaving the passenger compartment virtually intact. In addition, we were able to 'program' the rail crush in such a way that the suddenness of stopping the car—the deceleration pulse—is held to a minimum. This becomes very important to the passengers because it minimizes injury."

Aluminum Suspension Components. The next major task—again using computer modeling—was to concept out the 1984 Corvette's suspension system. Brian M. Decker, a native of Grosse Pointe Farms who holds his engineering bachelor's and master's degrees from the University of Michigan, had charge of the Corvette's powertrain and chassis design.

Chevrolet formally defines the Corvette's chassis as the bolt-in front crossmember, the front and rear suspension systems, with springs, brakes, wheels, and tires; also the entire drivetrain: engine, exhaust system, fuel system, transmission, and all driveshafts. States Brian Decker, "One of the suspension system's key features is certainly the aluminum content. Both front and rear suspensions are all aluminum, which is new for GM. We'd never done anything like it before. In fact, neither had any other domestic passenger-car manufacturer so far as I know. There are a few imports like the Porsche 928 that have suspension parts made of aluminum. But most of those parts are cast. We didn't want to cast ours because we feel castings

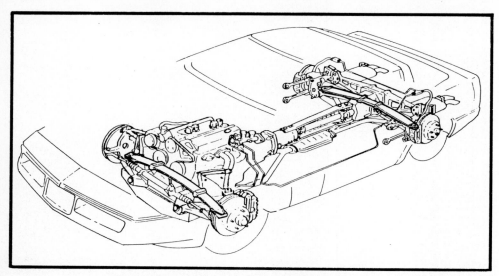

Liteflex fiberglass springs fore and aft save about 70% in weight, yet out-perform steel springs in terms of longevity, controllability, sag resistance.

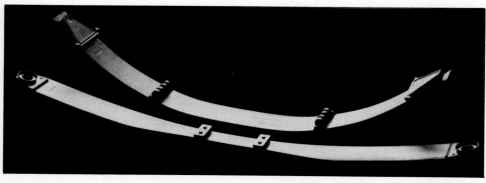

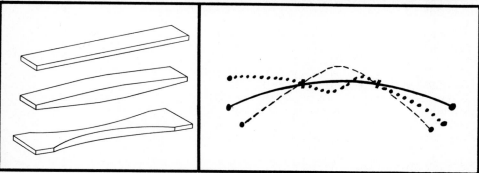

Tailoring both springs became a process of narrowing down infinite choices. Each spring doubles somewhat as a swaybar by trying to assume S shape.

really aren't proper for suspension components. Clearly forgings are better. They have more ductility. Lack of ductility is a problem with castings."

The 1984 Corvette contains approximately 375 pounds of aluminum, mostly the alloy 6061-T6, as compared with about 200 pounds in the 1982 model. Decker notes that, "...the reason for all this aluminum, of course, is that we were going after light weight. The '84 front suspension represents a 58% weight saving over the 1982 Corvette's. Less unsprung weight improves not just ride but wheel control and handling as well.

"We wanted maximum performance out of the 1984 car, and certainly weight is important for that. We wanted the lightest vehicle we could come up with. We wanted a car on the road, even with the V-8 engine, that weighed under 3000 pounds. That was our target."

There's talk, even at this early stage of the 1984 Corvette's production life, of an aluminum-block, 350-cid V-8. Whether an aluminum engine will become available to the general public, though, remains an unanswered question. An aluminum block might be offered for "off-road use" (which translates as "racing;" see Chapter 9).

The Beauty of Fiberglass Springs. "Another feature," continues Decker, "is the use of fiberglass springs. In 1981, we introduced the Liteflex transverse fiberglass leaf spring in the Corvette's rear suspension. The weight saving and technology in that are tremendous. It meant something like a 70% weight reduction compared to the previous steel spring. We carried that into the front suspension for '84. If you compare our fiberglass front monoleaf spring to a conventional set of coil springs, it weighs about ⅓. On top of that, it acts partly as a stabilizer bar. So the fiberglass front spring really replaces two coil springs and part of a stabilizer bar and weighs less than one coil spring.

"It's also totally corrosion-resistant and more durable than a steel spring. Any coil or metal leaf spring will eventually sag. The fiberglass spring won't. Also, if you compress a steel spring enough times—on a car or in the lab—after so many cycles it'll break; snap right in two. We can run these fiberglass springs, though, practically forever. We've run some rear springs up to eight million cycles in laboratory tests—full jounce to full rebound. As a comparison, the old Corvette's 9-leaf steel rear spring would break at something like 75,000 full cycles.

"Then, too, there's no interleaf friction, which gives us as good a ride as coils, with better road isolation. We can vary ride rate, roll stiffness, and load range by changing the thickness and width of the single leaf. So the reason we went to fiberglass is because it has the right properties to do the job: the most efficient storage of energy per unit of mass. It also packages very well in the car. It means light weight, so it all makes sense."

Was Henry Ford Right? The Corvette is probably the world's only current passenger car to use front and rear transverse leaf springs. In Henry Ford's day, more cars bounced along on cross springs than on any other type, but there's a world of difference between vintage Fords and today's Corvette.

The Vette's fiberglass-filament monoleaf springs contribute significantly to handling, and while I plan to cover this aspect in more detail in Chapter 5, I do want to mention the basics here.

The Corvette's Liteflex springs, made by GM's own Inland Div., incorporate some unique and interesting elements that apply to both the front and rear suspension systems. If you check out either spring, you'll notice that it's shaped for taper and camber. And at the front, the spring is attached to the frame at two widely spaced points. Now let's look at how the spring reacts during ride and then cornering maneuvers.

As the car goes through swells, both wheels travel up and down at the same rate and by approximately the same amount. The spring ends, therefore, also go up and down, but the center of the spring—between the two clamps—wants to rise and fall in the opposite direction from the ends.

Now, let's say the car enters a turn. At this point the body wants to lean or roll. Actually, the inside wheels try to go down and the outside wheels try to come up. Here, the monoleaf fiberglass spring also acts as a stabilizer bar, and the reason it acts as a stabilizer bar is simple to understand if you visualize the leaf spring trying to bend itself into an S shape as the body rolls. If the spring material were very soft and pliable, that's what it would do under hard cornering loads.

But it's the spring's resistance to bending into an S shape that helps minimize the Corvette's roll. Part of this roll stiffness is controlled by where along the spring you put the clamps or restraining mounts.

A coil spring gives no stabilizer-bar effect. One-wheel ride rate and roll rate from a coil spring are the same. In the monoleaf fiberglass spring, however, the spring stiffness in roll is 1.8 times the spring stiffness in jounce. In other words, the leaf spring gives 80% more roll stiffness than a set of coils with the same ride rate.

What that means in practical terms is that the Corvette's stabilizer bars can be skinnier and lighter. Originally, when the suspension engineers first looked at fiberglass springs, they hoped to eliminate at least the front stabilizer altogether. It turned out that they couldn't quite do that.

If you look, there's nearly twice as much distance between the front spring clamps as between the rear clamps. Theoretically, it's possible to tune the S bend in this type of monoleaf suspension system by simply moving the clamps in or out; also by varying the width and thickness of the spring at its center. But the Corvette engineers were locked in at the front suspension due to the locations of A-frame attachments, engine mounts, and steering rack. The spring-mount pivots were too close together to let the spring take over the full function of an anti-roll bar. Yet the front spring has taken over some of that duty, and this accounts for the new Corvette's smaller-than-normal front stabilizer. And in the future, Corvette engineers still hope to adapt the wide-based mounts to the rear so they can eliminate the rear stabilizer bar.

A monoleaf fiberglass spring is just a simplification of the conventional multileaf steel cross spring—the same type used by Henry Ford for 40 years. There are, though, considerable differences. The Ford spring, for instance, located the axles and wheels, which the Corvette spring doesn't do.

Also, a transverse multileaf steel spring can't follow the same motions as the single-leaf fiberglass spring, because there's no useful S-bending possible in a multileaf system. And the Corvette monoleaf's ride, handling, and static height characteristics can be changed considerably by altering the thickness of the spring, its taper or wasp-waist shape, and also by the distribution of fiberglass plies in it. It can take any complex shape: there's a nearly infinite variety of shapes, thicknesses, and compositions the fiberglass monoleaf can assume. So designing such a spring can be a complicated business.

Front Suspension Design. Chevrolet staff engineer James C. (Jim) Davis had responsibility for designing the new Corvette's front suspension system. In reviewing the history of this important aspect of the car, Brian Decker told me, "We looked at several different types of front setups—MacPherson strut, SLA, conventional stamped steel, iron knuckles, etc. We went through them all and decided that the SLA type, using forged aluminum members, was the way to go. We're extremely proud of the aluminum knuckles, forged aluminum upper and lower control arms, the aluminum UCA shafts . . . all forged aluminum . . . all the characteristics we wanted in terms of roll steer, compliance understeer, and less unsprung weight.

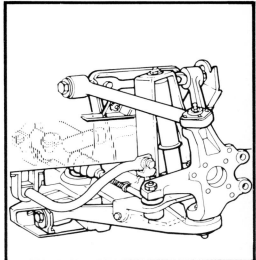

Front suspension tends to be fairly conventional except for use of forged aluminum. Alloy knuckle accepts steel spindle, which carries Girlock disc brake.

A solid stabilizer bar and leading-arm steering, both visible at top of photo, aid handling. Base car uses 24mm front stabilizer bar; Z-51 carries 25mm bar.

Corvettes with automatic transmissions get steel driveshaft and axle shafts, but in cars with Z-51, AG-9, or 7-speed manual gearboxes, these components are aluminum, as are brake dust shields.

Entire drivetrain, including the differential and cover beam, attach in only four places, are rubber-bushed.

"The front suspension has one additional feature that's unique to GM and probably to the industry," he adds. "It's what we call *caster offset*. In just about all other cars, the spindle axis intersects the kingpin axis. In this case, we've taken the spindle axis and moved it rearward from the kingpin axis by 12mm—half an inch. We've incorporated a normal 3° caster, so we have a combination of 3° caster plus 12mm of caster offset. That provides a great improvement in the car's on-center directional sense. It [also] affects the amount of roll steer you have per unit of ride steer. It's a feature that we've been looking at for quite a long time, and the Corvette is really the first car to put it into production."

Rear Suspension Design. Ron Crawford was the design engineer on the rear suspension. Crawford again emphasized light weight. As up front, most components in the rear suspension are forged aluminum, including the upper and lower trailing links, lower lateral strut rod, knuckles, and the wheel driveshafts for the manual transmission (or with power seats. Rear-wheel driveshafts are steel with the automatic transmission minus power seats.) It's possible that the aluminum propshaft combined with aluminum wheel driveshafts constitute a world's first for the Corvette.

The rear suspension is now a 5-link system instead of the old 3-link. Those five links (and you count them on one side only) consist of the two trailing links, lower lateral tie rod, rear tie rod, and the axle driveshaft itself. The twin trailing links allow great flexibility in setting up sideview suspension geometry in terms of swing arm length and slope, which determine anti-squat and anti-dive geometry.

Seen from the rear, the new suspension looks similar to the previous car's. Camber is adjusted by a cam-bolt arrangement at the inner end of each lateral strut rod, same as before. But with the new arrangement, you set toe by adjusting the rear tie rod without affecting other geometry. Steer characteristics are now controlled solely by the lateral components instead of the old trailing arm, giving essentially zero ride and roll steer.

Chevrolet put some extra money into the front and rear suspensions, but it paid off in terms of ride, handling, and adjustment flexibilities. And the fiberglass monoleaf

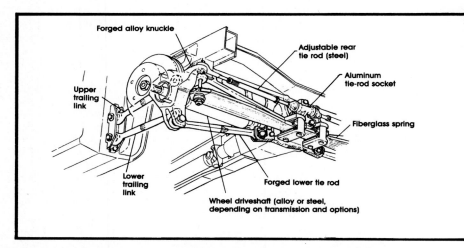

Upper and lower links pivot at both ends, whereas previous single trailing arm swung at the front only. This helps eliminate rear's tendency to steer itself.

springs represent an innovation that presaged other, similar GM suspension systems.

Tightening Up the Rear Suspension. The rear suspension continues to use U-jointed axle shafts, but unlike the previous design, nearly all of the compliance has been taken out. The old car suffered from lateral (sideways) axle movement and thus presented a similar deflection-steer problem at the rear (similar to the front). As the rear outside axle shaft moved inward during cornering, the outside rear tire toed out and caused oversteer. In the current car, though, Dana shims the axle shafts inside the differential housing to minimize lash. Lash is held to .010 inch. The shims are actually C-clips or keepers, and they vary in thickness from axle to axle.

The new twin trailing links put the sideview instant center up higher to improve the Corvette's anti-squat and anti-dive properties. They also eliminate the trailing arms and their front rubber bushings that used to cause even more steer compliance in the rear suspension system.

Steer control is now handled by the rear upper tie rods, which are basically a set of balljointed links which connect the knuckles to the differential case. That gives a very stiff path compared with the lower strut rod, which is rubber bushed. So the two stiff upper links (axle and tie rod) allow very little lateral movement or toe change at the top of the hub, while the rubber-bushed strut rod allows some outward camber change. This is compensated for, however, by the basic control-arm geometry.

Brian Decker makes this final point, "... the 5-link rear suspension gives us the greatest flexibility to tune all the compliance and steer properties to whatever we like best. We think we've set these properties up optimally, and it's something you can't help but notice when you drive the new car."

The Man Behind the Body. The Corvette began using fiberglass springs as recently as 1981, but its fiberglass body dates back to the very first Motorama show roadster of 1953. Not that Chevrolet claims America's only-ever polymer-bodied sports car; the Kaiser-Darrin and Bricklin come to mind, among others. Even the 1955-57 Thunderbird offered a removable fiberglass hardtop. But the Corvette remains the only domestic automobile that's carried fiberglass bodywork exclusively and continuously for over 30 years.

Robert A. Vogelei joined the Corvette engineering team on April Fool's Day, 1963. He's had a hand in developing Corvette chassis and body hardware ever since, but by the time I first talked to him in Feb. 1982, Bob Vogelei was the man in charge of engineering this newest fiberglass body. He's affectionately known as Mr. Plastic because of his high degree of expertise.

Born in Pt. Huron in 1926, Vogelei grew up helping his father rebuild tractor and auto engines in a small Eastern Michigan farm-community shop. His parents moved to Detroit at the outbreak of World War II and, in the summer of 1943, aged 16, Bob worked as an aircraft drafting detailer in the engineering department of Woodall Industries. His father, meanwhile, became a tank inspector at Cadillac.

"My ambition in life at that time," recalls Vogelei, "was to become an aeronautical engineer, so here I was, a kid of 16 working in Woodall's aircraft engineering department, and I thought I was on my way. When I finished high school, Dad came home from work one day and asked me, 'Where do you want to go to college?' I said, 'Maybe the University of Michigan or MIT;' you know ... the big names. He said, 'What about General Motors Institute?' And I said, 'What the hell is that?'

"He started to mention some people at Cadillac who'd gone through GMI and who were doing well; Ed Cole was one of the names that fell out. So I got some information about GMI, and next thing I knew I was enrolled. This was Sept. 1944.

"I attended GMI for four years, and like a lot of other people around here who've attended GMI, I got paroled in 1948. I had co-opped with, and then went to work for, Cadillac. GMI, which at that time was directly associated with General Motors, encouraged work-study programs. Specific divisions would sponsor students and, upon graduation, would hire them full-time. In 1950, I was shipped down to our Cleveland [tank] operation. Prior to that I did some postgraduate work at Wayne State University.

"We had an intensive program in Cleveland while I was there, and the projects I worked on provided excellent training. My work ranged from hull designer to mockup engineer. I designed everything from fire-control mechanisms to future armored vehicles."

In 1953, Ed Cole, who'd been manager of the Cadillac-Cleveland tank plant, was transferred back to Detroit to become Chevrolet's chief engineer. At that point, Cole began bringing some of his Cleveland staff to Chevy. "He felt obligated," says Vogelei, "to bring us back to Detroit since the tank operation had a questionable future. I got my invitation in the spring of 1955. At that time, the Corvette was just getting off the ground. I remember being asked by some of my Cleveland associates whether I was going to work on the Corvette, and I said no, although I thought it might be interesting."

Between 1955 and 1963, Bob Vogelei had assignments in Chevrolet truck, the engineering labs, the GM proving grounds, Corvair body, and Chevy II body. He went to Corvette on Apr. 1, 1963.

New Body Bonding Technology. Various points that differentiate the new body from the old one include: 1) the new panels are made from non-shrinking, low-profile resin systems; 2) there are no exposed bond joints; 3) all bonding is by urethane rather than polyester adhesives; and 4) all outer panels have molded urethane coatings.

Reminiscing about the 1984 body's development, Vogelei points out that, "We'd already developed a lot of the fiberglass technology, starting from the 1968 program on. Even that far back, we were wanting to do more plastic-to-metal bonding, and we challenged the adhesives industry to work with us. They were a little slow responding because of the Corvette's rather low volume. It took a lot of time, money, and R&D [research and development] to convince our suppliers to produce a special adhesive for only 25,000 cars a year. That's not many cars and thus didn't seem a wise investment to them at the time. But over the years, other cars started using plastics and needed new plastic bondings, so we now share those techniques with our other divisions.

"But our first task with the '84 car was to get ourselves organized to design a structurally sound, stiff, mass-efficient uniframe to carry the chassis and the body. Before, the conventional frame used to belong to the chassis group, and my guys did just the body. But for this new car, we inherited responsibility for the total structure, so the work has become more complex.

"I'd like to give you an example of what I mean. When Don Urban did the 1963 car, Don and four or five engineers did a whole brand-new body, and Walt Zetye plus a handful of engineers developed the entire 1963 chassis. In 1968, my staff put an updated, restyled body on that same '63 chassis; four engineers and I did that whole job.

"Today, for the 1984 car, I have three assistant staff engineers, 11 Chevrolet engineers, and an equal number of outside contract engineers supporting the body activity. It used to be that one of my guys or I would be confronted by a problem at 8:00 in the morning and, by 8:15, we could make a decision and be on our way and not worry about how it affected the emissions people or the safety people, etc.

"The design of automotive structures is kind of like the aircraft industry now — you have to be mass-efficient. We've tried to spring a little from aircraft background and techniques. They obviously don't have to worry about 30-mph barrier tests. We, on the other hand, not only have 30-mph crash tests but 5-mph bumper barriers to run, door side intrusion tests, plus passenger-compartment safety and several others."

That Great Big Hood. "We did use aeronautical computer programs very heavily," continues Vogelei. "A lot of work, for example, went into computer studies for the

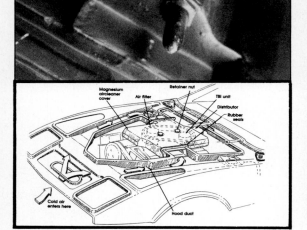

Rubber gaskets seal ducts to the air-cleaner; pins eliminate hood wobble.

Robert A. Vogelei

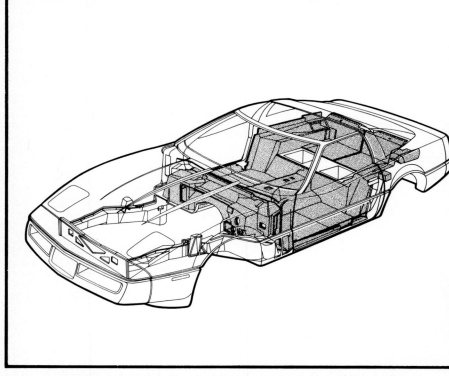

For heat and sound insulation, new Corvette contains full mass-back, 16-oz., cut-pile carpeting over urethane foam, amberlite, and other materials.

Corvette's hood. It's a huge, complicated structure, and we wanted to make sure we had a nice, strong, firm, solid hood. We wanted to do it with the least mass [weight] possible.''

Paul Huzzard, the man in charge of panels and trim under Vogelei, mentions that the clamshell hood is one of the largest one-piece automotive fiberglass structures ever made. Tom Delano, who works for Huzzard and who had engineering responsibility for the hood, adds, ''Just the size of the hood presented some problems. When it's open, for instance, it becomes a terrific sail, so we had to make both it and the prop structure strong enough to withstand stiff winds. I've heard people joke that when a Corvette owner runs out of gas, all he has to do is open the hood and head downwind to the nearest filling station.''

Huzzard adds that, ''We used *geometric tolerancing* in this car. Geometric tolerancing comes out of the aerospace industry. To explain what it means: In the past, we might simply make a hole for, say, a hood hinge or support and specify 1/32 inch. Geometric tolerancing takes into account what the hole is supposed to do—the relative importance of each dimension. It says, I've got three hood-hinge holes here that relate directly to another set of three holes over there. Those holes don't necessarily have to relate to the wheel openings, so you can emphasize dimensions that are critical—like the hood hinge holes—as opposed to those that aren't critical, like the wheel well. It's just a better way to spec and dimension a part.''

And Vogelei continues, ''The whole body was analyzed: door intrusion beams were studied in fiberglass and aluminum and steel, hood inner panels also considered in fiberglass, steel, and aluminum .... The body panels on our car are not really load-bearing members, unlike the panels of a steel-bodied car. We usually try to make every piece of mass do something, but that's not the case with the Corvette. I'm not saying the fiberglass panels aren't doing any work. The doors, door beams, and strikers, for example, add stiffness to the uniframe, and we especially beefed up that area when we got into our serious ride tests.'' John Schejbal acted as the Corvette's design engineer for door structure and hardware systems.

FRP, SMC, RRIM, and Alphabet Soup. As it now stands, the new Corvette's front and rear end caps are made of a soft, flexible plastic called RRIM, for *reinforced reaction injection molding*. The color-keyed front and rear fascias are supplied, surprisingly enough, by Oldsmobile Div. Design engineer for the front and rear bumper fascias was John Delmastro.

All of the Corvette's other outer skins — the hood, fenders, doors, roof, and decklid, are a fiberglass reinforced polyester (FRP) that's made into a material called *sheet-molding compound*, or SMC. The SMC material consists of a mixture of chopped glass fibers and resin made into a continuous sheet. The sheet gets cut into lengths and rolled up for storage. It can later be pressed into body panels. Each panel is made by charging a matched set of male and female molds with a given size and weight of SMC material.

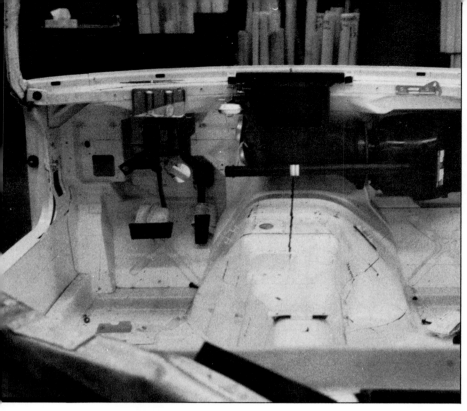

Tall rockers and huge driveshaft tunnel are molded into floor section. Multi-chambered climate control system occupies much space behind cowl.

Engineer Vincent K. Wagner checks out instrument panel assembly before installing it in prototype. This gives another idea of cramped quarters behind the i.p.

The FRP panels are molded by GTR Reinforced Plastics Co., an operating arm of the General Tire and Rubber Co. GTR, along with the Budd Co. and North American Rockwell, have been supplying Corvette body parts since 1964. In addition, Chevrolet Manufacturing began supplying body panels in 1983.

Upgrading the Finish. Another focal point turned out to be the Corvette's body finish. ''We tried to develop the best resin system we could for the best surface finish possible on this car,'' notes Vogelei. ''I think the customer expects it, deserves it, and when he sees this new plastic car, I think he's going to be pleased with it.

''I feel people are looking to us to be the leader in this industry, and I told all the suppliers we deal with, You'd better do a good job on this car, because everybody's going to be looking at it, and you're going to be remembered for it. I think people accepted yesterday's car with whatever surface imperfections there might have been. Even so, I don't believe the Corvette buyer is as critical of the body as we in engineering are.''

Vogelei points out that Chevrolet is doing a lot of things differently with this new car. GM and its suppliers have developed different resin systems to give a smoother finish. This development for the Corvette ran parallel with similar programs for the Fiero and other GM cars.

All the new Corvette's SMC exterior body panels have an *in-mold coating* on them. Explains Paul Huzzard, ''One of the problems we ran into previously with our fiberglass panels was porosity. There were microscopic pits that resulted from air trapped by some of the molding techniques. When the panel went through the painting process, it tended to trap volatiles in these tiny pores, and then when the panel went through the paint oven, the volatiles expanded and ended up with a cratering effect on the paint.

''Well, four or five years ago, GM Manufacturing Development, along with some of our molding suppliers, principally General Tire & Rubber's Chemicals/Plastics/Industrial Products Group, figured it might be neat if we could mold a panel, open the die up a few millimeters, inject a sealing material, close up the mold again, and heat-cure the panel. That way we'd end up with all the porosities sealed. The in-mold coating process was perfected in the late Seventies.

''So the 1979-82 car had removable roof panels that were in-mold coated. As were the 1980-82 Corvette hoods and front fenders. The coating might be five mils thick [0.005 inch]; it's relatively thin, and it has to be treated with care, because you can't do a lot of sanding. But if a bodyshop or fiberglass repairman has done his homework, he shouldn't have to do a lot of sanding anyway. By and large, in-mold coating provides a very successful means to improve the quality of the fiberglass finish. And as I say, the new car has all its SMC panels in-mold coated.''

Then, too, as mentioned in Chapter 2, the new car's body design specifically removed all exposed bond joints. That's important because, in earlier Corvettes, exposed bond seams had to be sanded by hand before spraying. This not only led to waviness and human error but created dust problems. Fiberglass dust had to be removed from car surfaces and filtered from the air before painting.

The new design takes a lot of the hand labor out of the plant and removes any chance of dust. "That's how the hood got to be one piece," observes Bob Vogelei. "Jerry Palmer and the people in Design Staff were very willing to work with us, because they'd seen so many bad cars with bad body joints. We changed the basic structure. Styling was determined to get the no-bond-joint design this time."

Corvette Doubles Corrosion Bogies. Thanks to its fiberglass body, rust has never been nearly the problem on Corvettes as with some automobiles. Even so, the Corvette isn't totally rustproof—its metal parts, like those of any car, can corrode.

Most metals tend to rust or, more properly, oxidize naturally even in normally humid air. It's a process that's speeded up by fog or rain, and it works most quickly in salt spray from de-iced highways. The new Corvette's metal parts add another dimension to the problem because any two dissimilar metals, like aluminum and steel, if they're in close contact, set up an electrolytic corrosive action when they get wet. And salt accelerates the electrolytic action between unlike metals.

So for this newest Corvette, the engineers made sure every metal member got that extra measure of corrosion protection, especially where two dissimilar metals touch or come in close proximity. For example, all nuts and bolts that connect two dissimilar metals in, say, the suspension system, are coated so they can't conduct electricity. All nuts, bolts, washers, and fasteners for the body, chassis, engine, transmission, drivetrain, and suspension are made of materials that resist corrosion or get special anti-rust treatment. All steel brackets, clamps, clips, and braces are especially coated or painted.

The uniframe, as mentioned, is totally galvanized on all inner and outer surfaces. The uniframe also gets totally immersed in a paint vat for extra protection. The front crossmember is made of aluminized steel, which is then dip-painted before installation.

All aluminum parts are left bare, but any bolts or fasteners that touch the aluminum get a special coating. The otherwise corrosion-prone magnesium rocker covers have a coat of epoxy paint over a coat of mag sealer inside and out. Paint likewise protects the inner and outer surfaces of the magnesium aircleaner cover. The engine oil pan is shipped into the plant already primed and painted. Parking-brake cables are either made of stainless steel or are sheathed in plastic.

Most cars' exhaust systems tend to rust out after 30,000 to 50,000 miles, but that's not likely in the Corvette. Its header-like exhaust manifolds are stainless steel, with an aluminized steel heat shield over them. Front header pipes are double-walled stainless, with the catalytic converter housing also stainless and the rest of the exhaust system aluminized steel.

Brian Decker sums up the Corvette's anti-corrosion stance this way: "We've really put some extra effort into making this a longterm car. People like to keep their Corvettes, so we do twice as much durability testing on the Corvette as on any other passenger car. Where a normal car runs one schedule, we run that plus another back to back. The Corvette has to pass both. All durability schedules are doubled. Same with corrosion bogies. The corporate corrosion bogie might be 10 years minimum of functional life. We make that 20 years. In other words, that member has to function perfectly and totally for at least 20 years."

From T-bar to Targa. As you know, partway through the body program, Chevrolet changed its mind and decided to go from a T-bar roof to the targa top—from twin removable roof panels to a single panel. This created an anxious moment not only for the body people but also for the ride-and-handling engineers (see Chapter 5).

Bob Vogelei reconstructs the situation. "We started by doing this car with a T-strut roof, like the previous Corvette's. We used the strength of the T in all our original structural analyses. Lloyd Reuss, before he left to become general manager of Buick, was leaning on Dave McLellan and the rest of us pretty heavily to get that T-bar out of there. He wanted the more open look; the targa openness and feel."

Adds Reuss, "I felt very strongly about the 1-piece roof, and there were a couple of others—Dave McLellan agreed with me. But there were *others* . . . . I remember sending Dave a Ferrari ad out of the *Wall Street Journal*. The ad said something like, 'If you dream about it, it can be done' . . . like that. I said, We've got to do this targa roof. It was a pretty arbitrary decision.

"My engineers came back and told me we'd have to add weight to compensate for the missing T-strut; that we'd have a big structural problem. I said, Yes, I agree with that, but it's such an important element in this new car to get rid of that T member that we'd better find a way to do it. It threw the whole program into a real tither there for a while."

And Vogelei adds, "Some of us resisted the deletion of the T-strut for a time, but finally, after we deepened the rocker sections and such, we changed our minds and agreed that we could take the central roof strut out and still get a good, sound car.

"But I think we overlooked a couple of variables earlier in the program. The first car we put on the road without that strut was pretty bad, and that worried me. It kept Fred Schaafsma and his development guys busy for quite a few months, but between us we identified the problems and managed to solve them."

Scratch-proofing the Roof. Vogelei pauses a moment and then goes on: "We also went through a heckuva program to develop the see-through plastic roof panel itself. It's acrylic as opposed to the glass panels we've used on our previous cars. Again, that's part of the mass-reduction move. Acrylics and polycarbonates aren't as heavy as glass. In glass, the single panel would have been pretty awkward to handle. We made it as light as we could."

Unprotected acrylics tend to scratch fairly easily, so the Corvette's see-through roof surfaces now carry a proprietary hardcoating that's put on by Swedlow, an aerospace company in California. Swedlow applies the hardcoating, which GM also uses on acrylic windows in buses. Bob Vogelei told me that, in case the acrylic roof didn't work out, he kept a lightweight glass program going as backup.

Chevrolet saved about 4.2 pounds by using acrylic instead of glass. The single acrylic roof panel's optics are better than that of glass, as is its light and heat control. Hardcoating protects the panel against anything except all-out vandalism. If an owner scrubs his top with steel wool, the surface will scratch, but the coating resists normal wear and even a fair amount of abuse.

Vogelei's body engineers bumped into some minor problems with the new Vette's large glass hatch, even though previous models had used similar pieces. PPG Industries, which makes the hatch, agreed to start with a relatively thin 5mm glass, again to take weight out. But the hatch was so flexible that the strut rods distorted the glass— actually bent it upward — and caused sealing problems. PPG upped the gauge to 6mm, but that still didn't solve the problem. So finally it was decided to overcrown the glass in the manufacturing process so that when it mounts in the body, under seal pressure and strut loads, it distorts *back into the designed shape*. That's one of the little gambits that veteran Corvette body engineers can call on to make things work.

The Untemperamental Chevy V-8. Turning now to the powertrain, anyone acquainted with older Corvettes won't find much unfamiliar under the hood. Except for the magnesium aircleaner cover, the engine dress and color scheme, the serpentine belt drive, and the electric cooling fan, this is basically the same engine as in the

1982 car. It's even the same V-8 that's so long been Chevrolet's gift to mankind and auto racing; the small-block that's reigned as an American standard since 1955.

One of the Corvette's great virtues lies in the fact that it's totally unexotic; 100% untemperamental. The Chevy V-8 doesn't play the practical jokes you so often find in other sports cars. Give the rest credit for multiple overhead cams, expensive alloy blocks, and jet-age fuel-injection systems; it all sounds just great until something goes wrong.

Developing Throttle-Body Injection. This book is being written in early 1983, in the heyday of twin throttle-body injection (TBI) and well before the advent of the Corvette's port-injection system. I've only heard port injection talked about. I understand that it might herald 265-275 horsepower from the 350 V-8, but I don't know this with certainty, nor do I even know when it's due. So I'll concentrate here on the 1984 twin TBI setup.

In my book, *Camaro, The Third Generation,* Chevrolet's chief engineer for engines and components, Russell F. (Russ) Gee, explained to me how Cross-Fire Injection came about. The following account comes from that previous book.

"I moved from Pontiac to Chevrolet on Jan. 1, 1979," Gee told me, "and in the middle of that month, a group of us had a brainstorming session on several vehicles. We sat down in my office and analyzed what we should be doing for the 1982 Camaro Z-28 and the 1982 Corvette.

"We'd been challenged by management to come up with a unique engine for the Z-28. Years ago, back at Pontiac, I'd been involved in developing the old Tri-Power setup—the triple 2-barrel system where you have one small carburetor in the middle of the intake manifold and two larger 2-barrels on the ends. I was really fond of that. We did a lot of work on it back in the GTO days under Pete Estes.

"What I particularly liked about Tri-Power was that you or your wife could drive around town five days a week and get excellent fuel economy with that very small center carburetor. Then, on weekends, you'd floor the other two carbs and had a real triple 2-barrel gangbusters engine.

"So when we sat down for this brainstorming session in my office," Gee continues, "it looked like we had three main alternatives available to us. One was to use a single 2-barrel TBI system as on the 1980 Cadillac. The second was the one I introduced, namely three staged single-barrel TBI's in a row, like the old Tri-Power. And the third was a ram-tuned intake manifold with two electrically controlled carburetors on it—an update of what the Z-28 had used so success fully back in 1968-69 for SCCA Trans Am racing.

"We worked these three programs out in the laboratory for some time. When we tried to combine the three single-point TBI's, though, it became evident early in the program that synchronization would give us some headaches. The triple TBI setup really wasn't in the cards.

"As you'll recall, Chevy's success with mounting two carburetors on a tunnel-ram manifold got them outstanding power, so we built on that idea. We married the concept of putting two TBI units on this ram intake manifold, and we've come up with what I feel is a very, very strong, unique powerplant. It has great airflow capacity and power performance. We also have the capability of tuning the V-8 to give very acceptable fuel economy."

And that's basically how the twin TBI setup came about. It was up to Rochester Products Div. to work out the details, which wasn't too difficult, but credit must go to Lauren I. Bowler, who refined GM's throttle-body injection system to make it practical. Today, of course, a great number of cars use TBI's, including the ubiquitous 4-cylinder Iron Duke, but it's still a relatively recent development. In fact, it wasn't until May 1980 that Chevrolet had prototype twin TBI manifold castings in hand for

For '84, Corvette sticks with iron-block 350 V-8, renowned for reliability and good performance. Rumor has it that an aluminum block might be in the offing.

Twin throttle bodies might also be replaced with port injection in the future. Single, always taut Poly-Vee belt won't fly off pulleys at high engine speeds.

Each throttle body directs a cone of fuel into manifold. Solenoids are pulsed by computer, which reads demand, optimizes fuel flow for power and economy.

Doug Nash Engineering, which supplies 7-speed overdrive manual trans, beefed main gearcase with extra bosses and put electric sensors on both shifter forks.

initial tests. Production units went onto the Corvette's 350 V-8 and the Camaro's 305 starting in 1982 models.

How Cross-Fire Injection Works. Most of you know how a TBI works, but for those who don't, here's a recap. Throttle-body injection has been called a cross between carburetion and port fuel injection, and that's not a bad description. Unlike port injection, though, TBI doesn't use high-pressure pumps, complex fuel-distribution metering blocks, or easily clogged injector nozzles at each cylinder. Nor is it anywhere near as expensive as port fuel injection.

Think of the TBI unit as a carburetor with the top part knocked off. The choke, air horn, venturis, float chambers, and all those upper-level jets and passages are gone. What's left is the throttle body: the bottom plate with the throttle butterflies. But above that plate there's a solenoid-activated nozzle valve that can be opened and closed very quickly electromagnetically. Electrical impulses open and shut this solenoid at very high speeds, like a vibrator. These vibrations are precisely timed to give just the right fuel flow.

Now, gasoline under pressure passes by the solenoid. As the solenoid valve opens and shuts — and it does this once with each cylinder firing — fuel escapes at the metered rate. It sprays down into the throttle bores in an inverted-cone pattern, at which point it mixes with in-rushing air, as it would in a carburetor. Swirl plates — little fans — in the bottom of the manifold cover help atomize the air/fuel mixture.

Pressure inside the TBI fuel lines isn't nearly so high as in direct port injection. In the Rochester TBI system, pressure ranges between 10.0 and 12.4 psi, whereas normal port injection fuel lines carry loads from 40 to 80 psi. With Cross-Fire Injection, a 2-stage, twin-turbine electric pump rests inside the fuel tank, and gasoline is forced through a loop system that ends up back at the tank. It uses regulators and bypasses to keep pressure to both injectors constant. The right-hand TBI, by the way, fuels the left bank of cylinders, and the left TBI feeds the right bank, which leads us to the term Cross-Fire Injection.

The electric impulses that tell the injectors how fast to vibrate and thus how much fuel to release are determined by an onboard computer called an *electronic control module* (ECM for short). The ECM takes information from various sensors. These sensors monitor throttle position, engine coolant temperature, road speed (mph), engine speed (rpm), and they also compare barometric pressure with manifold absolute pressure. An oxygen sensor monitors the amount of oxygen in the exhaust system ahead of the catalytic converter, and the ECM uses this information to check whether the engine is running too lean or rich. It adjusts the fuel flow (the amount of time the solenoids stay open) to maintain a stoichiometrically correct 14.7:1 air/fuel ratio.

The ECM-determined pulses are timed to engine speed. They're slowest and shortest at idle. As rpm picks up, so do the solenoid impulses. Then, depending on load and other conditions, the fuel bursts might become longer in relation to engine speed. At full throttle, the solenoids hold the injector nozzles all the way open for maximum fuel flow — a power-rich fuel/air ratio of up to 12:1.

The major advantages of throttle body injection are more accurate metering, thus better fuel economy, plus greater control of emissions. TBI's give better cold starts since they need no choke in the normal sense. And the system is self-diagnosing. It also incorporates what's called a failsoft mode which, if the ECM conks out, lets the engine start, idle, and run so you can at least limp home.

But unlike a carburetor, you can't alter a TBI's fuel-flow characteristics by changing jets. The ECM's factory settings pretty much determine performance for the life of the system.

Serpentine Belt Drive. Meanwhile, a great improvement in the V-8 — one that's not much talked about — involves the single, serpentine, Poly-Vee belt that drives the engine accessories. Ford introduced this type of flat, multi-grooved belt on the 302 Mustang. And Chevrolet engineer Frank Tenkel rode herd on it for the Corvette.

The Poly-Vee belt's main advantages are that it's automatically tensioned and that it doesn't tend to fly off its pulleys at high engine speeds. A normal V-belt really isn't much good at ultra-high rpm. Deeper pulleys aren't the answer, because no matter how tightly you tension a normal belt, its center of gravity, which rests below the outer cord layer, reacts to centrifugal force and tries to roll itself inside out at high rpm. As the outer plies flip down into the pulley, the belt stretches and eventually breaks. Broken fanbelts have been a major warranty problem for all carmakers.

With a flat belt, the center of gravity and the cords lie close together. No matter what the speed, the Poly-Vee stays on its wider pulleys and, because the pulleys are relatively broad, they give better adhesion, less noise, and don't build up heat.

There's only one belt to change and no adjustments to make, thanks to the single spring tensioner. Most of the Corvette engine's accessory brackets are aluminum, and it's interesting to note that the aluminum water pump rotates backward from normal, as do a few other accessories. A final advantage of the flat belt is that it can drive the smaller alternator pulley, which keeps the alternator's rpm up even at idle.

Doug Nash 4-speed With Overdrive. At this writing, the new Corvette lists two available transmissions. Standard gearbox is the Doug Nash 4-speed T-10 backed by a computer-controlled overdrive planetary gearset. Then, as in the past, you can order GM's own Turbo Hydramatic 700-R4 4-speed automatic with lockup torque converter, developed for the 1982 car.

Turning first to the manual transmission, it's basically the long-lived Warner T-10 gearbox, which Doug Nash now manufactures to Chevrolet's specifications. Nash bought all rights to this transmission from Warner Gear in June 1982 and builds it at his shops in Franklin, Tenn., near Nashville.

Corvettes offered the T-10 from mid-1957 to 1966 and again from 1978 through '81. For 1978, Warner Gear re-engineered the T-10 case to just about double its strength. Even so, changes to the Nash-built T-10 include beefing up the case and adding strength to the flanges. Nash likewise added more meat in the reverse pocket area plus casting in a couple of bosses at the back of the case to give adequate strength to support the overdrive unit.

"The reason for most of the strengthening," explains Gene McCrickard, Doug Nash's marketing vice president, "was Chevrolet's specifying the *spike test*. That's a test where we run the engine at specific rpm and then pop the clutch in both low and reverse gears. We do that three times at 2000 rpm, three times at 3000 rpm, and on up to 5000 rpm in each direction."

The infamous spike test showed that the strengthened T-10 case had to be beefed up for the 1984 car. One reason was that, since Chevrolet designed the new Corvette's transmission and rear axle as one rigid system, connected by a channel beam, the transmission case ended up handling a lot more up-and-down load than in the past. Previously, the weight of the rear of the engine, plus differential or torque reaction, were taken by intermediate crossmembers.

As Dave McLellan points out, "A good holeshot puts about 1200 foot-pounds of torque on the prop shaft. And the worst holeshot — one that just spins the wheels without moving the car — can deliver up to 2700 foot-pounds on the driveline. That's what breaks drivelines."

Where the Overdrive Came From. The hang-on overdrive gearset was derived from a unit that Doug Nash already had in the works. McCrickard told me that Nash had been developing an aftermarket overdrive for the Jeep CJ-7, CJ-5, and for the 203 transfer case for 4wd vehicles. That soon became the basis for the add-on T-10 overdrive gearbox.

"The reason is," says McCrickard, "that we could simply move faster with an existing overdrive in the timeframe Chevrolet handed us. We could never have developed a brand-new overdrive under normal lead times. But since we could develop it, we got the assignment of putting the T-10 4-speed and our nearly finished overdrive together; doing it with a target date that was realistic for both Chevrolet and us. But our whole program owes an awful lot to the GM test lab guys at the Technical Center and also to the fellows at the Milford proving grounds. Their help was priceless."

McLellan mentions that his powertrain staff, under Brian Decker, looked at several other overdrives before settling on the Doug Nash system. Decker initially tried to mate the T-10 with an ancient Warner Gear planetary overdrive (introduced in the 1934 Chrysler Airflow and used by Ford and Chevrolet as late as 1971). Decker also looked at the GKN/Laycock de Normanville overdrives sold in Europe and used by Volvo and Jaguar. But these lacked adequate torque capacity.

Finally, the Corvette engineers settled on the Doug Nash system, with Delco Electronics supplying the ECM. The Doug Nash setup provides overdrive ratios for the T-10's top three gears, resulting in what's essentially a 7-speed transmission.

Based on throttle position, gear selection, and road speed, the ECM decides whether or not to engage the overdrive. In normal starts, under mild acceleration, the transmission goes directly from first gear to second overdrive, then third overdrive, and finally high overdrive. If you're cruising along in fourth overdrive on the freeway and want to pass, the ECM senses throttle position at, say, 70% of wide-open and kicks down immediately. It then stays in direct drive until you back off. Or

Besides infamous spike test, Doug Nash overdrive underwent grueling laboratory trials. Main 4-speed section had previously been made by Warner Gear.

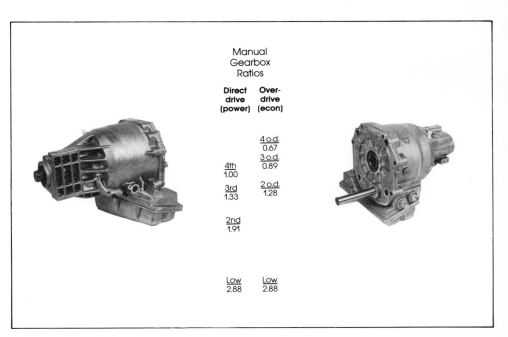

Manual Gearbox Ratios

Direct drive (power)	Over-drive (econ)
	4 o.d. 0.67
	3 o.d. 0.89
4th 1.00	
3rd 1.33	2 o.d. 1.28
2nd 1.91	
Low 2.88	Low 2.88

Nash originally designed overdrive unit for 4wd vehicles. Large ratio gap between low and 2nd o.d. is intentional. Overdrive saves gas, cuts engine wear.

Main gearcase and the overdrive combine to form one rigid unit. Each component has to withstand rigors of inflexible drivetrain under holeshot acceleration.

Overdrive innards consist of multiple disc clutches and planetary gearsets, all monitored by Corvette's main microprocessor, which also oversees fuel delivery.

at 110 mph, even if you're storming, the gearbox automatically upshifts into o.d. The normal upshift in fourth under mild acceleration comes at 32 mph.

Now, if you're moving briskly away from a stop, the transmission stays in direct drive all the way up. It will eventually upshift into overdrive when you ease off again on the gas pedal—or when you hit 110 mph. However, the ECM is programmed to downshift above 40 mph in second and above 50 mph in third no matter what the throttle position.

Why Overdrive Instead of a 5-Speed? Why didn't McLellan and Decker keep everything a lot simpler and just specify a traditional 5-speed transmission for the Vette? After all, even Doug Nash makes a suitable unit.

There's no question that the extremely tall 0.67:1 overdrive ratio was selected with an eye to fuel economy rather than performance. No one denies that. But McLellan gives good reasons for his decision to go with overdrive instead of a 5-speed.

"From an EPA dynamometer fuel-economy test standpoint," he says, "the best possible manual transmission is a wide-ratio 3-speed. I'm not saying it's much good for a Corvette driving down the road, but it's best for EPA numbers because of the way the EPA test is structured. EPA rules say you can't shift into second below 15 mph, into third gear below 25, or fourth below 40. And if you've got a fifth gear, you can't get into fifth until you hit 45 mph. If you run a 5-speed transmission with top gear for cruising fuel economy, you'll benefit the customer all right, but your advantage in the EPA highway cycle is only about half a mile per gallon. If, on the other hand, you've got only three speeds, you can get into your top gear a lot sooner, and that saves considerably more than half a mile per gallon.

"Anyway, in a Corvette, what you need for acceleration are four normal ratios. You need first gear to launch the car, with an overall ratio of 9:1 or 10:1. Anything lower than that will simply light up the tires. Any higher and the engine tends to bog. Then you need close enough spacing for the rest of the gears so you get satisfactory performance in terms of overlapping the torque curve with each of the shift points.

"So looking at our 7-speed overdrive package, we've essentially got *two 4-speeds*. We've got one 4-speed for performance driving, with the proper ratios for good acceleration. And then, to satisfy the EPA's city driving cycle, what we really have is another 4-speed made up of low gear plus the three overdrive ratios. You launch the car in first gear, same as before, and then if you're below the pre-programmed rpm, you shift into second, which basically signals the computer that you're not shifting into direct second for performance. You want second overdrive for fuel economy. It gives you a second gear that's 0.67 times the normal second gear ratio; it's really sitting above normal third. And you're in overdrive for third and high, too, which means you pick up considerably more than just half a mile per gallon overall." Brian Decker estimates that the Doug Nash overdrive, "...gives us about 2.25 mpg additional, compared with not having it."

For now, there are three unique, different equations or algorithms programmed into the overdrive ECM, one each for second, third, and fourth gears. The overdrive ECM logic, by the way, is incorporated into the same chip that regulates the TBI fuel-injection system and the LCD instrument panel.

I should mention, too, that the new car's shifter, supplied by Inland Tool, has been criticized as not being up to the standard of the old T-10 shifter. That's something Chevrolet is looking into. The new shifter is mounted to the body, not to the transmission, and that leads to linkage alignment problems. On the plus side, though, it also takes most of the vibration out of the shift mechanism and provides a clean in-car environment for the shifter.

Improvements in the Automatic. Let's now take a look at the Corvette's 700-R4

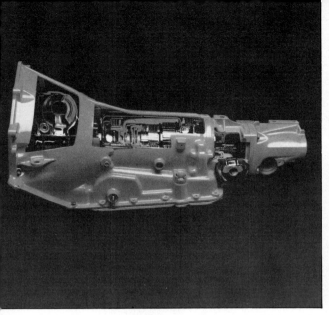

Buyers can also choose Hydramatic 700-R4 automatic transmission with new 2400-rpm stall ratio.

Twin master cylinders (top) add safety, and hydraulic clutch cushions rapid engagement.

Girlock brake calipers combine cast aluminum with iron for rigidity, light weight, plus good heat dissipation.

Turbo Hydramatic (THM). The aluminum case for this transmission got beefed up for the same spike-test reasons as the T-10's. In the automatic's case, though, the test consists of holding the brake on with one foot and applying full throttle with the other, then moving the shift selector between low and reverse. It's called a *rock-cycle* test.

And the automatic incorporates another set of important changes, as Dave McLellan points out. "The automatic transmission now has the high-stall Y5 torque converter: about 2400 rpm stall speed, which makes it good for much better 0-60 times. We've got enough fuel economy improvement so we can put a higher numerical axle ratio in the '84 car than we had in '82. We're looking at a Z-51 ratio of 3.31:l, up from last year's 2.87:l [standard is 3.07:l]. You have to look at that against a transmission that has a lot higher numerical first gear also, so it gives the new car a real leap off the line. And yet this transmission has good mid-range and high-speed performance as well.

"The shift pattern of the 4-speed automatic is now 1-2-3-4, all four fully available. Hydramatic Div. redid the valve body so the transmission will shift into fourth gear at around 110 mph at full throttle, whereas in the original transmission that was missed, because speeds above 55 mph weren't considered relevant. There was no full-throttle upshift. You were always in third gear at full throttle; never in fourth. But Hydramatic found a way to give that final upshift, so it makes for a lot better *Autobahn* cruising.

"We know more about the drag of the car, and we know the top speed is about 142 mph for both the manual and automatic transmission, because they're geared so much alike. With the lockup torque converter, in fact, overdrive ratios are nearly identical [0.70:1 for the automatic; 0.67:1 for manual]. So by juggling axle ratios, we could put our power peak at the top speed of the car."

Girlock Provides the Binders. The Corvette's brakes are unique in that they're pur-

chased from Girlock, Ltd., in Australia. The Girlock company formed when Girling and Lockheed combined. Delco-Morraine Div. usually supplies brakes for all GM cars, but the Corvette goal was to develop a lighter caliper with less drag friction that gave just as good stopping as before.

Notes Brian Decker, "Braking is very important for a car of this type, because part of its performance is having good stopping ability. The previous car had very good brakes in terms of effectiveness, fade resistance, etc. We wanted to maintain that kind of brake performance, so we looked at several different approaches. In mid-1980, we decided Girlock offered the best concept—the best design—for this car. The single-piston calipers are mostly aluminum, although the ring going around the caliper is iron. The caliper bolts directly to our aluminum knuckle. The dust shield is also aluminum.

"Girlock's approach is to combine aluminum and iron. It puts iron where we need iron. We need stiffness in one direction, to eliminate taper or uneven pad wear, and where we could use aluminum, we did to save weight. It's about comparable to Delco's all-aluminum system, but Girlock's features and the combination of iron and aluminum really turned out to be preferable."

The Girlocks still use 11.5-inch rotors, but they're thinner and lighter, with a narrower airgap in the middle. In all, the Girlock system weighs about 71 pounds less than the 1982 Corvette's Delco-Moraine disc setup, a principal advantage being less unsprung weight.

The aluminum master cylinder, vacuum booster, and parking brake also come from Girlock. The parking brake is a drum type, and the drums have a larger diameter than in previous Corvettes. The booster is different from normal GM practice in that the master-cylinder mounting bolts go all the way through the Girlock vacuum canister. In the GM system, the master cylinder bolts to the forward face of the canister only, which puts a stress on the entire booster housing. Girlock's booster can thus be more compact and lighter. □

Chapter 5

Ultimate Handling

Chevy Engineering set some very high handling goals for the 1982 Camaro. I'm talking now about the Camaro, not the Corvette. Tom Zimmer remarked to Fred Schaafsma at one point in the Camaro program that the Z-28 ought to shoot for .90g lateral acceleration. Zimmer meant this half as a joke, yet Schaafsma told me many months later that Tom might have been more serious than anyone suspected.

For the Corvette, the "joke" handling bogie had been set at a presumably unattainable 1.00g maximum lateral acceleration. Only all-out race cars have even approached 1.00g, and the sole streetable sports car in that range, until the Corvette got there, was the BMW M-1, which costs $95,000 and, if you've ever driven one, you'll probably agree that it's not very streetable at that.

So there was some question about 1.00g as a serious figure. If you aim high, though, you hit high. The production '82 Camaro Z-28, after a great deal of hard work, managed to corner consistently at .83g, just above the '82 Corvette's .826g.

Measuring Cornering Capabilities. To measure a car's g-force, or lateral acceleration, GM drives it around a 216-foot circle as fast as it'll go before it starts to slide sideways. One g is the amount of force equal to the pull of gravity. This means that if you're inside a car cornering at 1.0g, your body is pushing against the seat wings or door panel with as many pounds as you weigh. At .83g or .95g, the amount of force your body exerts is 83% and 95% of gravity — or your weight — respectively. At 1.0g, a car exerts its own weight sideways (laterally) as well as down (vertically) at the four tire patches on the road.

Not that ultra-high g's automatically mean a car handles well. High g's are one indication of good handling, but a high-g car sometimes gets beaten through the slalom by one with a lower g rating. That's because lateral acceleration is measured at a steady-state condition, where there's relatively little change in suspension geometry. In a slalom, though, a car's suspension angles change constantly.

The slalom makes a good measure of *transient response*, or how quickly a car can be put through a series of swerves from full left-g to full right-g. Slaloms have become a favorite way for car magazines to report on handling, because they're easy to run and report on in terms of average speed: the faster the better.

But General Motors has come up with a more scientific way to tell transient response. They measure yaw response by driving straight ahead at 60 mph and then suddenly flipping the steering wheel at precise angles to the right or left. Then, by recording the length of time it takes for the car to settle into steady-state cornering, they get a measure — in fractions of a second — of transient response.

Actually they break this measurement down into two components: *rise time*, which means reaching 90% of final turning speed, and decay, the time it takes to

Tire testing progressed throughout Corvette's development, with the target going higher as handling improved. In a leapfrogging process, the tire and suspension engineers tried to top each other.

Corvette corners at over 100 mph (above and opposite page) but shows virtually no lean. Chart below compares Z-51's steering response time with rival cars.

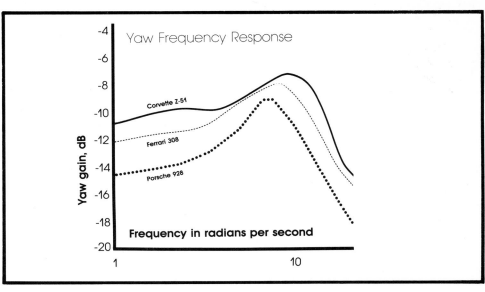

damp out any oscillations. If you look at the charts on page 65, you'll notice that rise time is fairly equal for all the cars compared, because it's dependent largely on tire characteristics. But the Corvette's lack of overshoot means there's essentially no oscillation-damping time involved, and this gives a big advantage in total response time. What this means is that, for any given steering-wheel input, the Corvette reaches the steady-state cornering condition in less than half the time of the next-best production car tested—the Porsche 928. And what this feels like is typical race-car response.

Handling development has become, without a doubt, one of the most complicated, jargon-loaded aspects of any car program and, for an automobile like the Corvette, it's even more complex than most. During the past 15 years, computer science has become increasingly important in making a car handle well, but despite the swift rise of computer analysis, the ultimate instrument remains, and probably always will be, the seat of the engineer's pants.

Ultimate Handling: The Z-51 Package. The Z-51 package makes the new Corvette the best-handling road car ever mass produced. Fred Schaafsma and his ride-and-handling engineers had the major responsibility for determining what the Z-51 package would consist of.

A complete list of Z-51 equipment reads as follows:
- 4 unidirection Goodyear P255/50VR-16 Eagle VR50 blackwall tires;
- 2 unidirectional 16x8JK alloy front wheels;
- 2 unidirectional 16x9JK alloy rear wheels;
- aluminum 16x4 spare wheel and T155/80-16 tire;
- higher front and rear spring rates—from 125 to 165 lb./in. front and 185 to 225 lb./in. rear;
- higher durometer lower control arm bushings front and rear;
- 25mm front stabilizer bar instead of the base 24mm (the Z-51 stabilizer was, at one time, going to be tubular and larger in diameter);
- 23mm rear stabilizer bar instead of the base 20mm;
- heavy-duty and recalibrated Delco shock absorbers (Bilsteins were being considered as this was written);
- 13.0:1 quick-ratio steering in place of the base 15.5:l;
- higher power-steering valve effort;
- 3.31:1 rear axle ratio instead of 3.07:l;
- engine oil cooler (after Apr. 1983);
- aluminum prop shaft;
- aluminum axle shafts.

The Corvette's optional Z-51 package marks the top handling level of an automobile that already stands among the world's best. Yet neither the standard car nor the Z-51 version came into the world handling the way they do. It took considerable work and some frustration on the part of the development engineers to bring the Corvette to its present state of handling sophistication. The fact that the car handles as it does and still rides comfortably and remains so liveable in other ways deserves some historical perspective, because it would be impossible to describe how the Z-51 package developed without explaining how the car as a whole evolved.

The Pre-Prototypes. Dave McLellan got GM's approval on Jan. 22, 1979 to go

Early pre-prototype chassis used conventional frame rails minus the integral birdcage. Suspension engineers experimented with various A-frame forgings.

ahead with what was then seen as the 1982 Corvette program. When the green light flashed on, McLellan and his staff, along with engineers and managers from the Bowling Green plant, got together at the Chevrolet Engineering Center in Warren, Mich., to oversee construction of the first pre-prototypes. At the same time, Bowling Green started looking at the best ways to produce the new car.

In any GM development program, the first iteration of a new design is the called the pre-prototype (or, sometimes, the *component car*). Next comes the prototype, then the pilot model, and finally production. I'll explain what each is and does as we go along.

The intent of the pre-prototype is to come as close to the final structure as possible, but with the understanding that anything can change. Pre-prototypes are mostly handbuilt, and they emphasize the mechanical and structural features of a new car: chassis, suspension, powertrain, steering, brakes, seating position, and overall dimensions.

There's not much emphasis on the pre-prototype's appearance and, in early versions, McLellan simply used 1979-80 Corvette bodies cut down to fit the shorter wheelbase and to approximate the new car's smaller size and lighter weight. Seeing one of these pre-prototypes on the street, most people wouldn't give them a second glance. They looked essentially like roughed-up production 1979-80 Corvettes. Later pre-protos began to take on fiberglass skins that looked more like the '84 car, but only in a rough way.

Early Refinements. The pre-prototypes gave McLellan a chance to move things around underneath and inside the car; to work out details and make refinements. For example, the backbone driveline beam began as a fully enclosed torque tube. It ended

Single trailing arm showed up again on initial rear suspension configurations, but handling complications led to double-link setup that became production.

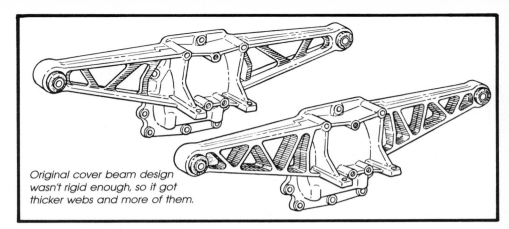

Original cover beam design wasn't rigid enough, so it got thicker webs and more of them.

up as an open C-section member mostly because it leaves the propshaft more accessible.

A big part of the pre-prototype program had to do with designing the uniframe—setting up target frequencies, getting load information at suspension points and drivetrain mounts, optimizing metal gauges in the uniframe, deciding whether to go with HSLA steel and other light metal parts.

It was also on the pre-prototypes that the engineers were able to work out the twin trailing links of the new rear suspension. Early pre-protos tried single trailing arms, fabricated from 1/8-inch flat steel sheet. These were similar to the trailing arms of GM's fwd X-Cars.

The pre-prototypes also used aluminum-block L-48 engines along with pre-production versions of the THM 700-R4. The aluminum L-48 V-8's marked an attempt to get total car weight down to the new Corvette's initial bogies. They weren't considered for production at that time, although as mentioned, an aluminum V-8 might be offered optionally later in this new generation's lifetime.

Another weight-saving idea that McLellan's staff tried was a graphite-fiber propshaft with aluminum ends. Aluminum splines were inserted into the hollow graphite-fiber tube and then either glued or riveted. Why this idea was abandoned I don't know.

Manual-transmissioned pre-protos carried the 1978-81 Warner T-10, but without the Doug Nash overdrive. It was at this stage, in fact, that Brian Decker tried to adapt ancient Warner Gear overdrives that he'd gotten from wrecking yards. Pre-prototype development continued from early 1979 through mid-1981. As individual prototype parts became available, they were incorporated into the pre-protos to make sure they fit and functioned.

Prototypes Come On Stream. Then, in Sept. 1981, McLellan and his people began to take delivery of the first true prototypes. Prototypes, by definition, are made up of the earliest "production" parts built off soft tools. In other words, a prototype car is hand-assembled, same as the pre-prototype, but it's made mostly from production-design parts, some supplied by the actual component manufacturers and others made by Chevrolet or prototype shops.

Prototypes were assembled at General Motors Assembly Research Center in Flint, Mich. They carried handmade bodies that closely approximated the final lines and shape of the production car.

By the time the prototypes arrived, a lot of the coarse computer work had already been finished. Trouble was, though, that much of it had been done for cars with the T-top roof. Suddenly, in 1979, Chevrolet decided to change from the T-top configuration to an open targa roof. This change, which sounds so simple in the telling, made for a totally different car and caused some painful teething problems.

Throughout the program, Chevrolet's engineering management kept an eye on the Corvette's developmental progress. They'd driven early T-top pre-prototypes, then the targa-top pre-prototypes, and they were now beginning to drive targa-top prototypes. Unfortunately, they found those earliest targa samples not to their liking. The cars didn't sound, feel, or ride as they should. More seriously, they didn't handle very well—didn't really show enough handling superiority over the Corvettes they were designed to replace.

McLellan and the Corvette's other top development engineers knew that handling refinement takes time. They recognized immediately that they needed more manpower. And it had to be manpower with very specialized knowledge. Here's where the car's accelerated handling development program began—at the transition from pre-prototype to prototype. Computers were about to play an even greater role than in the past.

Enter Fred Schaafsma. Tom Zimmer, who in those days had charge of Chevrolet's B- and F-Car engineering, suggested to his bosses, Ed Mertz and Paul King, that they reassign Fred Schaafsma from Camaro ride-and-handling development to the Corvette project. Schaafsma had just finished the program that gave the third-generation Z-28 its outstanding handling. He'd earlier been instrumental in bringing good handling to the downsized 1977 Caprice.

Today, Fred specializes in handling development, and I don't believe it's an exaggeration to say that he's the best in the business. Schaafsma has surrounded himself with young, bright, capable engineers, among them Larry Fletcher, Rick Darling,

Ride-and-handling engineer Fred Schaafsma came to the Corvette program after grooming the '82 Camaro. His work with structure brought the Z-51 to .95g.

Doug Ego, and Lee Mundy. Jim Ingle, who'd been the principal Corvette ride-and-handling engineer from the beginning of this program, stayed on alongside Schaafsma. Together they've become a self-contained handling clinic.

His parents brought Freerk Jetze (Fred) Schaafsma to America from Holland in 1962. He was 15. As a teenager, he liked to take things apart to see what made them work. He graduated from high school in Royal Oak, Mich., and entered General Motors Institute in Flint in 1965. Chevrolet sponsored him through GMI, and he officially went to work for the division in 1969.

"I got assigned to the Corvette project in early Aug. 1981," recalls Fred, "and I could tell immediately from the computer readouts that the pre-prototype's suspension and body frequencies were too close together. When we finally got the first prototype about a month later, it certainly didn't feel the way it should. So very quickly —within a week or two—we took the car to Mesa [GM's desert proving ground near Phoenix], where it was scheduled for cooling work, and we spent a weekend—Friday through Sunday—doing some preliminary structural probing.

"Now, the 16-inch tires are pretty stiff, as they have to be for good handling. The mass [weight] of the suspension is relatively low due to all the aluminum. That, in essence, gets the suspension frequency up higher than usual. Ordinarily you expect suspension resonant frequencies of 10-12 Hz [a Hertz or Hz is a measure of frequency equal to one cycle per second]. What you usually find is that the frequencies of the car's body are significantly higher—around 26-30 Hz. You want that gap, because if suspension and structural frequencies are too close together, the body gets too excitable. It drums or buzzes. But in the Corvette prototype, suspension and structural frequencies were each too close at between 14 and 16 Hz, which was not a good situation."

How do you separate these frequencies? The trick was to stiffen the Corvette's structure; not necessarily to make it stronger but to make it more rigid. This causes structural frequencies to go up and their amplitudes to come down.

"We also had a beaming frequency that was as low as 14 Hz," continues

Schaafsma. "And it was coupled with a torsional frequency. There was also a separate front-end beaming frequency; in other words, a discontinuity in the structure ahead of the front-of-dash. Then we had some more beaming frequencies in the 16-Hz range. Torsional frequencies were around 16 Hz, too; thereabouts. When I first saw that data on paper, even before we got the prototype, I said, Hey, we've got to do a lot of structural work. So that's what we've been working on since I got into the program, and we've come up with a structure for the Corvette that we feel is very, very good."

What Did He Just Say? I believe it might be appropriate here to explain what Fred's talking about. Think not of the new Corvette's uniframe but, for the purpose of illustration, imagine an old-fashioned ladder-type frame without a body on it.

If you drive this ladder frame over a rough road, the rails will bend a little as the suspension attachments move up and down. If it's a fairly weak frame, the middle of the rails might bow up and down appreciably. That side-rail bending action is called beaming.

Now if the frame twists as it goes over a rough road; that is, if the bending action stretches from a front corner to an opposite rear corner, it's called torsion.

These beaming and torsional motions can be simple or complex. For example, the side rail might not be just heaving up and down at its middle but might have a double heave, with the center of the rail staying relatively still and two smaller arcs moving up and down in a horizontal S shape fore and aft of that center point. Compare the frame with a violin string. You can pluck the string and it'll vibrate up and down just in the middle. But play the string with a bow and you're likely to get a whole series of little S-shaped vibrations all along it.

The shapes of beaming or torsional bends are called modes; engineers talk about *mode shapes* and *modal analysis*. To make things even more confusing, the point where the frame stays still—as at the suspension points or in the middle of the S—is called the *node*.

The bending motions of a car frame, like the vibration of a violin string, have natural frequencies. Motion sickness is caused by a frequency you might be familiar with. It's in the neighborhood of 5-8 Hz. You feel it in your gut. Rumble is caused by slightly higher frequencies that vibrate together.

Generally, handling frequencies are on the order of one Hz; ride frequencies range between 10 and 40 Hz, and acoustics are over 100 Hz. What engineers refer to as "noise and vibration" encompasses the range between 10 and 200 Hz.

Adding Stiffness to the Structure. Schaafsma's goal became, as with the Z-28, to get "handling via structure." You can't get crisp handling if the car's structure remains free to twist and bend. Weak structure is like Jello on wheels, where steering response becomes one long chain reaction of individual parts following each other through a turn. You want everything to move together as one rigid unit. Precisely. At the same split second. The greatest suspension system in the world can't work without a good, stiff, solid structure to bolt it to. So Fred attacked both problems—ride harshness and handling—at the structural level.

That first weekend at Mesa gave Schaafsma and his team a chance to do a quick structural evaluation, based on preliminary computer frequency analyses. They also "poked some sticks" at the structure, as Fred calls it, which meant putting a few crude fixes into the prototype. They installed K-braces behind the engine crossmember plus two other braces in the uniframe's front-of-dash area. These weren't intended as final; the engineers were simply looking for reactions. Nonetheless, the production K-braces turned out very much like those fabricated in Mesa that weekend, and the other two, while modified, also made it into production.

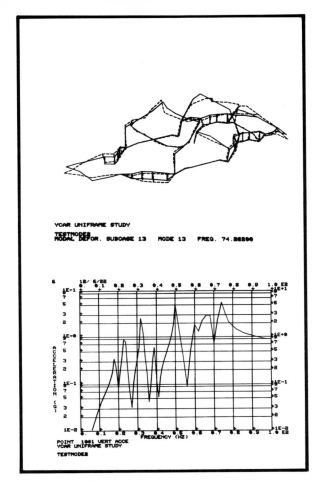

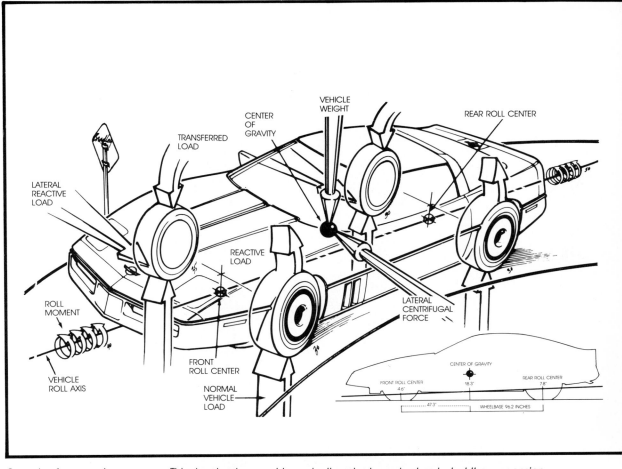

Using multiple, movable sensors, computer could analyze frequencies and wobbles over a real road.

Complex forces act on any car. This drawing is meant to make it easier to understand what the suspension engineers are talking about. Inset gives roll-center heights and locates the Corvette's center of gravity.

"The car began to respond," says Fred, "so then we brought the prototype into the lab and made shaker measurements." Making shaker measurements in this case meant setting the uniframe on inflated truck inner tubes, connecting mechanical shakers to the uniframe, and moving an accelerometer all along the structure. Then, using the accelerometer readouts, the computer is able to construct a simulated model of the car.

This computer model can be seen and read in several ways: as a moving cartoon on a video screen, as a printed line drawing with the beaming and torsional modes exaggerated beyond the real uniframe structure, as a chart whose spikes show the frequencies and their amplitudes, or as a long strip of numbers that only a computer technician can read. At any rate, the "pictures" drawn by the computer told Fred where to find the weak points in the structure.

"Based on that," notes Schaafsma, "we found where the discontinuities were. We knew that the large rockers were very, very stiff, because that showed up on the model. However, the front and rear frame extremities showed discontinuities. [*Discontinuities* are points between rigid and non-rigid members; for example, between the rockers and the front frame rails or between the windshield and cowl.] So based on that, we cobbled braces and gussets into the prototype car and tested it again in the lab."

Schaafsma hastens to add that his development group didn't work alone. Design engineer Walt Jaeger and structural analysis engineer Dolph Lohwasser continually modified and incorporated changes in the uniframe in concert with the development engineers' conclusions. Hal Nimer and Bill Parker from GMAD tooling also became involved because of changes that affected production assembly tooling. Everyone had to stay in close touch to keep the program rolling in the right direction.

Lee Mundy Discovers a Breakthrough. Shaker analyses in the lab proved a great asset. But then Lee Mundy got an inspiration — an important idea that no one had ever considered before. Lee Mundy, along with Doug Ego, worked out a system for evaluating and computer-analyzing an actual car as it ran down a real-world road. For the first time, they could instrument the car in its natural setting rather than just in the lab. In other words, the prototype could now be driven over a test loop at varying speeds, and its structural deflections could be measured at the same time. Now the inputs are natural and give a much better insight into how the car reacts to design modifications in the real world.

Using a relatively portable computer — a Hewlett-Packard Fourier analyzer — parked inside the Chevrolet garage at GM's desert proving ground, Mundy and Ego placed accelerometers all over the Corvette prototype's engine, body, and uniframe. I'm leaving out some details, but they selected roughly 40 sites per car, with one accelerometer moved around to each site, plus another at both front spindles to normalize or give reference points to the rest. The accelerometers broadcast tiny movements via radio signals to the Fourier analyzer, and the analyzer — linked by telephone modem from GM's Arizona proving ground to GM's Test Mode II computer program in Warren, Mich. — put together a picture of what the Corvette's structure was doing as the car ran again and again over the same pre-selected test loop.

GM's Test Mode II computer uses the NASTRAN program, developed by NASA in the Sixties for the space effort. It became available to private industry in the Seventies and has been used in developing every GM automobile since the 1977 B-Car.

Schaafsma continues, "I had a hunch the problem was a certain type of beaming. We drove the car over this particular road section time after time. By normalizing the accelerometers to the front spindles, we had a baseline. Since everything wiggled from there, Lee could construct what the structure's mode shapes looked like.

"Well, lo and behold, the mode shape I was complaining about was not a true beaming; neither was it a true torsion. It was a combination; almost a wobble, like a gallop. The uniframe was galloping down the road. Once we knew that, we learned how to attack it.

"Beyond that, Lee was able to take that modal, m-o-d-a-l, and turn it into a model, m-o-d-e-l. That was pretty significant, because then he could work on the model and tell us not only what was troubling us but what to do about it. We called it our what-if program. What if we put a certain gusset here, or a shear plate there?

"He'd tell me that he tried these what-if computer fixes on the model and, out of the 10 he tried, maybe two looked like they were worth pursuing. Doug built them into the car, and there wasn't a single time that Lee sent us down a blind alley."

The net result was that the Corvette prototype's structural development time went from a normal 18 months to something like six months. That's very significant.

Optimizing the Structure. Doug Ego mentions that, "We'd never analyzed a targa roof before, and when it was modeled on the computer, we had to make some estimates of the stiffness that would transfer load into the hatch roof from the quick-release latches. These latches were originally similar to the type we'd had on the '82 Corvette.

"When we got the prototype on the road, we found that those assumptions were way too stiff. The latches weren't able to transmit as much load into the hatch as the car wanted; they'd actually pop open.

"So we had to go from the quick-release latches to a bolt-on hatch roof. We measured the maximum load going through the latches and found it to be about half a ton."

The targa roof created other problems as well. The first versions leaked water, and sealing them proved more difficult than in conventional T-tops. Roger Schroeder and John Schejbal worked together to come up with good weatherstripping and rollup windows, which Ron Burns feels makes the Corvette "the best-sealed car of this type

Fourier analyzer at GM's Arizona test site allowed Mundy and Ego to break new ground in modal analyses. By "watching" an actual car bounce over a real road, they could suggest beefing up uniframe to make it rigid yet lightweight.

in the industry." Schroeder also worked out the roof hardware so that the attachments would not only carry the required loads but would meet buildability requirements and still let the driver remove the roof without too much hassle.

Fred continues the narrative: "We still felt we were structurally below where we wanted to be, but we did want to keep the open targa roof. So we decided that maybe we ought to bolt the roof panel in instead of using the latches. That made a tremendous difference, and although it makes the roof a little more cumbersome, we think it's worth it.

"Up front we added what we call a *wonder bar*. Because of the open roof, we needed to control some of the front-end torsion, so there's now the wonder bar—the torsion tube ahead of the engine crossmember. The wonder bar increases front frame stiffness.

"Why do we call it the wonder bar? That's a little inside joke. One of our draftsmen couldn't understand what the wonder bar was trying to accomplish, so he wondered what the bar was. Others said, Gee, that bar does wonders!"

The structural engineers also turned their attention to the big aluminum differential cover and beam that connects the rear axle housing to the aluminum rear frame rails. The beam went through several design changes before it was deemed stiff enough. The earlier versions used relatively thin webbing in V and I shapes, while the final rendition has thick, W-shaped webs. Likewise, the bushings that fasten the beam to the frame rails became stiffer as the program went along, as did the engine mounts.

Wouldn't Allow Scarring Surgery. Fred encouraged Chevrolet's development engineers, including his own staff, not to deface the prototypes. So often, when a brace or gusset goes into such a car, the mechanic or technician simply cuts a hole in the skin and bolts or welds the piece in place, often without patching the hole. That's why they call it *cobbling*.

"I felt," says Schaafsma, "that it would be bad for morale to mess up the prototypes unless we absolutely had to. I feel a car in good condition makes people prouder to work on it, and it surely looks better in those sneak photos."

Resuming his explanation of specific fixes, Fred continues, "We also added triangulating braces to the aluminum cross brace under the instrument panel. The aluminum member pulls together the hinge pillars. In addition, we put vertical shear plates ahead of the instruments and similarly, another shear plate at the right-hand side of the dash. Those were installed mostly to reduce lateral shake between the windshield pillars and roof rollbar, but they helped us with handling, too. The front-of-dash now acts essentially as a shear wall. We filled in some holes in the bulkhead behind the seats for noise reduction, and added gussets at the rear tub crossmember.

"The doors in our early prototypes had plastic side impact beams. Doug Ego convinced the door guys to replace those with steel beams to help strengthen the doors. There was also an aluminum door pin mechanism that we ended up replacing with steel and using to tie the body structure together better at the door opening."

Fine-Tuning the System. Fred Schaafsma offers several anecdotes in the area of fine-tuning the Corvette's ride-and-handling, and I feel they bear repeating, especially since they illustrate the care and attention that went into optimizing the car. The first story involves suspension bushing durometers.

"The bushing for the front lower control arms are the same size as for the rear," begins Fred, "and you can't tell the difference by just looking. We specified different rates for those bushings, but the supplier split the difference and sent us bushings with the same rate for both ends of the car.

"That wouldn't be a big thing with most suspension systems, but if we'd wanted the same rate, we would have asked for it. We specifically asked for different rates.

After Schaafsma and Fletcher broke 1.0g at Milford proving ground, Goodyear placed this full-page announcement in AutoWeek.

When we got the pilot models with those bushings installed, we could tell something was wrong. It was basically there, but not quite. We check everything as a matter of course—check the durometers of all the bushings and other rubber components. So we found the problem and asked the supplier to go with our original specs."

Another example arose during pilot assembly. "We dug in our heels when Bowling Green wanted to improve access to a specific bolt by notching the right-hand K-brace. We ended up moving the brace slightly, but we managed not to compromise stiffness."

Going for the Big One Gee. "We were now at the point where we're very happy with the basic structure," recalls Fred Schaafsma. "I could take the roof panel out and get a level of handling that I'd certainly be willing to live with. We had recently begun running lateral acceleration tests on the car, and I knew the figures were going to be high, but I was a little surprised when we found out it was .95g. I figured it would be over .90g, but .95g is really right up there:

"When you're up at .90g-.95g, although I don't feel that's an indication of a car's overall handling capabilities, it does become awfully enticing to see what it would take to break 1.0g. It's one of those things you can't leave alone.

"We had a lot of work to do aside from handling, so we didn't get to the skidpad tests until the week before Thanksgiving 1982. In fact, Larry Fletcher ran the test that Wednesday night — the day before Thanksgiving. We'd wanted to run it out in Phoenix, but they'd just resurfaced the skidpad. The coefficient of friction had been coming up as the pavement was curing, but it wasn't high enough yet, and I couldn't even duplicate my .95g on it. So I said, Nuts, I'm going to ship the car back to Milford, which I did, and the car got there Tuesday night. Larry had gotten in the

Roll Gain

Roll angle in degrees

5°	
4°	Ferrari 308
	Porsche 928
3°	
2°	Corvette Z-51
1°	
0	0.8g 0.9g 1.0g

Lateral acceleration in gravity (g)

Corvette's roll gain (or lean) near limits of adhesion remains well below that of rivals. And while most low-roll cars compromise riding qualities, Chevrolet engineers managed to avoid that sacrifice.

night before, so he was at work, but the skidpad in Milford was iced over due to freezing rain the day before.

"We were going to be there just for the day — a Wednesday — because the next day was Thanksgiving, and Friday we were due back at the desert proving ground to prepare for the Corvette's long-lead press preview. I got off the red-eye from Phoenix around 9:00 a.m. Wednesday, went home, took a shower, napped for a while, and when I got up, Larry told me the skidpad had ice on it. But around 4:00 in the afternoon, the ice had melted, and we got the green light.

"We put the 9½-inch wheels on the front and rear of the car. The only thing I wanted to be sure of was that we run the car with full tread-depth tires, not shaved. And we concocted what we felt we needed in terms of suspension alignment, which was 5° caster instead of 3°, plus about 2° negative camber. Fletcher ran the tests, playing with tire pressures until we got a final reading of 1.01g. It was like breaking the sound barrier!

"By the time I got home again, I was higher than a kite. I told my wife, You won't believe what we did: We got 1.01g! And she said, Oh, that's great! She knew I was very excited. I was thrilled. It was interesting, because I called [Tom] Zimmer at home, and I said, I gotta tell you this. We pulled 1.01g. I really felt so good about it. That's what we did out there."

Suspension Tuning. The previous Corvette was truly not a bad-handling car, especially when you consider that its suspension design harks back to the very early Sixties. According to *Road & Track,* the 1982 car with the FE-7 suspension could pull .826g on the skidpad with stock (and very good) 255/60 Goodyear Eagle GT tires, and that's better than the Ferrari 308-GTsi, Porsche 911 and 944, or Audi Quattro.

Even so, 1963-82 Corvettes have a reputation for several quirks that McLellan, Decker, and the other suspension engineers managed to get rid of. For example, older Vettes have a notorious reputation for rear roll oversteer and compliance, or "give," induced by a combination of deflection in the rear-axle halfshafts and the rubber anchors of the single trailing arm.

And up front, because the previous steering tie rods stood behind the axle centerline, the 1963-82 Corvettes suffered from deflection oversteer. This came about when side forces in effect shortened the control arms more than the lateral steering linkages and caused the tires to steer inward during hard cornering. Deflection oversteer gives the feeling that the car wants to cut more sharply into the turn than the driver wants it to. It's harder to control than deflection understeer, both in development and during driving.

The new Corvette's front suspension benefits by having the steering tie rods ahead of the axle centerline. There's no way to get rid of all deflections, but with the steering linkage ahead of the axle, the toe changes now point outward instead of inward and cause *deflection understeer,* which is much more predictable and easier to control. Instead of trying to turn more sharply into a corner, the new car tries—in a very mild way—to keep going straight, which simply means the driver cranks in a little more steering angle to correct the situation. It's easier, in fast cornering maneuvers, to twist more lock into the steering wheel than it is to judge how much to back off.

Controlling Ride Steer. We talked in Chapter 4 about the front spindles' 12mm offset. The main reason for this offset has to do with the new Corvette's handling, and its effect is best explained by first imagining an ordinary automobile's conventional front spindle location.

Normally, the front spindle is in line with the upper and lower balljoints. The angle

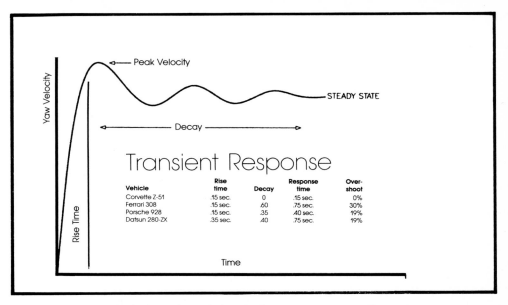

This chart gives a typical sports car's transient response curve, with peak showing overshoot, then some wavy decay oscillations leading to steady state.

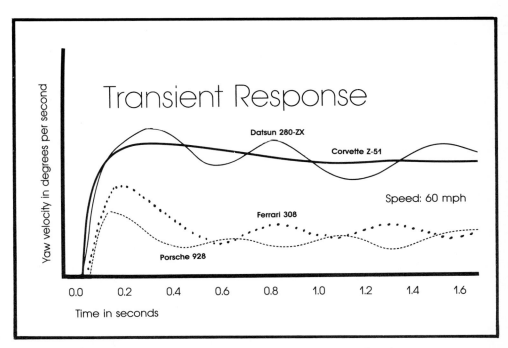

Corvette's transient response curve shows no overshoot at all, and there's no oscillation. Z-51 suspension allows for an easy ride with cornering tautness.

of this line from vertical is the caster angle, and the intersection of this line with the ground locates the trail distance from the middle of the tire patch on the road. The principal virtue of caster is that it makes a car track straight, but more angle is not always better, because it can make the steering feel heavy. Also, as you decrease caster alignment with a front-steer knuckle design, you also increase ride steer, because the steering-arm angle changes.

"One thing I did when we got those first prototypes," says Schaafsma, "was to redesign the front knuckle. We stuck with 3° caster, down from the initial design of 5°, rather than going down to maybe 1.5°, which I personally would have liked. And we stuck with the 12mm offset. We'd been experimenting with 12mm offset for years. The combination of 3° actual caster plus the 12mm offset gives us enough trail to equal 5.5° effective caster without any of the drawbacks of a lot of caster. And by correcting the steer-arm position, we've managed to get almost zero ride or roll steer with no reduction in straight-line stability."

Some Words About Roll. Body roll not only looks ungainly, but it's bad because it keeps a car from pressing all four wheels firmly against the ground. A car whose body rolls a lot eventually puts the tires at angles to the road.

Chevrolet's engineers managed to get the new Corvette to roll very little in turns: only about 2° per g. Most other streetable sports cars have a roll angle of 4° or more, and 2° is normally reserved for all-out competition cars. Competition cars get their low roll angle by sacrificing ride but, as you've noticed, the Corvette hasn't sacrificed riding qualities. So how did the ride-and-handling guys do it?

One way was to use relatively soft rubber spring mounts. These bushings take up the first fraction of a degree of roll. Then the springs, which are fairly stiff, come into play and hold down the rest of the roll rate.

Another factor that holds down body roll is the positioning of the suspension's roll centers in relation to the center of gravity (cg). Front and rear roll-center heights are among the first determinants of oversteer/understeer of any car, and they also have a lot to do with roll angle. To explain, let's take a hypothetical case.

Let's say that you engineer a car with identical spring rates fore and aft. Types of springs and suspension systems don't matter; the only given is that it's a 4-wheel independent setup. Now let's exaggerate again and say that both the front and rear roll centers stand 36 inches off the ground. In this example, the car's center of gravity

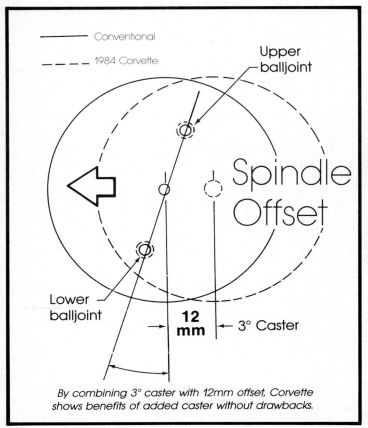

By combining 3° caster with 12mm offset, Corvette shows benefits of added caster without drawbacks.

Corvette engineers interrupt prototype testing to swap opinions and make adjustments to engine, suspension, and instrumentation.

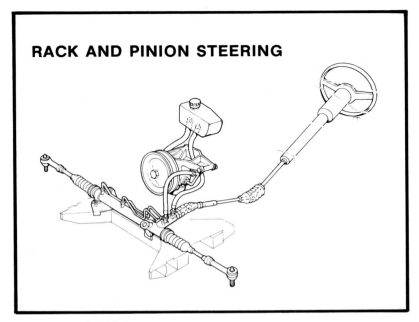

RACK AND PINION STEERING

Steering U-joints are sealed to prevent corrosion, and they're also set to take full advantage of natural fast/slow positioning. They're fastest on center.

Modified X-Car rack and pinion rides ahead of front axle, which helps lower the engine and eliminates previous model's undesirable oversteer bump steer.

would have to be *below* the roll center, and the car would bank in the *opposite* direction from normal—into the turn. Sounds great, doesn't it? After all, the car's now creating its own banking. But unfortunately, you really can't have that, because your suspension arms would be so inclined that ride travel would be severely compromised.

Now, if the roll center were at ground level and the center of gravity were *above* that, the car would roll very heavily *out* of the turn. Lots of body roll. But if you had your roll center front and rear at exactly the same height as the center of gravity, the car wouldn't roll at all.

So you can begin to see that the height of the roll center, in relation to a car's center of gravity, is a means of resisting roll without involving the springs. It's one of the things you have to take into account when designing any suspension system, and it's always a tradeoff. You'd like to have the roll center high to resist roll, but the higher you get it with independent suspensions, the more negative camber you get in a turn — a phenomenon called *jacking*. It occurs particularly when a car's roll axis is inclined, and it makes the tires come up on edge. They tend to dig in, and the car, in effect, tries to polevault over them.

At any rate, Corvette engineers have kept the front roll center pretty much the same since 1963. It's been at about 4.4 inches for all these years. But at the rear, it was 7.5 inches in 1963, then 4.7 in 1968 to get less jacking, and for 1984 Chevrolet raised it back up to 7.9 inches.

Now the question remains, How do you raise and lower a Corvette's rear roll center? You do it by changing the angle of the lower lateral strut. The axle shaft will always assume the same horizontal angle, so the outer location of the lateral strut is always fixed. But the inner mounting location is relatively easy to change. By mov-

ing the inner mount up or down fractions of an inch, you determine the rear roll-center height and thus, to a large extent, the car's roll angle.

Solidifying the Steering. The Corvette's rack-and-pinion steering is very similar in design to the X-Car's, which is also aluminum. Aluminum, as you know, has an inherently lower modulus of elasticity than steel; it's only about ⅓ as stiff. That meant that the aluminum steering rack had to be tied down as solidly as possible to the front crossmember. It also meant that the crossmember attachments to the uniframe had to be made tremendously rigid, which they weren't when Fred Schaafsma and his people received the first prototypes.

"We did quite a bit of nailing down of the rack," mentions Fred. "We couldn't mount the steering gear completely solid, because the steering wheel would be so buzzy you couldn't stand it. But we put a bushing in the mount that's basically solid. It has just a 3mm thickness of rubber—very, very thin. We wanted barely enough rubber to give us some isolation and take care of valve hiss. Then on the right-hand side, we've got an aluminum strap-type mount."

The intermediate shaft in the steering column has two U-joints to allow for offset and, as Fred puts it, "A U-joint is inherently a speed-up, slow-down member unless you've got a double joint at each location. So I suggested we take advantage of that. Ideally, the fastest U-joint action should come right on center. We fussed with it and had a little trouble, but Rick Darling managed to set the steering up that way, and I think it's very important.

"Another thing we contended with," continues Fred, "was the stiffness of the bearings inside the steering column: making sure they weren't sloppy. We wanted to make sure the sliding feature of the telescoping column didn't get sloppy in the rotational direction due to the looseness it needed to slide up and down." □

Chapter 6
In the Driver's Seat

This being a driver's car, the interior becomes extremely important. And, as anyone who's folded himself behind the new Corvette's steering wheel knows, there's an awful lot going on inside this automobile.

I'd like to use this chapter to talk about the LCD instrument panel, the standard and Sport seats, and especially the Delco-Bose sound system.

The LCD Instruments. "We were always committed to an electronic instrument panel," reflects panels-and-trim engineer Paul H. Huzzard, "and I have to give great credit to Dave McLellan for that. Dave said from the beginning that the car should have visual impact when people first see it, and when they open the doors, they should be just as impressed. Dave was very much a driving force behind the electronic system."

Most electronic instrument panels on the market at the time of the Corvette's creation — those in the Lincoln Continental, Toyota Supra, Datsun Maxima, etc. —

were not liquid crystal displays (LCD) but rather used light-emitting diodes (LED). A third type of electronic display, namely the vacuum fluorescent tube (VF), has also been used in cars and was considered for the Corvette. All three have advantages and drawbacks, but LCD's can do things that LED's and VF's can't.

For example, LCD offers a much broader range of colors and graphics. That's important to the designer, who wants as much latitude as possible. LED and VF come in only two or three colors, and the colors are hard to combine. Second, LCD tends to be easier to read in bright sunlight; doesn't wash out as readily as LED and VF. Finally, LCD's draw very little current, and they're easy to control with a microprocessor.

However, at the time General Motors began looking into LCD technology, liquid crystals also showed some rather awkward problems. For example, large LCD's didn't work well under temperature extremes. Corvette engineers found that Arizona's summer heat would build up inside a parked car and made the displays go

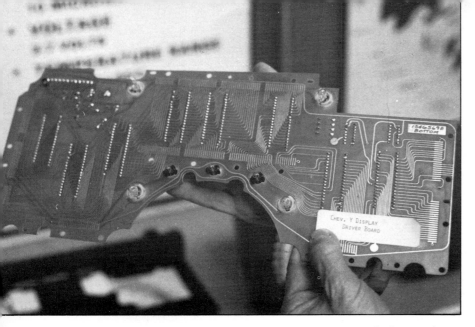

(Above) Printed circuit behind liquid-crystal panel powers displays and contains small lamps for backlighting. *(Right)* The secret to understanding how an LCD works is to focus on firecracker-shaped molecules in center of drawing. Unenergized, they twist 90°. Light follows this twist and can't pass through rear polarizer. Energizing straightens them out so polarized light goes through.

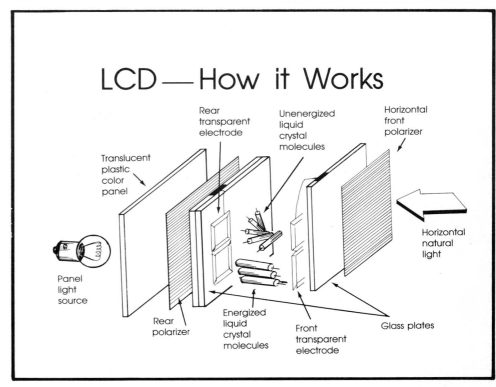

LCD—How it Works

blank or "blind." Then in Minnesota, below-zero cold slowed down the LCD's rate of display movement, so that the numbers and telltales didn't keep up with actual events. In very cold weather and before the car's interior warmed up, the LCD speedometer in an accelerating automobile might momentarily register only 40 mph when the car had actually reached 45 mph.

Development of automotive LCD displays at GM began in 1978 and, in the Corvette's case, became the responsibility of General Motors' AC Spark Plug Div. in Flint, Mich. Because no one knew for certain that an LCD instrument panel and its manufacturing processes could be perfected in time for Corvette production, AC developed a mechanical gauge cluster as backup, just in case. We touched on that in Chapter 3.

How an LCD Works. LCD's are used, as you're aware, in digital wristwatches, certain hand-held calculators, and most recently in the light-metering monitors of 35mm cameras. The only other automobiles sold in the U.S., though, that offer LCD instruments (at this writing) are the Mitsubishi Cordia and Starion.

Before we examine the Corvette's LCD panel in detail, it might be interesting to see how liquid crystal displays work. They're not terribly complicated.

An LCD operates on the principle of electric polarization. Imagine millions of tiny, crystalline, firecracker-shaped molecules suspended in a very thin layer of oil. The oil is held between two parallel sheets of glass that stand a mere 0.0005 inch apart. The glass is sealed on all sides so the liquid crystal solution can't leak out.

In their natural state, bundles of these firecracker-like molecules assume a 90 twist. It's as if you tied a string of them together around their middles and then

twisted the string so the front firecracker ends up lying horizontal and the rear one ends up being vertical.

Now let's say we place twin horizontal polarizers in front of and behind the two glass plates. That means that light enters the front polarizer, but it's twisted 90 by the liquid crystal molecules, so when it hits the rear polarizer the light ends up being vertical. A vertical polarizer against the horizontal polarizer blocks the light and, in effect, makes the front surface look black.

Now we come to the crucial quality of liquid crystals. The individual firecracker-like molecules have the capacity to act like tiny dipole magnets. Each one is polarized itself; not to light but to electricity. We can call one end of the firecracker "plus" and their other end "minus."

If you place two sets of transparent, virtually invisible electrodes on both inner surfaces of the glass and create an electric field between them, these firecracker-shaped molecules will stand on end—arrange themselves with their plus ends pointing outward, perpendicular to the glass. And when that happens, the molecules no longer reflect or twist the light. You're now seeing them on end, not their side surfaces. You can see right through or past them.

What makes a liquid crystal display arrange itself into numbers or letters or graphic patterns is the fact that the engineer has etched these invisible conductive strips to the inner surfaces of the glass and then selectively run current to the electrodes. These electrodes, or conductive strips, look like clear cellophane, but they conduct electricity and can set up an electric field. Current is brought in from the edge of the glass, where conductive rubber strips make the connection to the driver electronics and eventually to the microprocessor circuitry.

To compose numerals, there's the traditional pattern of seven segments made up of these clear, conductive strips. Each segment can be energized separately, and when they're all energized together, the figure 8 appears. The numeral 1 needs only two segments energized, 3 needs five, and so forth. And that's basically what makes a liquid crystal display work.

Light and Color. One of the beauties of this system is that the dipole crystals normally react very quickly to electricity. The instant the electrodes are energized, the liquid-crystal molecules turn on end, and you see through or past them. In the case of your wristwatch, the numerals appear black, because you're seeing a black background.

In the case of Corvette instruments, there's a translucent sheet of colored plastic behind that second polarizer, with little light bulbs beyond that, illuminating the display from behind. That's why you see colored figures and patterns. If the Corvette LCD weren't backlit through the colored plastic film at night, all the displays would appear clear against a black background, and you wouldn't be able to see them very well. During the day, the ambient light hits the color sheet and combines with the backlight to provide the necessary brightness for good visibility.

Now there's another clever aspect to the Corvette system that you might not be aware of. Up near the left-hand corner of the dashboard, there's a tiny photocell. It's a lot like the light receptor on a camera—the one that tells the aperture to open or stop down. This photocell measures the ambient light inside the Corvette's cockpit and adjusts the brightness of the little bulbs behind the display panels. In daylight with the roof panel off, the photocell will give the bulbs full power so they'll over-come the washing-out effect of the sun. At night, the photocell will dim the bulbs just enough to make the instruments visible but not annoying. And it's receptive to all light conditions in between, even making quick adjustments as the car passes, say, under a bridge in daytime or past a brightly lit building at night.

You can also dim the instrument cluster manually, of course, anytime the headlights are on. Furthermore, if you forget to turn on your headlights at dusk, the photo cell gradually dims the instruments to remind you to turn the headlamps on.

Instrument Panel Details. The Corvette instrument panel consists not of one big LCD but of three smaller, individual ones. From left to right, these separate displays are: 1) speedometer, 2) driver information center, and 3) tachometer. Each is distinct from the rest and replaceable as a unit.

They're all driven from an 8K computer (microprocessor) that takes its information from fairly standard sending units. If you're familiar with, say, the engine-mounted senders for normal oil-pressure and temperature gauges, you'd certainly recognize those same sending units on the Corvette. The notable difference is that, before the signal gets to the computer, it's digitized by an analogue/digital converter within the unit. The computer then takes that digitized data, reads it, and calculates what the LCD's should read.

Some Subtle Functions. The computer itself has been programmed to recognize abnormal and dangerous conditions. "It's a lot smarter than your average idiot light," says Chevrolet electrical design engineer Kenneth T. (Ken) Milne, Jr. "For instance, take our oil-pressure sensor. Normally, the instrument engineer has to pick

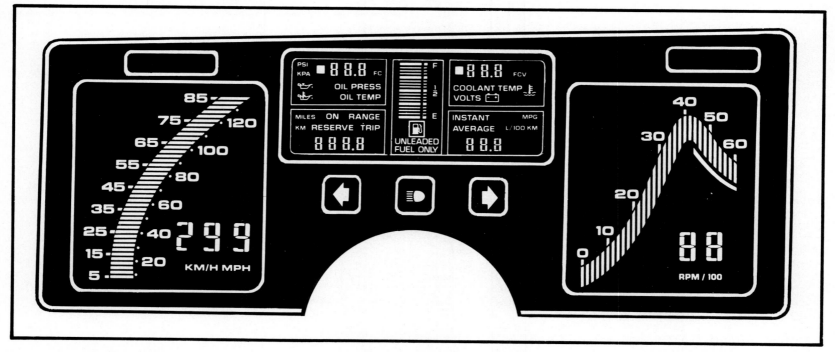

Switch panel above the console controls digital readouts (shown opposite) in metric or English.

AC Custom Cruise III senses speed off transmission, shares turn-signal lever with dimmer switch.

Window switches flank primary mirror regulator, with mirror, optional seat controls down in recess.

Leather-wrapped manual shifter attaches to body rather than trans. Collar below is reverse lockout.

Console storage comes with tape tray, coin holder, and pushbutton release for the glass hatch.

Aerodynamic outside mirror adjusts electrically and can be heated to melt away frost and ice.

Nameplates adorn the Corvette's brake pedal as well as the big breadloaf ahead of the passenger.

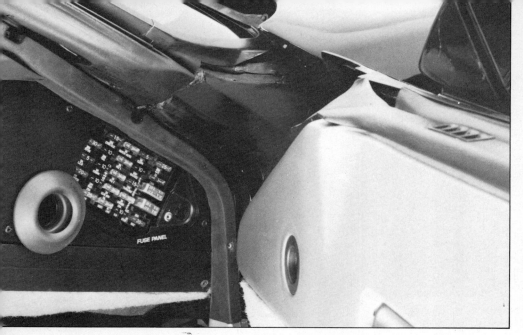

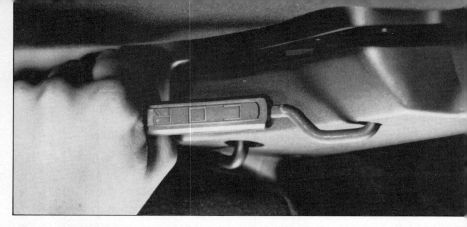

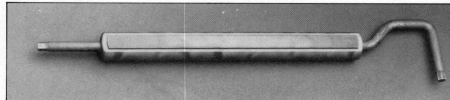

Duct next to very accessible fuse panel feeds warm air to outlet atop window sill. This demists side glass so that driver can use the outside rearview mirror.

You need a special tool to remove or tighten lift-out roof panel. Curved end gives greater mechanical advantage, while opposite end speeds twisting.

a certain pressure that turns the telltale on. In most cars, we turn it on when the pressure drops below about six psi.

"But at 3000 rpm, if the oil pressure drops below 20 psi, you're probably going to wipe out every bearing in the engine. So we program the microprocessor to compare a value table we've given it to what the sensor tells it. Then, if oil pressure drops to 20 psi at 3000 rpm, the telltale lights up. At idle, though, it still lets oil pressure drop to six psi before it illuminates the telltale. So we've been able to sharpen up these warning lights and make them much, much more than idiot lights.

"Then, too," Milne continues, "when the microprocessor sees these abnormalities, it not only lights the warning telltale but it also brightens the instrument cluster lights slightly at night, because that's another way to attract the driver's attention.

"Another computer function involves fuel range. Using the approximate mpg and how much fuel is onboard, we calculate a driving range. But we don't calculate the range to an *empty* tank. We calculate it to a tank that's ⅛ full. At that point we say the range should read zero. And at *that* point—the ⅛ tank mark—we turn on a low-fuel warning light. We warn the driver that he's low on fuel. We also light up a signal that says *On Reserve,* and we switch over from computing range to telling the driver how many miles he's gone since the *On Reserve* light came on—when we first warned him of low fuel. Now even if he doesn't see the *Low Fuel* light come on at first, he can look down later and sees how long ago we began warning him. The system has a built-in memory.

"So now he realizes, Ohmigosh, it's been 30 miles, and I know I only had ⅛ tank 30 miles ago. I probably can't drive more than 50-60 more miles, so I'd better get some gas fast. Or if it's happened just a mile or so ago, he might make it to his neigh-

borhood station. I think it's a great feature that people will like as soon as they discover it. But they probably won't read about it in the owner's manual until the light comes on."

Niggling Problems. It's one thing to produce a relatively small LCD wristwatch, which usually operates next to a constant 98.6° F. heat source. But it's another challenge to make much larger LCD's like those used in the Corvette instrument panel, simply because it's tough to hold a consistent .0005-inch gap between two parallel sheets of glass. Nor is that the only remaining problem.

We talked about the effects of extreme heat and cold. LCD's also sometimes have a tendency to form *Newton rings*. Newton rings are similar to the rainbow discoloration you see when oil droplets float on water. They're caused when the two glass sheets of the LCD don't stay perfectly parallel. (You can see now why the surface of the Corvette's instruments are so uncurved.)

General Motors also had to test the LCD panels for unexpected reactions to different sorts of microwaves, radio waves, sound waves, and voltage surges. What happens, for instance, when someone uses the cigar lighter or jump-starts another car? The system has a built-in watchdog circuit to compensate for extreme changes in current and puts the panel on a failsoft mode if the battery goes completely dead or gets disconnected.

Maximum Potential. The Corvette's speedometer registers to 157 mph or 255 kph (kilometers per hour), depending on whether you flip the console switch to English or metric. The tachometer reads to 6000 rpm, with the graphic tach display peaking at 4200 rpm: the point of maximum engine horsepower. Speedometer and tach bar

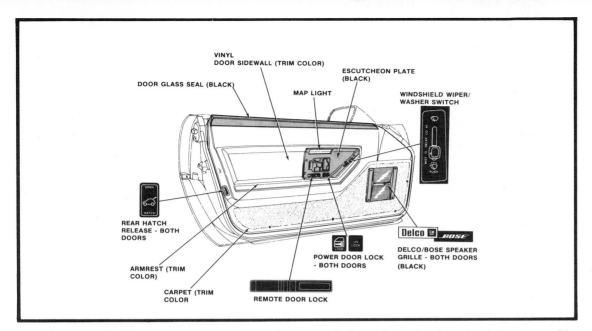

VINYL
DOOR SIDEWALL (TRIM COLOR)

DOOR GLASS SEAL (BLACK)

ESCUTCHEON PLATE
(BLACK)

MAP LIGHT

WINDSHIELD WIPER/
WASHER SWITCH

OPEN
REAR
HATCH

REAR HATCH
RELEASE - BOTH
DOORS

ARMREST (TRIM
COLOR)

CARPET (TRIM
COLOR)

REMOTE DOOR LOCK

LOCK UN LOCK
POWER DOOR LOCK
- BOTH DOORS

Delco BOSE

DELCO/BOSE SPEAKER
GRILLE - BOTH DOORS
(BLACK)

Multi-function door switch panel houses wiper/washer, power locks, and speaker. Door has to be opened to get at hatch release, which means glass liftback can't be popped up accidentally or when doors are locked.

Once driver gets used to switches, he can "touch-type"—find them without looking.

graph inputs are updated 16 times a second, but their digital displays (the numbers) are updated only twice per second.

The odometer stands outside the LCD system. It works mechanically, but not by a conventional rotating cable. The display consists of cogged wheels turned by an electric motor. "The main reason we went to this system," observes Ken Milne, "is that we were a little afraid of the erasability of a purely electronic display. We don't have any doubt that we could make a mileage recorder that would be as hard to erase or change as a mechanical system. But ours would be different, and there would be ways to trick it. We knew that, and while the ways of tricking an electronic and a mechanical odometer are different, the methods of tricking a mechanical system are established and accepted. So we were frankly afraid of being criticized by people who said our system was easier to change."

The Corvette instrument panel also uses three ordinary flashing lamps. These are for the two turn signals and the high-beam indicator. AC decided to use them because, at low temperatures, an LCD telltale won't turn off quickly enough between flashes. Same with the high-beam indicator if you flip it several times.

Milne mentions that the computer used for the instrument panel has the potential for many additional functions. "We have capacity in our microprocessor to do a lot more tasks. Right now the computer's an extremely fast worker, and it doesn't have enough to do. So we've started looking for other microprocessor work around the vehicle. I'm sure we'll find it.

"We can take any of the inputs we have and, at any particular temperature or pressure or time or speed or rpm, we can send the signal to some device and tell it to turn on or off. Or slow it down or light it up or whatever. Once we've digitized all the information, we can just open the gates when we reach a certain point. We can do all

these things at very little additional cost. We have a number of tasks we're thinking about, aiming at the next sizable change. And we feel other cars will soon use the LCD technology that the Corvette has pioneered. We're just beginning to scratch the surface."

Adventures in Seating. The new Corvette offers two types of seats: the standard bucket and the optional Sport seat. The base seat comes upholstered in cloth, with hefty lateral restraints (wings), and a manual back-angle adjustment. The pads and trim all snap into place.

One thing that distinguishes this seat from most is its wool fleece comfort liner. Wool padding underneath the upholstery absorbs body heat and lets moisture evaporate.

You can also order the base driver's seat with a 6-way power adjustment (RPO A-42) and/or leather trim (B-16). The power seat tilts, moves up and down nearly 1.5 inches and fore and aft 6.5 inches. Leather seats also have the wool comfort liners.

The Sport seats use the same centerline as the base seats, but they have electric fingertip controls for the following functions. First, there's a triple-segmented pneumatic lumbar adjustment that uses an electric pump to inflate three bladders. You pump them up tight and then let out as much air as you want with three little bleed-down buttons below the pump switch. This switch stands on the right-hand bolster.

Second, the seatback lateral restraints have electric motors and a hinge mechanism that move these wings inward or outward up to 15°. Third, another electric motor powers the backrest itself through a 12° arc. Finally, you can order the same 6-way power option for the driver's Sport seat as for the standard bucket.

The seatbelt harness is interesting, too, in that it has a "cinch" button at the top of

the lapbelt housing that lets you strap yourself in tight for very hard cornering. Ordinarily, the harness works on the principle of a motion-sensitive pendulum lock. In other words, you can move around in your seat or even tug on the belt without it restricting you. But hit the cinch button and you become part of the car.

That Fabulous Sound. The Corvette offers four different sound systems. We'll show pictures of the lesser ones elsewhere, but I'd like to talk at some length about the Delco-Bose option (RPO UQ-4). I want, in fact, to let Dr. Amar Gopal Bose tell us about it, because no one can give us, I feel, a better introduction to his rather unorthodox and highly successful ideas. I asked him to begin our phone interview by telling me a bit about himself.

"I was born in Philadelphia in Nov. 1929," he told me. "My father came from India—an importer of handloomed fabrics—and my mother was born in America, a schoolteacher. During the war, when I was in high school, I got very interested in radios. The people who ordinarily repaired radios were all away in the service at that time, so at about age 13 I taught myself how to repair radios, and I opened a repair shop.

"My father had dealt with a number of retail stores in Philadelphia — hardware and a few department stores, but when the shipping stopped, there was no import trade, so we had an income problem. My mother's teaching salary wasn't adequate

Corvette for '84 offered three seat/upholstery choices. Sport seat with lumbar controls and more pronounced wings stands at top. Below it is the leather option, the only seat available in red. All levels came in five different colors, each with a fleece interliner beneath upholstery to promote air circulation.

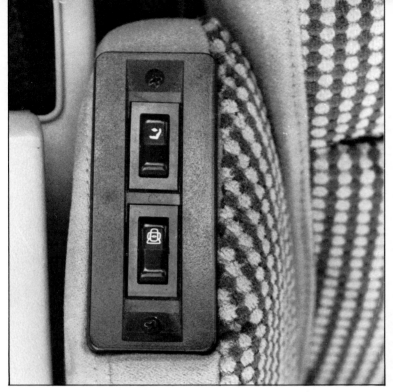

Buttons on left side rail allowed driver to adjust Sport seat's wings and backrest angle. Those on right controlled lumbar support.

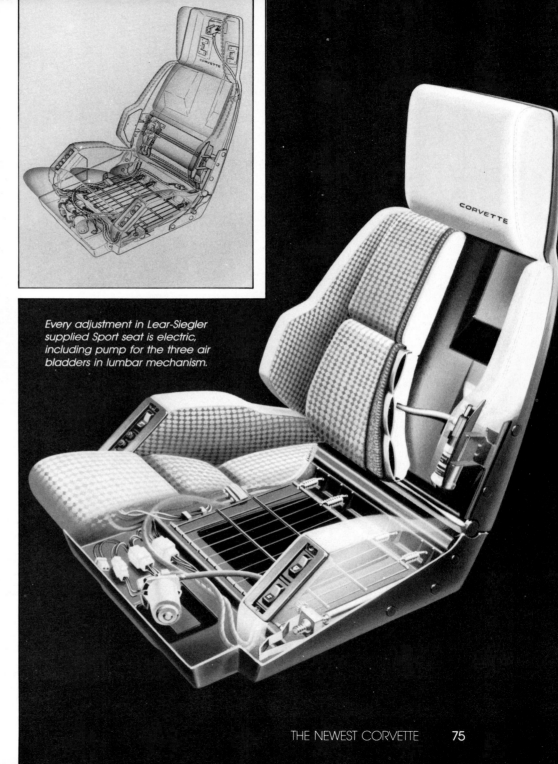

Every adjustment in Lear-Siegler supplied Sport seat is electric, including pump for the three air bladders in lumbar mechanism.

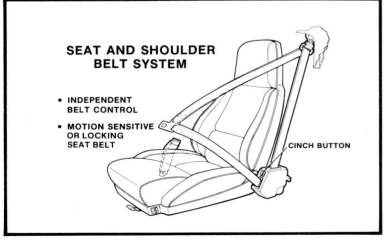

SEAT AND SHOULDER BELT SYSTEM

- **INDEPENDENT BELT CONTROL**

- **MOTION SENSITIVE OR LOCKING SEAT BELT**

CINCH BUTTON

Driver can push cinch button to lock himself tightly into seat for rough going. Otherwise, motion sensor leaves harness loose.

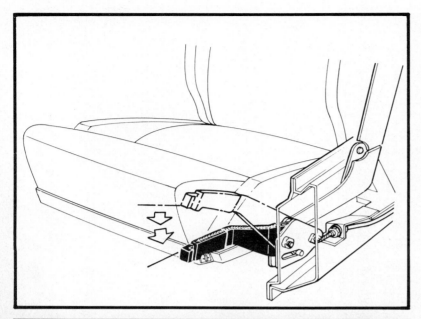

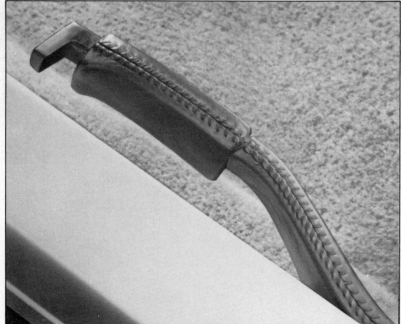

Leather-wrapped emergency lever returns toward floor so it doesn't interfere with entry or exit. Stainless cable and Teflon sheathing prevent corrosion.

Color and Trim Selections

For 1984, interior trim colors were: blue, bronze, graphite, gray, dark red, and saddle. Of those, the leather-seat option could be ordered in all colors except blue. The cloth buckets came in all colors but dark red.

Three 2-tone exterior paint combinations were offered for '84: 1) light with medium blue metallic; 2) light with dark bronze metallic; and 3) silver plus gray metallic. Recommended interior colors for those combinations were (respectively): blue, bronze, and graphite or gray. The dark red leather interior was allowed only with the silver/gray 2-tone but wasn't recommended.

The '84 Corvette also came in 10 solid exterior colors, seven being non-metallic. The non-metallics were black, red, and white. The metallics were light blue, medium blue, light bronze, dark bronze, gold, gray, and silver.

Specific interior colors became available with specific exterior colors. The Corvette color charts listed them either as "R" (recommended) or "A" (allowed). Colors <u>not</u> listed as "R" or "A" had to be ordered under RPO D-60, meaning that the dealer had to tell the plant that these color combinations reflected the buyer's personal tastes and not those of the Corvette's designers.

—Black could be ordered with any interior color except blue.
—With a light blue exterior, Chevrolet recommended a blue interior or allowed graphite.
—For medium blue, same as above.
—For light and bronze exteriors, only the bronze interior was recommended.
—Gold paint called for a saddle interior, with bronze allowed.
—Metallic gray got a recommendation of gray or graphite seats, with dark red allowed (leather).
—A Corvette solid red exterior called for dark red, saddle, or graphite interiors.
—Silver paint went with gray or graphite recommended, or dark red was allowed.
—White exteriors came with any interior color, with bronze being the color simply allowed. All others were recommended. □

for the family, so we got the idea that I would repair radios. My father went to the stores he used to deal with, and they put up signs saying *Radio Repair*. They kept 10% of the customer invoice.

"This grew into one of the larger radio repair shops in the Philadelphia area. I taught a number of my high-school friends how to test tubes, replace parts, etc., and it got to be quite a business before I left in 1947 for MIT.

"Tinkering with radios," continues Dr. Bose, "led to my great desire to study electronics at MIT. Nine years later, I'd finished all the research work toward my

Generous cargo deck incorporates security shade, whose handle is visible at right above the carpeted rear wall. B-pillar lamps illuminate the rear area, and

trap doors open above storage bins. These plastic bins can be removed to expose a deeper cavern underneath. Seatbacks tilt forward for easier access.

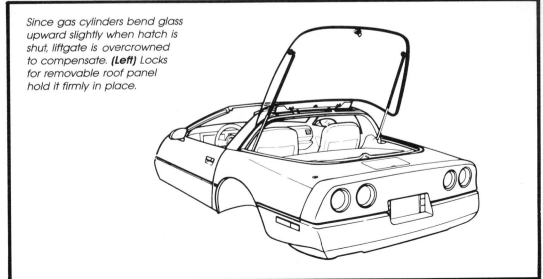

Since gas cylinders bend glass upward slightly when hatch is shut, liftgate is overcrowned to compensate. *(Left)* Locks for removable roof panel hold it firmly in place.

doctorate and had come to the process of writing up a thesis. That's the boring part, so I decided to reward myself by buying a hi-fi set.

"I had studied the violin for seven years, and with my nine years at MIT I thought I understood all the electronic and acoustic specifications. So I went out to buy a hi-fi as an engineer would—reading all the spec sheets and feeling confident that I understood them. I bought a system strictly on the basis of specifications, brought it home, hooked it all up, bought some violin records, and was absolutely appalled when, for example, an ensemble of violins playing up on the E string gave a shrill, screechy sound that had virtually nothing to do with a live performance.

"I thought this system was actually defective, and I marched it back downtown. This time I started listening in the store, and I found that this kind of artificial sound was present even in much more expensive systems. I remember asking the salesman, What happens when a musician comes in? He said, Hah! Musicians! They only play the music. They don't know what it sounds like out in the audience. This is what it sounds like in the audience!

"Of course, that answer already implied that musicians must have criticized the systems before I did. But more important than that, it was as if somebody dropped a puzzle in my lap. I went home and thought, My God, the specifications are so good! By everything I know in engineering, this should be fantastic, and yet my ears tell me it's terrible.'

Searching for Answers. "In June 1956, I received my doctor of science degree from MIT and was appointed to the faculty. I was granted a year's leave of absence to accept a Fulbright scholarship to teach in India, but I asked MIT for permission to stay that summer with no pay so I could use their equipment to make measurements on commercial acoustical products. I borrowed hi-fi systems from local stores."

When Dr. Bose returned to MIT the following year, he taught electromagnetic field theory and the statistics of communications. But nights and weekends he continued his personal research into acoustics.

"Finally," Dr. Bose goes on, "in 1959, a lucky thing happened. Jerry Wiesner—Dr. Jerome Wiesner, who later became president of MIT—passed me in the hall one day, and he said, Bose, I noticed in your office a very strange-looking thing: an eighth of a sphere with 22 small loudspeakers on it. What's that got to do with the statistical theory of communication . . . ?

"So I started to talk to him right then and there, and to tell him about what I'd been working on these past couple of years in evenings and weekends. It turned out that, before coming to MIT, Dr. Wiesner had worked in the Library of Congress, studying problems of sound recording and reproduction. So the conversation struck a responsive chord.

"At that time, 1959, we were able to show that what was in all the textbooks and, amazingly enough, still is now, on how you should design a loudspeaker was wrong. We could show it was wrong, but at that time we couldn't replace it with anything better. We didn't know what was right.

"Dr. Wiesner took a great interest, and he said, Look, the purpose of MIT is not to develop a product, but it certainly is to develop knowledge and to replace incorrect information with correct. So he said, I think we should make this an official project.

"Well, that turned out to be a pivotal discussion. I'm sure I wouldn't be talking to you today by phone had that not happened, because that made funding possible for research. Up until then, I'd funded it all myself—I bought any equipment that MIT didn't have.

"Another interesting point: Had that conversation in the hall not happened when it did, it probably wouldn't have happened at all, because the following year, 1960,

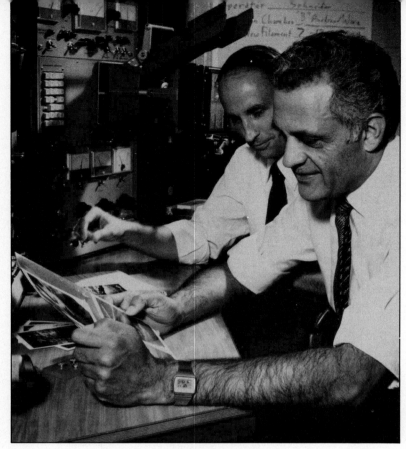

Dr. Amar G. Bose (foreground) confers with an aide.

Kennedy came into office, and when Kennedy came in, he called Jerome Wiesner to Washington as his science advisor. Weisner stayed for the life of Kennedy . . . ."

The Bose Corporation Formed. That chance conversation launched Dr. Bose's very intensive program at MIT, which garnered him several patents and ran until 1968. MIT reserves the right to choose whether it will pursue a faculty member's patents or whether it turns them over to the originator. They chose the latter in Dr. Bose's case, for developments in both electronics and acoustics.

"So in 1964," reflects Dr. Bose, "we took that big leap and I, with one student, Sherwin Greenblatt, formed the company. I stayed on at MIT, as I hope I always will, because without MIT, there would have been no company. They've been incredibly supportive. I've had the great pleasure now of observing and working with my own students for almost 20 years. Many of them are in the company, and I ask myself regularly, Have we done the best for them? And, What should we have done differently?

"As our research at Bose Corp. progressed, we realized that the environment in which a loudspeaker is placed plays a very important role in the sound we hear. That environment not only affects the sound once it comes out of the loudspeaker and bounces around the room, but it affects actually what comes out of the loudspeaker. In other words, if you take a loudspeaker outside and hang it up in a tree and make measurements, like anechoic [non-echoing] chamber measurements, you'll find that you get one balance of, let's say, high notes and low notes—the different tones. If you bring that same speaker into a room and put it in the middle of the floor, you'll get a different balance. I'll explain why in a second.

"Now, if you set it against a wall, you'll hear yet a different tonal balance. And if you put it in the corner, you'll get still another one. Basically, what happens is this. Think of a loudspeaker as a paper cone with a coil that moves the cone forward. As it moves the cone forward, the air exerts a pressure on it, clearly. The cone feels that pressure.

"Well, how much pressure it feels depends on the immediate surroundings of the loudspeaker. If it's out in free space, the sound can travel all around, and there's not so much pressure on the cone—at low frequencies, particularly.

"If it's in the corner of a room, the sound is more constrained, and there's much more pressure. That causes the cone to radiate different frequencies with different intensities. And if you place any loudspeaker down on the floor in a corner, it sounds like a jukebox. It'll give big, boomy sounds; obviously too much bass. If you place the same loudspeaker out in the middle of the room on a table, it'll sound very thin—not enough bass."

Physical and Psycho Acoustics. "So all loudspeaker design up to that time really hadn't adequately considered the environment. The environment affects two things: l) the balance of tones coming out of the loudspeaker, and 2) how these different tones are attenuated after they leave the speaker. Some rooms will absorb some frequencies more than others.

"We began to take that into consideration in our research, and that's what we call *physical acoustics*. These are elements you can measure; they deal with physical phenomena. Physical acoustical research led us to design the speaker enclosures for the new Corvette, for example, with very specific shapes. These enclosures are tailored to the speakers themselves and also to the car's interior environment. We'll talk more about that in a moment.

"However, there's another whole field which hadn't come into speaker design at all: the field of *psycho acoustics*. Psycho acoustics is basically the science that relates human perception to the physical parameters of acoustics that we measure.

"For example, you've heard the term *frequency response*, I'm sure. That has to do with the balance of tones that might be measured at your listening position. Well, how far can frequency response be off before you perceive it? Or what should it be for good sound reproduction? Those are questions involving psycho acoustics.

"Basically, psycho acoustics raises many questions, an important one being whether traditional audio measurements, such as transient response, are relevant to human hearing in terms of sound reproduction systems. In the case of transient response, the answer is no. We can forget the transient response totally if we're careful about other parameters that are important.

"Another example involves distortion. Today you can buy amplifiers that have .01% distortion; perhaps even lower than that. People pay considerably more money for .01% distortion, but in fact, if you had .5% instead of .01%, you couldn't hear the difference on any music or speech signal.

"So, without the psycho acoustics discipline brought into the design, engineers continue to 'improve' parameters. If there's a parameter called distortion, each year they make better electronics to minimize it, but they tend not to ask whether the result makes an audible difference. They produce better specifications, which makes for

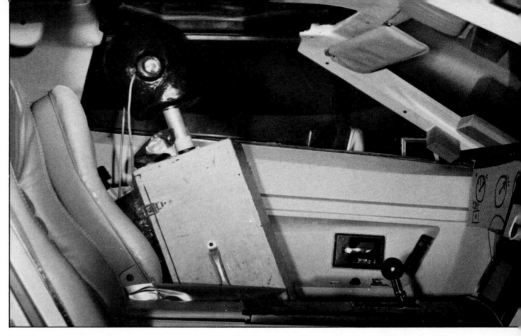

Refinement of the Delco-Bose sound system for the Corvette began early. Here Morgan sits in an old buck that still uses T-top and primitive interior detailing.

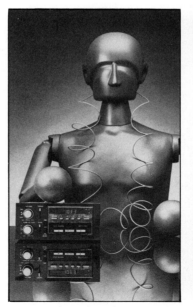

An acoustic dummy, Morgan approximates human hearing electronically. GM lab sent Morgan's signals to Bose headquarters in Massachusetts for analysis.

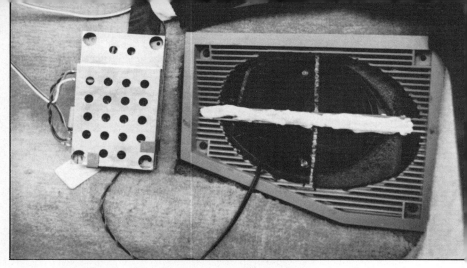

Although they'd done a lot of work with interior bucks initially, final refinements came when Delco and Bose engineers were able to work with a real

car. Precise speaker placement angles, baffling, and other nuances had to take into account upholstery materials and actual hardware inside cockpit.

good marketing literature, but it might only cost more without producing listener or consumer benefits.''

Quantifying Psycho Acoustics. I asked Dr. Bose how he and his staff go about quantifying psycho acoustics. He mentioned that the basic approach involves setting up listening experiments in which only one parameter at a time changes. Then he can measure the minimum change that a person can hear.

For example, he might play pure tones of slightly different pitch alternately. By taking averages of a large number of repetitions, it's possible to measure the minimum pitch difference that the average person can hear.

He also told me that other aspects of psycho acoustics, while researchable, aren't so neatly quantified. He cites what he calls the cocktail-party effect. When you stand in a room full of chattering guests, it's not hard to focus on one particular conversation. If Dr. Bose records this conversation, though, with the best microphone at his disposal and then plays it back over his best loudspeaker, that conversation might be totally lost. Psycho acoustics, then, enters to study the process by which the human brain analyses the acoustic signals at the person's two ears to focus on that elusive conversation. ''Knowledge of psycho acoustic processes help us design better sound systems,'' says Dr. Bose, ''tailored to specific environments, such as automobiles.

''But let me add one more point of interest, because that will lead us into the new Corvette. As a result of work in psycho acoustics, we learned the great importance of the spatial aspects of sound. This had been largely neglected. By spatial aspects, I mean how does the sound arrive at your ears? From what angles?

''In the course of our research, we learned a very fascinating fact that most people don't realize. Amazingly, if you sit in a music hall, about the same amount of sound comes to you from every different direction in a horizontal plane. As much sound arrives at your ears from each side and even from the back of the hall as from the front.

''You can tell that the orchestra is out in front of you only by the fact that the first sound that hits your ear comes directly from the musical instrument. Your brain recognizes this, even though that direct sound's intensity may be less than that coming from the sidewalls by all the multiple reflections.

''Until we realized the importance of reflected sounds, hi-fi systems had been been radiating sound directly, like flashlight beams, from a loudspeaker straight toward the listener. We discovered that, by redesigning loudspeakers to bounce sound waves around the room in certain patterns while preserving a little direct sound, we got more of a spatial dimension — the effect you get in the concert hall. That's what we went after for the Corvette.''

It Began With the 901. That initial research led Dr. Bose to the company's first home loudspeaker, the 901, which got better reviews than any speaker before or since. The 901 really built the Bose empire. Bose now has subsidiaries in 13 countries. In the U.S., Bose employs about 1000 people in its two Massachusetts plants — one in Framingham and one in Hopkinton. And they also have manufacturing facilities in Canada and Ireland, plus wholly owned marketing subsidiaries.

In 1977, Bose began developing an aftermarket automotive sound system. That led to Bose's interest in the Detroit OEM field, because instead of designing car speakers in the laboratory, the company started to look at automotive interiors. ''I think we took 90 different cars,'' recalls Dr. Bose, ''and studied all those environments; all aspects of their acoustics. And we soon realized that there was incredible variation among cars.

''Many people have said that a car isn't a good acoustical environment, but we don't believe that. The studies we've done have shown us that it's just a very different one. What we realized is that there was no way that anybody, as far as we can see, could ever make an optimum system for that environment unless the system were tailored specifically for a particular model car and unless we, as manufacturers, could get involved with the carmaker to control some of the acoustics and the speaker placements.''

Dr. Bose points out that the design of the speakers, along with their placement, is absolutely critical. In a home, the listener can sit anywhere, and he might place the speakers anywhere, too — in the middle of the floor, high up on a wall, in a paneled room or in one with heavy rugs and drapes.

Not so in a car. Placement and acoustics inside a car are totally predictable. You know where the driver and passengers have to sit; you can control where to put the speakers; you even know what the upholstery materials are. Dr. Bose thus realized

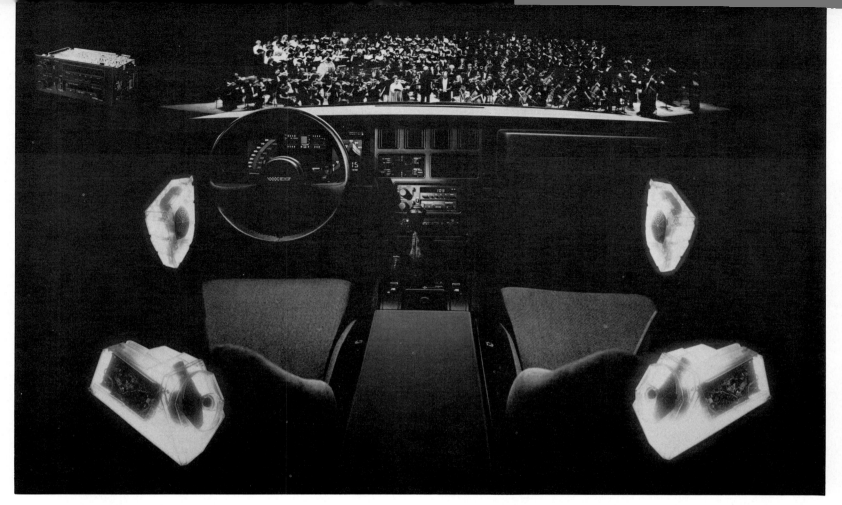

that if his engineers could get together with the car's interior designers, they could design the entire sound environment together.

The Delco Link. Meantime, in their analyses of different cars for the aftermarket, Bose had aligned and tested radio receivers made by various manufacturers. What they found was that, according to Dr. Bose, the best radio reception available came from Delco Electronics Div of General Motors.

"Delco wasn't then and isn't even now thought to be a top-quality manufacturer of car radios," acknowledges Dr. Bose. "People say, How can a car company make good radios? It takes a hi-fi manufacturer to do that.

"Well, our engineers thought that, too; in fact, so strongly that, in the first round of testing, they didn't even include Delco radios. Then, when they did, they tested them twice, because Delco turned out to have the greatest ability to pick up weak signals and to reject strong interfering ones. Delcos also had functions that were far ahead of the hi-fi industry. For example, hi-fi car receivers, even today, have blend switches. A blend switch changes the receiver from stereo to mono because there's less noise on a mono signal when you're going into a fringe area. Well, Delco for

years has had blend switching all in a chip that automatically changes from stereo to mono as the signal weakens. They also had the best noise rejection circuits.

"The reason, perhaps, why Delco and other factory radios hadn't had a good reputation was that the audio sections and speakers in all cars were pretty poor. People naturally judge the entire system what they hear.

"In the process of testing all these receivers, we came to realize that designing a car hi-fi receiver tends to be a lot tougher than designing one for the home. For one thing, the receiver sits next to 25,000 volts of spark generation in the ignition. Then, too, the antenna runs down the road at 55 mph. It soon became clear that we had to find a partner with expertise in that part of it, because we couldn't learn all there was to know in a short time.

"That's what led us to believe that we ought to approach General Motors. GM is the only automaker that has its own captive solid-state facility. They start right from growing the silicon crystals in-house, and they end up making their own special integrated circuits.

"So when we made these tests, we concluded that GM's Delco Electronics Div. was the partner we ought to have, because we wanted the best front end we could get. I went to Jerry Wiesner and told him that I thought we had an incredible opportunity

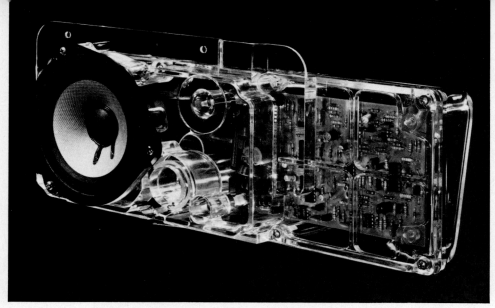

This is not the exact speaker decided upon for the Corvette's front doors, but it's very similar, including the 2-state modulation amplifier on the right.

Delco-Bose rear speakers tuck out of harm's way at extreme rear corners of cargo deck. They ratiate the sound toward glass, which bounces it forward.

to achieve this spectacular sound, and that GM looked like the right partner because of Delco radios.

"Relations between GM and MIT are very good, so Dr. Weisner arranged for us to make a presentation at Delco, which we did on Sept. 19, 1979. We made a 4-hour morning presentation on the possibilities of a new concept in auto sound.

"And then came another very great stroke of fortune. GM corporate vice president Edward Czapor, an incredible person, was Delco Electronics' general manager at the time. He basically had the vision, the courage, and the ability to see that there was something in this and to make it success. If there's a father to the Delco-Bose program, and if it ever gets recorded, Ed Czapor is that man. He really made it all possible. Another amazing thing in this whole activity is that no lawyers got involved. The whole arrangement took place on a handshake."

Overboard on Quality. "What I learned subsequently is that Delco Electronics has a higher level of quality control than I've seen in any American, Japanese, or European company. It's much more like work we'd done for NASA .... Unbelievable standards of quality control. And they taught us these standards. I'll give you an example.

"If you go into our place now, or into Delco at any time, you'll find that people putting sensitive integrated circuits into printed circuits are grounded. They wear a ground strap around their wrist, and it's connected to earth. I don't think anyone else really knows about this. What happens: Delco makes about 20,000 radios a day. As an experiment one day, they built 10,000 sets without grounding the assemblers and 10,000 with. Then they tracked all those radios by owner for two years. And they found out that, at between one and two years, the failure rate was much higher in sets put together by ungrounded assemblers than those assembled by grounded workers. That's because of static charges on the ungrounded workers."

Who Builds What. Delco produces the front end: the radio receiver and cassette player. The low-voltage signal produced by the front end is then taken over by Bose equipment to be distributed to the four amplifiers plus two front door speakers and two rear speakers in the hatch area. Bose produces the amplifiers, speakers, and custom enclosures.

The amplifiers are what Bose calls *2-state modulation* amplifiers. They've never been used before in homes or autos. They need no heat sinks—those finned aluminum boxes that dissipate the heat from conventional amplifiers.

Bose realized they couldn't put an ordinary amplifier, with its large heat sink, inside a car door, because the temperature inside the door would get too high. To do an adequate job, the heat sinks would have to be so big that there'd be no room for the window mechanism, impact beam, etc.

"Interestingly enough," explains Dr. Bose, "this 2-state modulation technology is something we'd developed early on at MIT. It had been used in the military by us, but it had never come into any consumer application. The devices that make it practical also were very high priced until recently.

"The 2-state modulation amplifier uses no heat sink at all. It works on a principle of the home light dimmer switch. Imagine a light that you're able to turn off and on very quickly: 100,000 times a second. You wouldn't see the light flicker, but since it would be off half the time, the bulb would be dim.

"Just as you control the intensity of the light by the amount of time it's on or off, you can also control the audio signal generated by the 2-state-modulation amplifier. It switches on and off around 100,000 times a second. There's a minimum of power dissipated, because when it's off there's no current flowing through the transistors. When it's on, there's no voltage across them. It turns out that power dissipation is proportional to the product of these two factors: voltage and current. Zero times zero is zero.

"The other unique element of the Delco-Bose system is that, where the Corvette's speakers look into different environments, they send out different tone balances. The Bose amplifiers are different front to rear, because they look into different physical environments. They balance the tones differently."

Corvette speakers are adaptations of the Bose 901. And they're unusual because, first of all, each coil uses rectangular wire instead of round wire. This eliminates spaces between the turns on the coil, making the highest density of voice-coil metal in the industry. The speakers are also capable of handling an amazing amount of power: 25 watts per channel, for a total of 100 watts.

Morgan on the Road. The first cars to make the Delco-Bose system available was the 1983 Cadillac Seville and Eldorado, along with the Buick Riviera and Olds Toronado. The 1984 Corvette became the fifth GM car to offer it. Each, of course, has been designed specifically for the individual auto's interior.

For the Vette, Bose engineers wanted to be sure that, at curbside or at top speed, the occupants would be able to hear the sound system's full *dynamic range* — the ratio of the loudest signal to the noise background. Dynamic range has to be much greater in an automotive system than for the home and greater for the Corvette than most other cars.

To measure such elements as dynamic range and other parameters of physical acoustics, Bose uses an anthropomorphic dummy with microphones at each "ear." One of Dr. Bose's students at MIT named the dummy *Morgan,* and that's what he's been called ever since. Morgan sits in the driver's or passenger's seat and picks up signals. Those signals are analyzed by a computer whose program takes into account the ways in which the human ear processes sound before sending it to the brain.

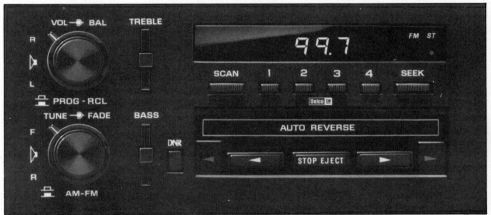

"We've looked at the processes by which a person senses spaciousness, for example," explains Dr. Bose. "The computer processes such factors and then gives us information that lets us judge more accurately when we have a good sound system."

All Engineers are Musicians. At Bose, all the engineers working on this project are also musicians. Some have been professional musicians. The ultimate decision of what sounds best has to be subjective, and Dr. B. feels a trained musician can make better judgments than non-musicians. But in the end, there's no science that lets anyone say, unequivocally, This is correct; this is a live performance or it's 10% away or 20% away.

"That doesn't exist," concedes Dr. Bose. "I think we've pushed the science further than anyone, but we still have to spend hundreds and hundreds of hours with any one car model, listening.

"It all boils down to subjective opinions, but that's part of what's been wrong in the field up until now. People think they can make a few simple quantitative measurements and get a good hi-fi set. You just can't do that.

"I do remember," concludes Dr. Bose, "that, of all the GM cars we became involved in, including the Corvette right from the beginning, the attitude of the designers was very, very progressive. They said, You tell us all the things that will make it optimum. We'll consider those along with other design constraints and will try to meet as many as we can.

"In fact, they built us a handmade mockup of the Corvette interior— a buck—a couple of years ago so we could make the first acoustical evaluations. The results have been far beyond our expectations. People who never thought music mattered in their lives get into one of these cars, and it spoils them for anything else. That's perhaps the worst thing about this new sound system." ☐

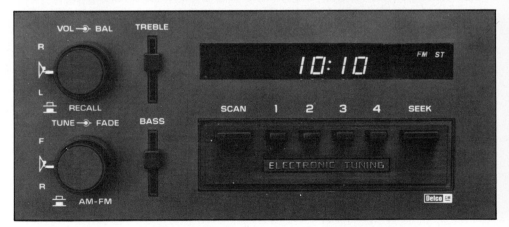

Corvette's standard AM/FM Delco 2000 ETR (bottom) could be replaced with RPO UM-6 that included cassette (center), or UU-8 Delco-Bose system (top).

Chapter 7

Making It!

In chassis subassembly area, the engine and drivetrain are mounted on front crossmember along with brakes and front suspension. Meanwhile, rear suspen- sion goes together upside down in another part of chassis room, and these sub- assemblies are married via channel beam and exhaust aboard Towveyor.

The Corvette simply outgrew the St. Louis plant and, in 1981, GMAD gave the car a new home in Bowling Green, Ky. When the plant moved, so did about 1100 workers and their families—men and women who otherwise might have been without jobs. This 300-mile trek marked one of the largest industrial relocations in American automotive history.

Nearly all the hourly employees now at Bowling Green made the move from St. Louis. The self-proclaimed wagon master was Jack Gerbic, an ex-Marine, the father of nine, and a 35-year GM veteran who himself went from the assembly line to management in 1952. Jack was the St. Louis plant's general superintendent of Corvette and is now Bowling Green's production manager.

Recalls Gerbic: "People came to Bowling Green looking for a new lease on life. Most of them wanted to come, and most are glad they did. But for some it's been a traumatic experience. Unless you've lived it, you can't really understand it. To move from a big city like St. Louis into a small community like Bowling Green.... A few still haven't made the transition."

The move took place early in 1981, and Bowling Green produced its first Corvette that June 1. Longtime residents helped find homes for the new families, but everyone had to pay his own moving expenses. Local people participated in GM's self-help programs, some even going to St. Louis to talk to the GM workforce about Bowling Green; to explain what to expect, what housing and other facilities were available.

Plant a Focal Point. In all, the Bowling Green Corvette plant projected a manpower requirement of about 2100 people to work both the first shift and an anticipated sec- ond shift. For those 2100 positions, GMAD received 10,000 applications. Most of the early jobs were filled by workers who tranferred from St. Louis.

At the time, Bowling Green was basically a quiet college town, population 47,000. It's sometimes difficult to be accepted into such a community, but GM and local leaders tried to ease the burden. The move of GM people to Bowling Green took extensive planning, and the company set up social facilities in the plant to make the transition as gentle and easy as possible.

Gerbic himself had been in Bowling Green since 1979. He helped plan the move and set up relocation programs inside the plant. By and large, the move went very smoothly, with the vast majority of both townfolk and workers pleased with the out- come. For Bowling Green, it meant revitalizing not only the old Chrysler Airtemp factory but making use of housing that otherwise might have stood empty. For Cor- vette assemblers, it meant keeping their jobs—jobs that, in many instances, they'd grown very fond of.

Says Gerbic, "We've tried to make the plant a focal point. We let the hourly employees bring their wives and husbands in; we let relatives use the plant for meet- ings. They take their families through and show them their workplaces. We devel- oped a training program and want to have more people involved in the plant's day-to- day activities.

"We initially held a 48-hour orientation class here in Bowling Green; called it our Votech training program. We instructed people in behavioral and communication skills. From that we established an employee awareness group." Actually, anyone who wanted to take the Votech training program could, and some prospective

Uniframe main rails enter "Pac Man" automated weld area for addition of birdcage. The Corvette's uniframe, chassis, and body get subassembled separately.

Fluids for power steering, brakes, and clutch are added as chassis moves along on Towveyor. Components travel more than 7 miles on various conveyors.

Trimshop worker assembles rear speakers. People swap tasks freely whenever jobs get monotonous.

Subassembler adds hinges to prepare door for attachment to uniframe a little farther down line.

Fuel tank pressure test checks for leaks. Tank fits in place just before the rear body goes on.

employees who weren't hired at Bowling Green did. But since the course prepared them for jobs in other GMAD plants, it helped even those who didn't get Corvette jobs.

"There aren't too many places to go in Bowling Green, so people do get more involved with the plant," Jack continues. "The plant is much more social than it would be in other places. You can't walk around town without meeting GM employees, so we participate in the community. We're making our mark."

St. Louis Got Mighty Crowded. GMAD's St. Louis plant began producing Corvettes for 1954, at a time when cars were still fairly simple. By the Sixties, though, automobiles had gotten more complicated, and each time another major accessory or option came along, it meant adding one more work station. To install power steering or an air-conditioning system required more space on the assembly line. Yet there was no room in the plant to expand the Corvette line. Everything just got crowded closer together.

Body engineer Bob Vogelei amplifies, "Crowded line space got to be a terrible problem at St. Louis, both in the bodyshop and on the chassis line. I can't give you exact numbers, but when I joined the Corvette group back in '63, we were producing 5-6 cars an hour. By 1981, St. Louis was producing 10 cars an hour—cars a lot more complicated than in 1963. Doubling capacity meant adding more people to the line, so it became very crowded for space and led to poor working conditions.

"Also, every time you wanted to make a change in the car, it became very traumatic, because we had to figure out where in the line we could fit this thing in. It was already so tight and compact. Many choices never happened because they were physically impossible."

St. Louis, though, remained a multi-car plant, and at the time of the Vette's move to Bowling Green, St. Louis was producing 102 vehicles an hour: 10 Corvettes, 35 trucks, and 57 passenger cars. In 1979, Corvettes were still being built in the same relatively small corner of the St. Louis plant where the 1954 models were born. And by the late Seventies, demand far outstripped production capacity. That fact became the key to the Bowling Green move and the next-generation Corvette.

New Plant, More Cars. So in 1977, Chevrolet Div. and GMAD decided to look for new quarters for the Corvette. The search became part of a 5-year plan, and a task force was set up to find a plant that had the potential to produce the new Corvette in the quantities Chevrolet was projecting. The former Chrysler Airtemp facility looked ideal.

The plant at that time enclosed 750,000 square feet, to which GMAD soon added 250,000, making it an even million—23 acres under one huge roof. Before the plant could be rebuilt, though, every inside wall came down, and a lot of the concrete floor had to be ripped up to accommodate Towveyor tracks and underground facilities.

Chevrolet and GMAD began to formulate plans for the new plant *and* the new Corvette together. The original intent called for moving production of the then-current Corvette into Bowling Green but at the same time incorporating whatever changes would be necessary to produce the 1984 car (which, at that time, was still presumed to be the '82 model).

Says Dave McLellan: "It wasn't until we had Bowling Green's additional capacity

(Right) Huge press at GTR (General Tire & Rubber) in Ionia, Mich., molds the industry's largest fiberglass automotive component in 2500-ton Verson press. The Vette hood's outer skin is then bonded to its more intricate inner panel.

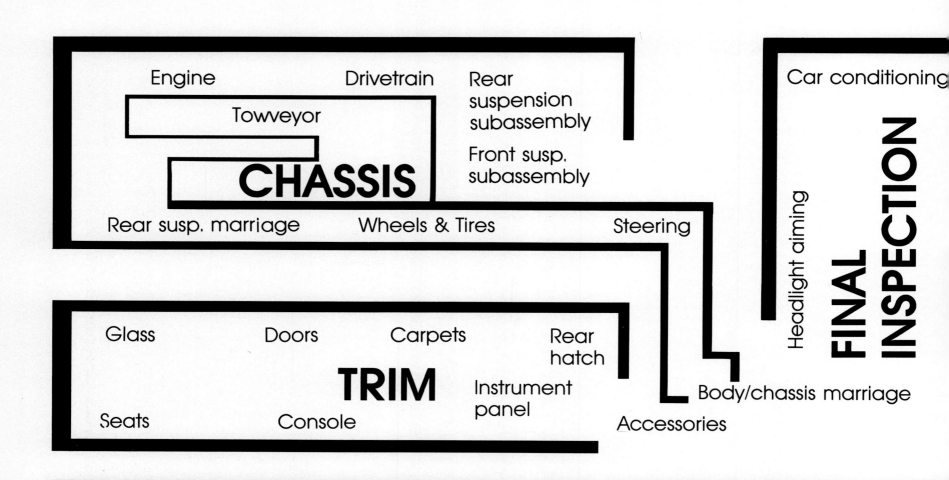

CHASSIS

Engine

Drivetrain

Rear suspension subassembly

Front susp. subassembly

Towveyor

Rear susp. marriage

Wheels & Tires

Steering

TRIM

Glass

Doors

Carpets

Rear hatch

Instrument panel

Seats

Console

Accessories

Body/chassis marriage

FINAL INSPECTION

Car conditioning

Headlight aiming

UNIFRAME

Pillars

Body sides

Torque boxes

Weld area

BODY ASSEMBLY

Radiator

Pedals

Plenum

Uniframe sealer

Polish area

Schematic map shows the main work areas of GMAD Corvette plant in Bowling Green, Ky. Component and final assembly works its way systematically. from the left of this map toward the right, with finished cars emerging at the top, center. Paint and bodywork areas account for ⅓ of floorspace.

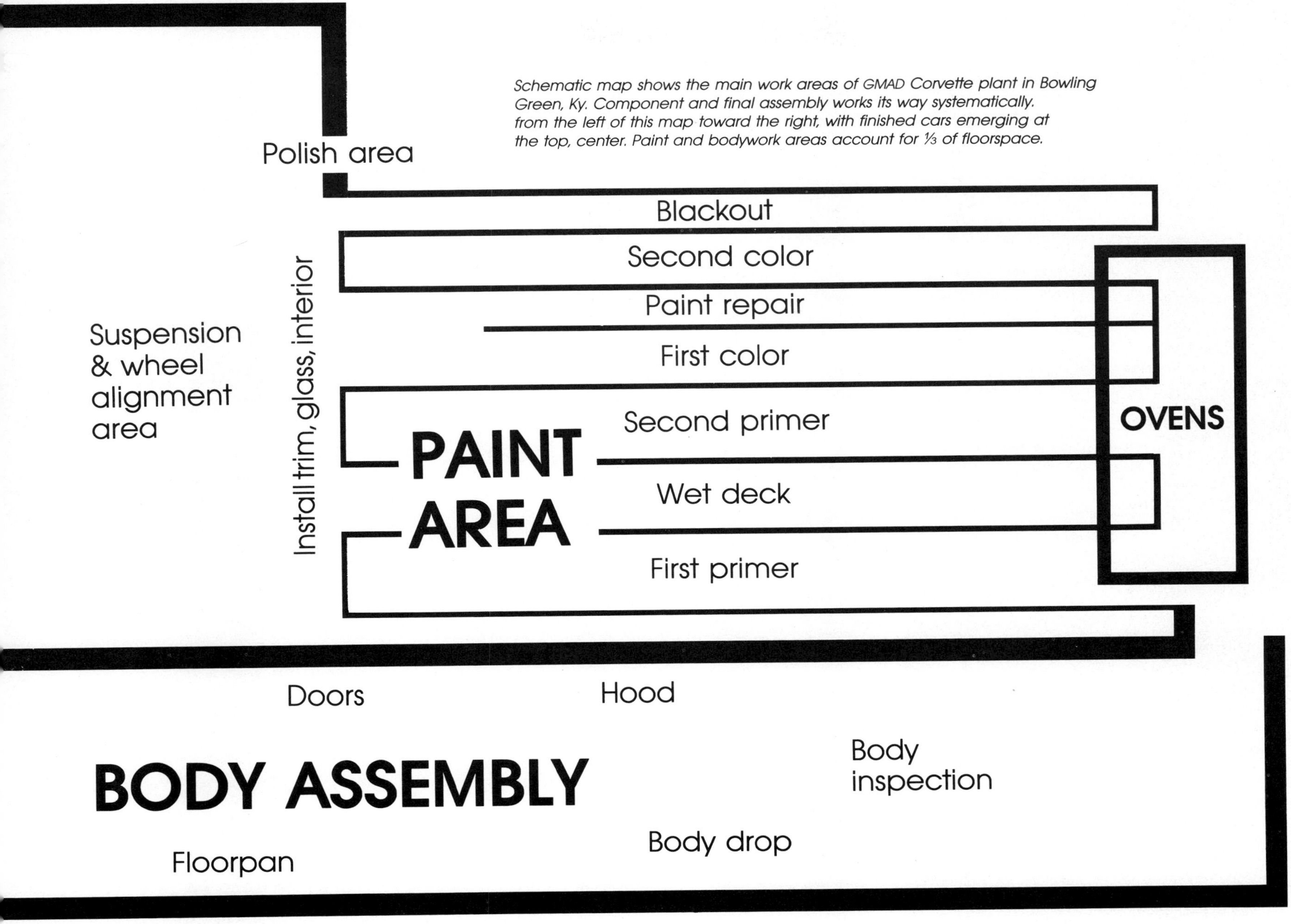

Blackout

Second color

Paint repair

First color

Suspension & wheel alignment area

Install trim, glass, interior

PAINT AREA

Second primer

Wet deck

First primer

OVENS

Doors

Hood

BODY ASSEMBLY

Body inspection

Floorpan

Body drop

Chevrolet
GM Assembly Division
Bowling Green, Kentucky

CORVETTE

The Bowling Green plant site covers 212 acres and has a million square feet under one roof (equal to 22 football fields). Parts arrive each week in 40 railcars and 200 trucks from 827 vendors across America. This plant builds only Corvettes at the rate of 15 an hour, and it began by working 2 shifts.

that we could say we'd be able to satisfy the market demand. The volume increase we got with Bowling Green's production capacity really helped us sell the new Corvette program."

Birdcages and Robots. The man charged with mobilizing the new Corvette plant was Earl Harper. Harper has since been transferred, but a great deal of credit is due him for making Bowling Green what it is today.

The major differences in the way the 1982 and '84 cars were engineered had to be reflected in the way the plant went together. Chevrolet and GMAD wanted to make the changeover as painless as possible. For example, the '82 car's engine was top-loaded; that is, it dropped down onto the frame from above. The '84 car's engine loads from the bottom. It's bolted to the front crossmember along with the suspension, and then the uniframe comes down to meet it.

Another significant change has to do with the new uniframe itself, which is totally

Just over 2100 people work for General Motors at Bowling Green. Many moved from the Corvette's previous home plant in St. Louis, Mo. Considerable plan-ning went into this move to make it as untraumatic as possible for the workers and their families. Bowling Green is basically a small college community.

unlike the separate, bolt-together, frame/birdcage that preceded it. The planners who laid out the plant had to take this major difference into account, and the area that previously served to weld up the original bolt-on birdcage now serves to weld up the entire uniframe.

This section currently uses four robots, a 6-stage welding fixture, and 133 individual weld guns. It takes various subassemblies and *toy-tabs* them together. Toy tabbing means exactly what it sounds like—Tab A fits into Slot B: actual tabs in the

subassemblies go into slots of other subassemblies. This allows enough movement for the fixtures to hold them dimensionally correct before and during the 2-stage automatic welding process. The main welder, by the way, is fondly called *Pac Man*, because it looks like the video gremlins nibbling away at the steel pieces.

Daily Emphasis on Quality. There's never been more attention paid to the Corvette's overall quality than now at Bowling Green. Everyone participates. Workers

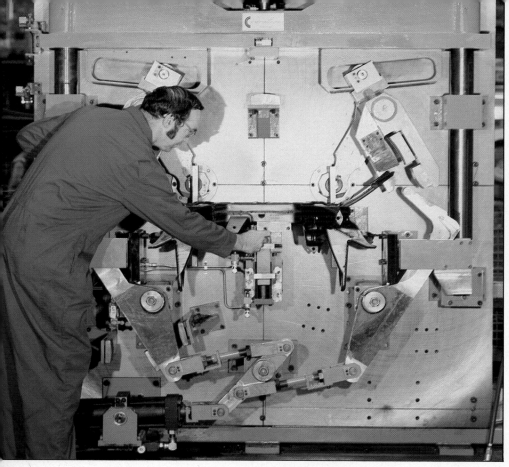

Spring twist fixture tensions fiberglass leaves before they're installed on the chassis. Large hydraulic rams bend the springs, and machines fasten them.

(Above) Technician assembles and adjusts Girlock disc brakes on subassembly. **(Below)** Instruments undergo electrical test before installation. This particular unit showed an odometer malfunction, so that part had to be replaced.

are allowed to drive new Vettes home so they become more familiar with the total car and not just the specific part they work on.

Plant manager Joseph J. Dell'Ario mentions some of the ways in which he and his staff encourage and foster the idea of quality. ''We begin with an audit of a certain number of cars every day. By audit, I mean we check them in great detail and give them scores. Then, in order to get both salaried and hourly working people involved, we let them take the cars home. This means coming face to face with a car, as opposed to a stream of cars and, if something is wrong, the person really notices it. If there's a long line of cars, a fellow figures, Well, so this one seat is wrinkled, so what? I'll get the next one.

''But now he comes face to face with one car standing still. The guy comes back, and he has to give us a little talk at 9:00 in the morning. He's had the car out the night before. And he'll say, Yeah, I've worked for GM for 20 years, have been on Corvette for 15 years, and this is the first time I drove one home. My family just loved it, and my kids wouldn't get out .... We let about four people take cars home each night.''

Quality Audits. The corporation has long had a system for auditing or grading the quality of all its cars in the various plants. This is an internal system, "...and it can be misunderstood by the media," adds Dell'Ario, "but it's just a way of trying to identify the slightest little speck or pop in the paint or a glue run or a molding out of place; whatever. Right now we're taking five cars a day and going over them in great detail. It's not just a walkaround. The cars go up on the hoist, and each member of the group has a fat packet of papers. He checks every little thing—the movement of the rearview mirror and the tightness of the side glass, routing of the wires, all that good stuff. And we give each car a score.

"Then the next day we have an audit area in the plant over by the hourly entrance. Everybody goes to this area, and at 9:00 a.m., which is break time, we set up a review. We review the cars that were audited the day before. We talk about whether something happened to the paint, and we check and have the people who work on the car comment. How could that happen? What do they think? And they'll go back and check—the cars are still standing there by the entrance. Someone on the line might not have been aware of his own mistakes. And we'll see if there's a trend.

Quality audits involve everyone who's worked on previous day's cars.   Each morning at 9, assemblers critique each vehicle, suggest quality improvements.

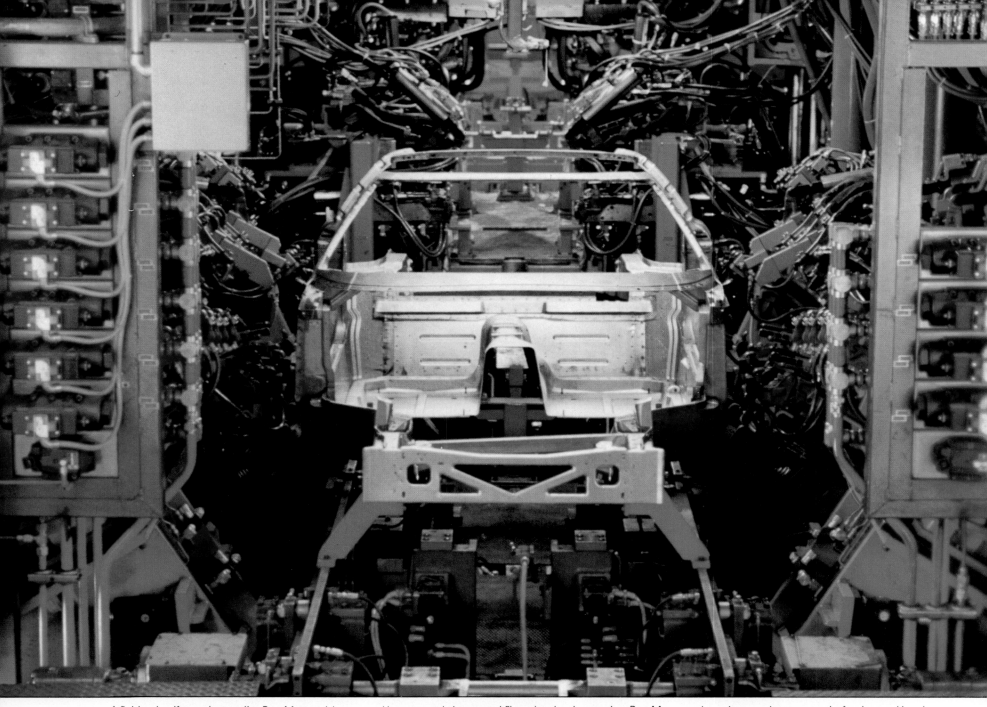

A finished uniframe leaves the Pac Man weld area and is now ready to accept fiberglass body panels.   Pac Man creates a tremendous amount of noise and heat.

"Everybody's there—staff people and the hourly people. We make a big show of it. We encourage everyone to take part and know what's happening. Then the people who've driven home cars the night before . . . we have a microphone, and they come up and tell us what they thought of the car. We do that every day.

"What we're trying to do is get the line worker as excited and enthusiastic about the Corvette as the rest of us. We do that by keeping them informed. If they don't know what's going on, they can't do a decent job. We have employee awareness groups getting together, and we try to have them become more and more involved.

"By the same token, I worked very hard with the salaried people to understand that we're not involved with heads. Some people call the workers *heads*. How many heads do you have? They're not heads. They're people. We'd all better understand that they're people with responsibilities, and many are leaders in the community;

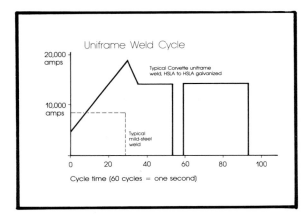

Uniframe weld takes two hits at twice the current of normal mild-steel welds—a new technique.

Fiberglass tail section takes on special urethane bonding adhesive before it's mated to uniframe. Various panels are bonded and riveted in position.

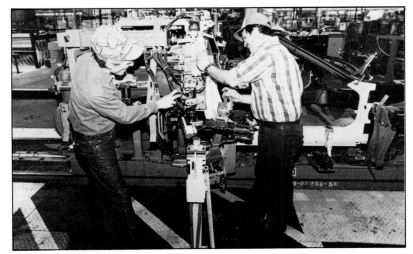

Special fixtures along the body bonding area assure accurate fits and alignments. These two men are setting up the fixture that will set the rear panel.

they have families and concerns. Just because some are hourly and some are salaried doesn't mean they're different.

"The key thing I'm trying to do is get the people more involved, so they want to do the job. We can't force them to do a better job than they want to do. We can't watch them every minute. And we're trying different things. For example, I've asked the guys to get into smaller groups, like in the i.p. [instrument panel] subassembly area. This involves about five people. The guys are going to try to decide who does what. Let them decide, but let them help each other to make sure they ship that i.p. only when it's all perfectly ready. If one guy gets in trouble, I want the rest to help him. Or if he gets bored or tired of doing one job, let him switch around."

Shine a Foot Deep. Corvettes began using a new painting process called basecoat/clearcoat (bc/cc) when GMAD moved into the Bowling Green plant in mid-1981. Base/clear enamel has all the advantages of lacquer without any of the disadvantages: a deep, penetrating, mirror-like shine without the cracking and yellowing or short road life.

GM's German subsidiary, Adam Opel AG, began using bc/cc several years ago, as did Mercedes-Benz. Mercedes made base/clear an optional finish and even today

Here's where they install the door weatherstripping. Like vital engine fluids, adhesives come down from overhead hoses and are applied via special nozzles.

Driver's door gets aligned and is held on by another fixture. The next station will shoot bolts to the hinges, and the passenger's door mounts similarly.

charges about $700 extra for it. In the U.S., Lincoln and Chrysler have offered bc/cc in recent years, but the Corvette is the first and only U.S. General Motors car to use it. Metal-bodied GM vehicles are scheduled to get bc/cc around 1985.

According to R.H. (Dick) Groesbeck, the Chevrolet project engineer with responsibility for the Corvette's paint process, "Base/clears with lacquers had been used in the past for a number of coating systems where durability wasn't a great concern... mostly in custom paint jobs. Durability with clear lacquers has always been a question. They just don't stand up very well for long periods.

"But base/clear lacquers do give a real pearlescent, candy-apple look that's very attractive. It also has a high gloss, and it gives you the ability to use metallic colors without worrying about dulling or mottling.

"So when we decided to spend the money and move the Corvette plant to Bowling Green, we got the opportunity to do two things. First, we upgraded the total paint system for the car and, second, we set up a new finishing system that would let us get the appearance we all wanted." Bowling Green has set aside a large portion of the plant to the new painting process.

GM uses finishes developed mostly by outside suppliers, and in this instance — starting in 1979 — Dick Groesbeck and his staff worked with duPont, PPG, and Inmont to perfect a bc/cc system compatible with fiberglass and the inmold coating process. Inmont got the final nod. The Inmont system, of course, uses enamel instead of lacquer because, as Mr. Groesbeck points out, "All carmakers are having to get out of the lacquer business because of air-quality standards. The EPA requires reduced hydrocarbon emissions, which means going into acrylic enamels."

Nuances of Base/Clear. There's a trick to applying base/clear enamels that doesn't make the process easy to automate. Basecoat/clearcoat isn't a high-speed process, because it demands a lot of hand labor. At the beginning of production, all spraying

Once major panels are affixed to uniframe, sanding begins. Much sanding has been eliminated as compared with previous car, thanks to lack of bond seams.

was done by hand in a section of the plant set aside as a *clean area*. The actual shooting and baking took place in special *clean rooms* that cover nearly half the floorspace of the plant itself. No one goes in or out of the clean area without authorization, and everyone entering has to wear special lintfree, dustfree, anti-static white clothing. If you peer through the clean-area windows, it looks like an operating room with a lot of doctors inside.

But even though the early production cars were painted totally by hand, Bowling Green had been looking into robots for applying primers, and by the time you read this, those primer robots might already be in place. If not, they soon will be.

All 10 colors initially offered on the 1984 Corvette were base/clear. Even non-metallic black, red, and white profit in depth and luster from the base/clear process. Solid colors have less hiding quality than metallics, so they're put on a bit thicker. And thicker paint always increases the possibility of sags and runs. The range of film thicknesses for the metallics is 0.7-.9 mil for the basecoat and 1.5-2.0 mils for the clear. Solid-color basecoats are just over one mil thick. One mil equals .001 (one thousandth) inch.

Aluminum is one of the best hiding pigments available. Metallic or metalflake automobile finishes consist of billions of tiny aluminum flakes suspended in the pigmented paint solution. The aluminum flakes give the metallics their good color coating qualities. Metallic colors cover the body surface easily and consistently with less than one mil thickness per coat.

The Corvette's base/clear finish uses two coats of color plus two coats of clear, with a *flash* between all four coats and oven bakes between primer, base, and clear applications. Flash means a wait of 2-10 minutes to let the solvents evaporate. The two color coats go on practically dry, and they look dull or flat before they're covered with clear. It's the clear that gives the finish its deep gloss.

One beauty of the clearcoat is that it buries the aluminum metalflakes under two mils of clear. This means the flakes never become exposed to the air. With other metallic finishes, when the surface sealer wears away, the aluminum flakes corrode as oxygen seeps in. That's why you often see early dulling and staining with conventional metallics.

Another interesting point is that the new Corvette's soft front and rear RRIM fascias are now painted with the same "unibase" basecoat as the body. The clearcoat on the fascias, though, is different from that used on the body. It's more flexible so it can bend without cracking. The flexible clear is also softer than the body clearcoat, so it tends to scratch and become dull if you wash it with a brush too many times (as in a commercial carwash).

How the Finish is Applied. "About half our problem on the previous Corvette had to do with bond seams," comments Dick Groesbeck. Body bond seams meant a lot of sanding, and fiberglass dust in the air tended to make the painting process very difficult.

Since the new Corvette has no bond seams, sanding time is cut considerably, and cleanliness isn't the problem it used to be. The car still requires a fair bit of handsanding, but this means sanding between the paint coats. It doesn't mean sanding the basic body.

To give you an idea of what's involved in the total painting process, I've asked Floyd McKee, Bowling Green's paint foreman, to give us a run-through.

"When we get the body-in-white from the bodyshop," explains McKee, "we alcohol-wipe it down for dirt and dust. Then we look at the total surface for any small

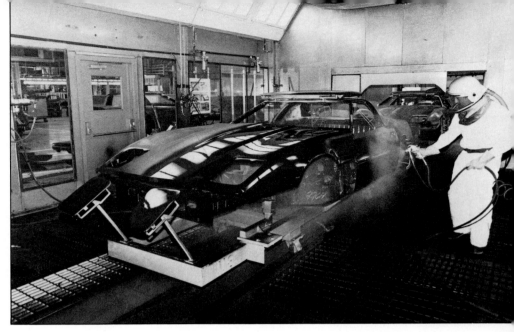

First color coat follows polane primer. All finishing operations take place inside "clean rooms," where everyone wears white, lintless clothing and masks.

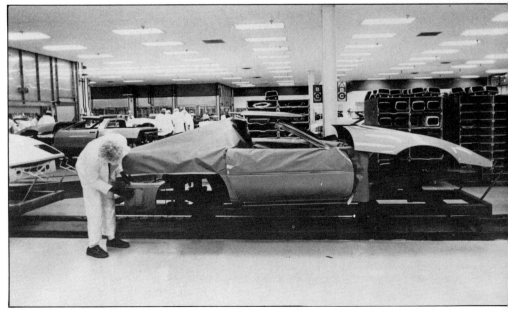

When customers order special 2-tone paint schemes, the top portion of body is finished first, then it's masked off and a second color is applied to bottom.

Once painted, workmen mask off all edges and apply "blackout" under hood, to cowl and other semi-hidden areas. Lamp doors rest on stands ahead of hood.

The finished chassis arrives aboard a Towveyor, and the freshly painted body drops down on it from above. The car has its interior and glass at this point.

defects. With the inmold body-panel process, there's a lot less chance of imperfections than there used to be. But if we find any, we handsand them with 400-grit paper.

"The body then goes through our ionized blow ring. This is in an area that takes any static-electric charge off the body. And it's now ready to go into first prime, where it's sprayed with Sherwin-Williams polane primer.

"After that initial primer coat, the body moves into an oven for 30 minutes at 250° F. After the body goes through the first oven, we re-inspect it for pops and imperfections, and it's again wet-sanded with 360-grit paper on the wet deck."

Second Prime and Color. "It now goes through what we call a *mud wash* to get all the sludge off," continues McKee.

"Then the water is drawn out of the body crevices with a narrow-nozzle vacuum. Next it goes into another oven at 250° for another 30 minutes to dry out. After that, any dirt that happens to have gotten on the body is wet-sanded off. The car is again blown off and tacked down before it goes through another ionized blow operation.

"At this point, it's ready for the second prime coat, after which it goes into another 250° oven for 30 minutes. When it comes out, we inspect it for dirt and lint, and any defects are hand wet-sanded out. This is followed by a tack and blow with ionized blow guns, and the body passes through an ionized blow ring once more.

"Now the body finally gets its first color coat. This is applied by two men with hand sprayers; it's not automated. The car gets one coat of base, they give it a minute to flash, then on goes another coat of base, another minute's flash, on goes the first coat of clear, a minute's flash, and then the final coat of clear. After that, it gets about 10 more minutes flash time."

At this point, the body passes through a new radiant oven where the heating elements skim over the top of the clearcoat. This is again a 250° oven for 30 minutes, but there's very little air inside this oven, which means that whatever dirt happens to get inside isn't likely to swirl around. If any does fall on the clearcoat surface, the skimmer traps it on the top so it can be rubbed out later.

"When it comes out of the skimming oven," adds Floyd McKee, "the body is again inspected. Any foreign matter is rubbed or sanded out. At this point, the paint foreman decides whether that body meets the established quality standards, and if it doesn't, any problems are repaired in the line before the car gets delivered to the trim shop. Last year, we were running about 80% okays, and 20% had to go back for repainting. This year we're doing a lot better than that. If the body needs spot repairs, it goes back to the second color booth."

Touchups, Repaints, and Two-Tones. There's no way to spot-touchup small areas with the bc/cc process. If the body gets rejected after the clearcoat goes on, it has to be handsanded down to the panel surface, and the whole panel has to be done over. But that doesn't happen very often.

If the job calls for one of the Corvette's three 2-tone paint combinations, the body goes into a special 2-tone booth. Here, the top color is taped and masked off to the molding seam. The bottom half is sanded and goes through the base/clear routine one more time.

Finally, after the body is totally painted, it goes into what's called *blackout*. That means that underneath the hood, inside the fenderwells, and along areas where weatherstripping and other moldings go, painters spray flat black so there's no color behind the moldings. The non-blackout areas get taped off by hand, and the flat black is sprayed very carefully. The body then goes through another 250° oven to dry out the black. After that, the body is ready for trimming and installation.

When I asked Dick Groesbeck whether local bodyshops would have any trouble repainting cars involved in scrapes or accidents, he said he thought not. Most van

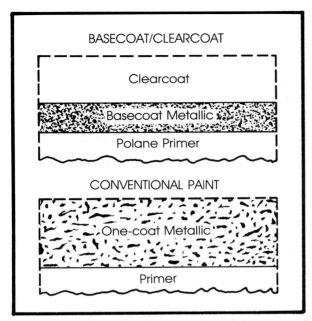

BASECOAT/CLEARCOAT

- Clearcoat
- Basecoat Metallic
- Polane Primer

CONVENTIONAL PAINT

- One-coat Metallic
- Primer

Normal metallic finishes leave aluminum flakes exposed while base/clear protects them from sun and oxidation.

Final body and mechanical adjustments take place just after the body drop, such as attaching front A-frames, setting aircleaner in place, and hooking up the underhood wires.

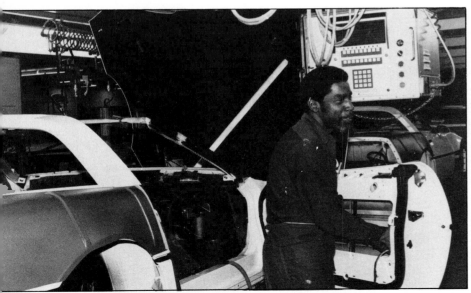

Inspector tests electric windows with an overhead power source and monitor. Instrument panel, seats, carpeting, and rear hatch still need to be installed.

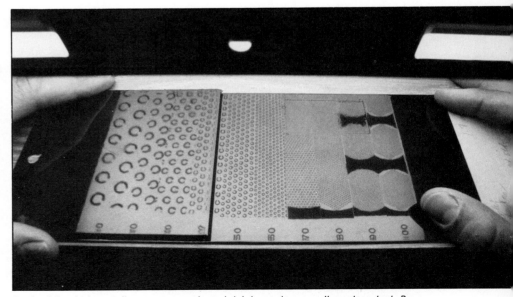

In final body inspection area, each paint job undergoes the gloss test. By using this device, the light-reflective quality of any surface can be measured.

conversion firms have used bc/cc for years, and almost all automotive refinishers have access to systems and equipment that are compatible with bc/cc.

The 1983 and '84 Pilots. Chevrolet, of course, decided to skip the year 1983 and go straight into '84 with its model-year designation. While all first-year production Vettes carry 1984 VIN (vehicle identification number) tags, 33 pilot models and 10 prototypes were built with '83 VIN's.

According to Fred Schaafsma, "Cars with 1983 numbers were never sold, because although they were built off production tools, they weren't really productions cars. We used the first 19 to do handling and durability testing, emissions certification, and so forth. Although they cost Chevrolet around $500,000 each, the 10 prototypes and 33 pilots have all been scrapped."

After the first 43 "1983" models, Chevrolet built 69 engineering cars that became a test of the plant. They all carried 1984 VIN numbers and were used to help the people at Bowling Green "go up the learning curve," as Dave McLellan puts it. These

Every Corvette undergoes a water test when it's finished, but some cars get two wet checks. Paint is buffed to a high luster in the final polish area (above).

69 engineering cars were numbered sequentially, starting not with VIN #001 but with #002. This run ended with #070, and #071 became the first true 1984 production Vette that left the plant for sale to a customer. According to Bowling Green traffic manager Donald W. Thomsen, it was shipped—along with 678 other Corvettes—to California during the week of Feb. 24, 1983 for the West Coast dealer introduction on Mar. 24. Of those 679 cars, 15 went to GM's Van Nuys assembly plant to await distribution, 151 were shipped to Fremont, and 513 to South Gate.

For the record, the 1984 VIN #002 left the line on Jan. 6, 1983. The "official" VIN #001 was built after #070 and was raffled off by the National Council of Corvette Clubs for their 1983 spina bifida fund raiser.

Most of the first 69 1984's assigned to Chevrolet Engineering did end up in private hands. Some were used for engine development, so the engineers could change any altered items back to stock, and Chevrolet then sold the cars. The first 19 "1983" cars that Fred Schaafsma received couldn't be sold because, as Fred saw it, "After we ran our durability cars for 50,000 miles, they were in no shape for the public to enjoy." □

Road and roll-test pit at end of final line keeps one inspector inside car and another man under floor making adjustments based on computer inputs.

Plant manager Joe Dell'Ario (left) was on hand when Rick Nagy bought Corvette # 0071 from Bob Rubino of Cochran & Celli Chevrolet in Oakland, Calif.

Chapter 8

Hands Across the Sea

Several years ago, Chevrolet decided that America needed to *export* cars for a change, so to launch a serious export effort, the division set up a new group of engineers and marketing people whose function it would be to pursue Chevrolet exports only; nothing else.

The first car in Chevrolet's export push became the European Camaro Z-28E. Introduced at the 1982 Geneva auto show, the Z-28E sold very well from the start and has been a smashing success in Europe ever since. The second car to gain export status was the 1984 Corvette.

Various countries in Europe, the Mideast, and the Far East have different requirements for safety, lighting, instrumentation, emissions, and other aspects of the cars sold there. It's now the job of Chevrolet's export facility to monitor those laws and then make sure that cars destined for other countries incorporate the required non-U.S. equipment and design changes.

Chevrolet assistant chief engineer Fred C. Porter coordinated the domestic and export versions of the car from the beginning of the 1984 Corvette program. "We have two major functions here," he told me in Feb. 1982. First, my engineers try to convince the engineers designing the U.S. car to build in as many features that comply with export requirements as they can. In other words, if we can get the U.S. car to meet overseas standards from the start, great. If we can't, then we redesign the part to meet the overseas requirement."

Three Major Export Packages. For the new Corvette, Porter's people came up with three all-encompassing packages that would legalize the car in three specific areas of the world. For Europe, there's the VD-1 package; for Japan the VE-1; and for unregulated areas like the Mideast, the export Corvette takes on the VT-7 package.

All exported Corvettes arrive at their destinations with two mandatory options included in the base price. These are the Z-51 handling package and the THM 700-R4 automatic transmission. For 1984, you couldn't get a manual transmission with any of the three export packages, but this restriction was lifted after the first year.

The overseas Z-51 package differs slightly from the domestic version in that it

Chevrolet hopes to sell significant numbers of Corvettes overseas and has developed three special packages to conform to European, Japanese, and international requirements. All three get the Z-51 option, but with 8.5-inch wheels all round. Exhausts exit straight out instead of down toward the road.

specifies 8½-inch rims all around. The 9½-inchers don't meet European requirements that call for wheel arches to fully enclose the tires. The 9½-inch wheels leave about ⅛ inch of rear tread exposed.

The export Z-51 package also uses the 15.5:1 steering ratio because of the sustained high speeds these cars are expected be driven at. Speeds over 100 mph can make steering corrections with the 13.0:1 ratio feel a trifle fast.

The European VD-1 package originated the engine oil cooler. The cooler wasn't slated for U.S. cars until Chevrolet decided to make it standard on exports. The VD-1 also desmogs the V-8 by removing the closed-loop emissions system and catalytic converter. A resonator replaces the converter.

Additional VD-1 changes include removal of the fuel-tank restrictor so the car can use leaded fuel, installation of European headlamps and tail lights, special shoulder harness webbing and retractor, specially tempered tinted glass, spacers to raise the rears of the seats, rear hatch defogger, flag-type outside mirrors with electric adjust-

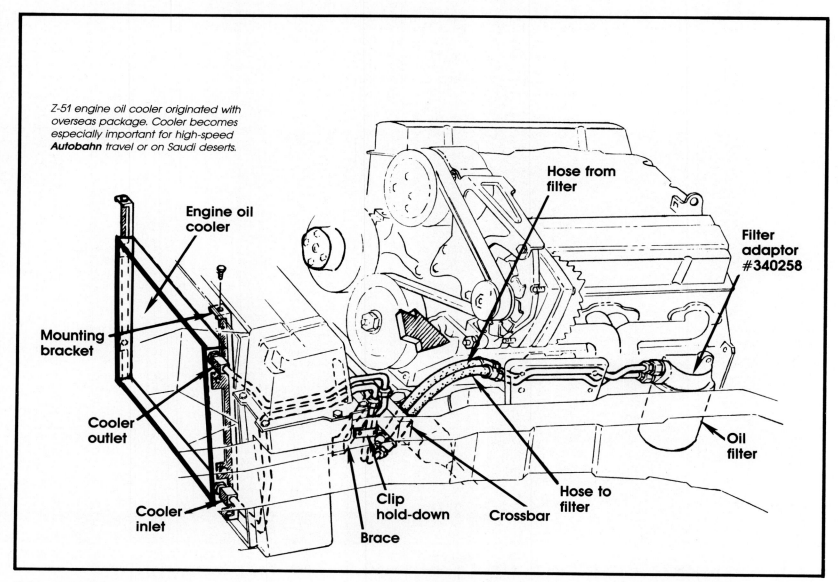

Z-51 engine oil cooler originated with overseas package. Cooler becomes especially important for high-speed Autobahn travel or on Saudi deserts.

Engine oil cooler

Mounting bracket

Cooler outlet

Cooler inlet

Hose from filter

Filter adaptor #340258

Oil filter

Clip hold-down

Brace

Crossbar

Hose to filter

Design mockups for overseas Vette tried to retain 9.5-inch wheels by using black wheel-lip moldings. Some countries don't allow tread beyond edge of body. Other readily visible differences include flag mirror, split lamps in grille. Rear lenses stand nearer surface, flank wider license receptacle.

ers, the cassette radio with European frequency band, European horn, special labels, wider license brackets, a red hazard warning switch (instead of black), and all-metric symbols on the instrument panel.

The Japanese VE-1 car comes with the California emissions package and requires exhaust shielding and temperature warning light for the catalytic converter. The Japanese car further incorporates specific lamps, the same flag mirrors as required in Europe, the radio set up for Japanese broadcast frequencies, the European horn, plus Japanese shipping labels. Japanese law also mandates a flashlight mounting bracket on the instrument panel and an over-speed warning buzzer for the speedometer.

The VT-7 package for Mideast export includes nearly everything required in Europe, but with Japanese tail lamps and no smog equipment.

A Corvette buyer in Europe, Japan, or the Mideast can order additional RPO options if he wants, but not all those available to Americans and Canadians are sold overseas. Sport seats, leather trim, the 6-way driver's seat, power door locks, 2-tone paint, and cruise control are available in all countries. Unavailable items include the acrylic roof panel, dual heated sport mirrors, lighted vanity mirror, and the UM-6 sound system. Other options depend on where you place your order.

Some of the Tricks. Chevrolet's export experts got into the Corvette program fairly late, which meant there were a number of export requirements they couldn't incorporate in the domestic design. Seatbelts are one example. European seatbelts have different webbing and retractor requirements.

Export Corvettes also have an entirely different lighting system. Headlights, tail lamps, reflectors, and sidemarkers are totally different and even vary from country to country. The export Corvette's rear fascia, for instance, had to be fully redesigned. That happened not only to accommodate the wider European license plates, but the tail lamps had to be moved outboard to comply with overseas lighting laws. The export lenses, in fact, are almost flush with the rear fascia, not recessed.

Where fog lamps appear in the domestic car's grille, export versions incorporate a dual-function lamp that's split horizontally. The upper half is what the Europeans refer to as a *position lamp* — we call it a parking lamp. The lower half becomes the turn signal. Sidemarkers are not only not required but are illegal in some parts of Europe. And European headlamps are non-Sealed Beam.

Overseas Corvettes run with straight-out tailpipes, because pipes that point downward aren't legal in most countries. They tend to kick up dust.

Fred Porter adds, "What doesn't show up in the pictures is that this will be GM's first car that complies with European interior projections and exterior fittings. Essentially, Europeans are starting to set some standards that call for specific body radii and the toning down of interior projections. It's extremely difficult to meet these, because they're design standards. They're not performance standards. For example, all radii in the vicinity of the bumpers have to be 5mm. They're very arbitrary. I don't know where they came from or why they exist. We worked with Paul Huzzard and the design guys and made sure, when they were drawing their drawings, that all the radii were right. It was extremely difficult to do."

Packages Aid Ordering. Chevrolet developed the three Corvette export packages for two reasons. First was to make the car legal, but secondly, in the past the division had problems with dealers overseas not understanding the car. "We'd get oddball

The European Vette made its debut at Geneva auto show in Mar. 1983, where it attracted large crowds. When a GM overseas engineer drove a car around Ger-many soon afterward, more crowds gathered at every stop. GM has been exporting the Camaro Z-28E since 1982 and plans to export other cars in the future.

orders," mentions Porter. "For example, there might be a dealer in Saudi Arabia who fails to check off heavy-duty cooling. Then the customer comes back complaining about overheating."

All exported Corvettes except those going to Japan have the Z-51 engine oil cooler. Nearly any car, if it's driven at top speed for more than about five minutes, will suffer from overheated oil. This shows up on German *Autobahns* and Italian *autostradas,* where there are either no top speed limits or very generous ones. It can also be a problem in some of the Arab states, where desert heat plus long, straight roads do their best to cook high-revving engines.

When this book was written, Chevrolet hadn't yet made the engine oil cooler (RPO KC-4) available to North American Corvette buyers, which means that early Z-51 cars were delivered without them. But all Z-51's, domestic as well as export, were equipped with oil coolers after Apr. 1983.

In conclusion, Fred Porter points out, "We know that the Corvette's overseas volume will be low at first. This is going to be a relatively high-priced car in other countries, because when you add shipping, duties, taxes, and the rest of it, the Vette's base price is going to be right up there with the Ferraris and Maseratis. And yet I have no doubt that we can compete in that market.

"Another reason that early export volumes will be low is because our dealers overseas are going to have trouble getting a share of production. We're going to be very limited in how many export cars we can build. We expect no more than 1000-1500 the first year.

"We didn't export the Corvette for many, many years due to the competing North American demand. It was exported long ago, but that tended to be a hack job. If you go to Europe now and find one of the earlier cars that GM overseas dealers imported, you'll see all sorts of cobbled items that look like they came from a mail-order catalogue. Chevrolet would rather not have its products look like that anymore."

The export Corvette made its official European debut on Mar. 8, 1983, at a press conference before the Geneva auto show in Switzerland. As in the U.S., the car won the acclaim of the press and public alike. □

Chapter 9

The Corvette
Goes Racing

V ince Piggins devoted his 27 years at Chevrolet to making the division's name synonymous with winning. Piggins' career with Chevy spanned the glory days of the small-block V-8, and Vince, more than any other man, made that engine the most popular and widely run in every type of motor racing—worldwide.

Piggins came to Chevrolet in 1956. He'd been *the* factory liaison for Hudson in the Hornet's successful NASCAR years. His earliest assignments at Chevrolet teamed him with Zora Arkus-Duntov, first helping Duntov win at Pike's Peak and soon afterward setting up factory-aided stock-car endeavors plus a 9-car NASCAR team effort called SEDCO. SEDCO (for Southern Engineering & Development Co.) operated out of Atlanta, Ga., and was managed by racing great Jim Rathmann.

Vince also helped Duntov with various Corvette racing projects in early 1957, adding a Corvette to the SEDCO stable. This car was to have been crewed by Red Byron and driven by SCCA champ Dr. Dick Thompson, but with the AMA racing

Vince Piggins

Designer Randy Wittine sketched early 1984 Corvette race car in Jerry Palmer's studio. Both these men oversaw clay development at Diversified Glass Products.

Scale clay model helped shape race car's aerodynamics in GM's windtunnel. It was also employed by Palmer and Wittine to explore various graphic treatments.

ban that June, Chevrolet disbanded SEDCO and dropped all direct factory participation in racing.

Soon, however, as head of Chevrolet's product promotion engineering department, Vince began making it possible for outside Corvette builders and drivers to get competition parts and, at times, engineering assistance. In fact, Vince and his staff saw to the design, development, production, cataloguing, and sale of every competition part Chevrolet has turned out over the past two decades. Vince, along with associates John Pierce, Bill Howell, Wes Yocum, and Ron Sperry, wrote and published *Chevrolet Power*, which has been the racer's bible since 1975. It's available at Chevy parts counters.

In addition to furthering the Corvette cause, it was Vince Piggins who fathered the 1962 Impala Z-11, the Mark II Mystery Daytona engine, the Z-16 Chevelle 396, and the Camaro Z-28, including the 1969 aluminum ZL-1. Vince played an important role in bringing the 1968-69 SCCA Trans Am championship to Chevrolet through the Z-28 and the efforts of Roger Penske and Mark Donohue. He was also instrumental in conceiving the various V-6 and V-8 turbo versions of the Corvette and the Corvette pace cars.

The purpose of Vince's department—product promotion engineering—has always been to put Chevrolet in the forefront of any sort of wheel-to-wheel competition. Vince retired as head of Chevrolet product promotion engineering on Apr. 1, 1983, but not before he'd set up a competition program for the 1984 Corvette. I don't mean to imply that he did this alone (and he'd be the last to claim credit anyway), but over the years Vince has shown an uncanny knack for recognizing the best race-car designers, builders, drivers, and backers and bringing them into Chevrolet's fold.

Into the Breech. Once a team gets Chevy's attention, product promotion engineering puts it in the honored and privileged position of receiving not cash—never cash—but something far more valuable. It amounts to a piece of Chevrolet's research, development, design, and technical capabilities.

As parts and processes are proven out in the lab and on the race track, everything that's developed initially for one team is made available to everyone. This is done through Chevrolet's (and now GM's) vast off-road parts network, so what you'll read about here either is or soon will be available at your local dealer's.

Chevrolet's product performance engineering staff had been anxious to field a 1984 Corvette racing effort from the program's inception. In early 1982, they began searching for likely candidates to put together a lead team. Sifting through various applicants, they settled on Blaine Ferguson, who'd approached Chevy with what looked like a winning program.

Ferguson, a Coloradian and former manager of professional racing with the Sports Car Club of America (SCCA), teamed with race-car designer/builder Lee Dykstra of Grandville, Mich., and received assistance from California businessman Jerry Brassfield. Brassfield's son, Darin, was scheduled to drive the first car produced, but Piggins and Ferguson also kicked around the names of other drivers, among them Al Unser and Mario Andretti.

Lee Dykstra is considered one of America's great race-car designers, having

Bob Birchmeier, whose Diversified Glass Products, Inc., produced and marketed the finished race-car body panels, stands alongside the full-sized clay created

by Palmer and Wittine. They shaped race car's clay over a fiberglass prototype of the production car. Female molds were then taken directly from this.

Aero Tuning the Race Car

	Bhp needed to maintain 130 mph	Total lift or downforce in pounds
Stage 1: Production 1984 Corvette	97	203
Stage 2: Race-trimmed plus underbody enhancements but minus airdam and rear spoiler	88	17
Stage 3: Race-trimmed with 150mm airdam clearance and 55mm rear spoiler	100	-213
Stage 4: Race-trimmed with 125mm airdam clearance and 75mm rear spoiler	106	-284
Stage 5: Race-trimmed with 75mm airdam clearance and 125mm rear spoiler	118	-374
Stage 6: Race-trimmed with max aero loading, 50mm airdam clearance and 162mm rear spoiler	129	-427

Note that horsepower requirements rise at a greater rate than downforce.

Aerodynamic Data at 130 mph

	Bhp needed to overcome air resistance at 130 mph	Front lift, lbs.	Rear lift, lbs.
1984 Corvette	97 bhp	148	55
1980 Corvette	126 bhp	155	24
1979 Corvette	143 bhp	220	183
1963 Corvette	108 bhp	254	163
1982 Camaro	111 bhp	239	40
1982 Porsche 928	138 bhp	232	173
1982 Toyota Supra	109 bhp	290	57
1982 Datsun 280-ZX	111 bhp	174	116
1981 Isuzu Impulse	108 bhp	238	158

Explanation: The lower a car's CdA, the less horsepower it takes to maintain a given speed in still air. Factors of front and rear lift affect steering and tire adhesion. In this chart, everything was measured in the General Motors Design Staff windtunnel at a simulated 130 mph.

Comparing Aerodynamics

	Cd	Frontal Area	CdA
1984 Corvette	.341	19.28	6.57
1980 Corvette	.443	19.43	8.61
1979 Corvette	.503	19.43	9.77
1963 Corvette	.402	18.30	7.36
1982 Camaro	.363	20.90	7.59
1982 Porsche 928	.445	21.10	9.39
1982 Toyota Supra	.381	19.51	7.44
1982 Datsun 280-ZX	.387	19.51	7.55
1981 Isuzu Impulse	.389	18.90	7.35

Explanation: Cd stands for coefficient of drag, which is one measure of aerodynamic efficiency. A more complete measure is reflected in the CdA, which multiplies the Cd times frontal area (in this case expressed in square feet). The lower a car's CdA, the less power needed to move it through the air.

The controversial Brassfield/Dykstra car became the first 1984 Corvette to appear in competition. Its Ryan Falconer-built engine delivered around 525 bhp from 305 cid. Exhaust routes into square rocker seal.

Lee Dykstra fabricated nearly every part of this car, including A-frames and tubular control arms.

Weismann 5-speed gearbox uses cooling coils embedded in floor, as does Franklin axle (not shown). Aluminum floor sandwiches 500 lb. of lead ballast.

Brassfield car would be under SCCA weight requirement without ballast. ATL 32-gallon fuel cell rests inside aluminum housing at rear of the tubular chassis.

In its first race, with rookie Darin Brassfield driving, Corvette #11 completed 12 laps before being edged off the track. This led to front suspension damage.

put together everything from Al Holbert's highly successful IMSA Monza to Bob Tullius' Jaguar GTP and Bobby Rahal's Indy machine. Dykstra's car builder, John Bright, a Lola factory-trained Britisher, constructed—among others—Brian Redman's Lola GTP.

With the effort underway, Ferguson arranged to work with Goodyear's Leo Mehl and Jim Alexander to develop race tires for SCCA Trans Am series. This became an independent effort, not tied to the production VR50 tire, and it was to be keyed initially to the Dykstra car, although these tires were soon made available to all comers.

Plotting "Ground Effects." Once battle plans were drawn up, Piggins called another meeting to talk strategy. John Pierce joined from Vince's staff, plus Ferguson, Dykstra, GM aero lab engineer Max Schenkel and, via telephone, Corvette design-studio head Jerry Palmer. Between them, they decided to make blueprints and sketches, reserve time in GM's windtunnel, and put together a quarter-scale model based on a melding of Design Staff's styling renderings and Dykstra's specifications.

Once Chevrolet product promotion received Dykstra's initial suspension dimensions, Piggins asked GM's fiberglass fabrication department to take a master mold off Design Staff's one-and-only existing Corvette quarter-scale model. This master mold was copied to accommodate different specifications and body outlines as they evolved. The project of making a duplicate scale model took several modelmakers two weeks to complete.

Dykstra's specifications laid down all the critical dimensions of body height, width, and length so it would fulfill not only the SCCA's requirements but would also accomodate the race-car's totally redesigned suspension system, its oversized tires and wheels, the rollcage, and re-routed exhaust system.

Then came the critical underbody area. The race team had decided early on to make this—as nearly as rules and practicality would allow—a ground-effects machine; that is, to tailor the floorpan so its aerodynamics would help press the car down against the road. This wasn't a new concept, but it's one whose time had come. Lee Dykstra hoped to tailor the shape of his car's floor so it would create, in combination with

Feeling slighted by Chevrolet Div., the Brassfield team decorated the Corvette with Ford Motorsports signs—behavior that also left Ford Motor Company miffed.

Meticulous Dykstra workmanship reflects in all interior details. There's not a wire or hose out of place. Far left-hand gauge is for fuel pressure, and the

tach redlines at 8600 rpm. Clutch uses Lakewood scattershield. Twin reservoirs located on passenger's side are for brakes, with electric kill switch to their right.

the road surface, a venturi effect as the body rushed through the air. This venturi, like the venturi of a carburetor, would set up a negative pressure, or "suction," underneath the car that would help press the moving body down harder the faster it went.

The idea sounded great, but the challenge was to make it work. Dykstra drew up several different underbody configurations. One by one, these were incorporated into the quarter-scale model for windtunnel evaluation.

The Shape of Things to Go. Max Schenkel conducted aero lab tests for the race car at the same time he was finishing up the production 1984 Corvette. As background, Max not only helped design GM's windtunnel but, on his own, has long been active in numerous racing projects. He's no newcomer to auto competition and has been able to study ground-effects both in theory and practice.

Schenkel and company got the race Corvette's underbody configuration down to a set of basic shapes and angles. The engine became totally enclosed in its own carefully vented compartment, and behind the engine, the bottom of the firewall, when seen in sideview, had a gently curved leading bottom edge. This blended into the floor beneath the driver's feet and then, immediately, the floor began to rise up toward the bottom of the rear bumper.

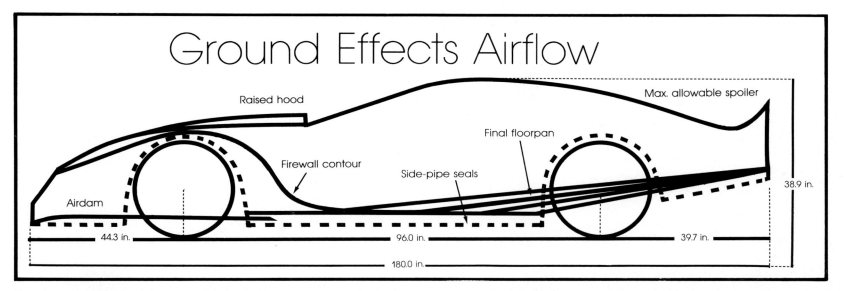

Ground Effects Airflow

Raised hood

Max. allowable spoiler

Final floorpan

Firewall contour

Side-pipe seals

Airdam

38.9 in.

44.3 in.

96.0 in.

39.7 in.

180.0 in.

Drawing aerodynamic data gleaned from windtunnel tests, several new Corvette race cars incorporate what can best be described as a venturi in their underbodies. By-rushing air is compressed beneath cowl and then allowed to expand again as it moves rearward, thus helping "suck" car toward the ground.

In other words, as the car moved over the road, the forward section of the floor tended to "compact" the air in a relatively tight, narrow space. Then toward the back of the car, the floor tilted upward or moved away from the track surface, creating the venturi effect and "sucking" the floorpan of the car downward. This, in essence, explains the working principle of the ground-effects phenomenon.

In addition to this underbody development, Schenkel also had to be concerned with overall aerodynamic lift, downforce, and drag at high speeds. He found, for example, that at a scale 130 mph, the stock-bodied production Corvette registered an overall 200 pounds of lift. But in its final racing form, the Dykstra Vette with all its "aero loading"—the 50mm (2.17-inch) front airdam ground clearance plus the 162mm (6.4-inch-tall) rear spoiler—ends up with a total *downforce* of about 420 pounds (see charts on page 111).

Downforce, of course, helps put more traction and cornering power on the ground at higher speeds. But it also exacts a penalty. The penalty expresses itself in the amount of horsepower drawn off to provide that downforce. Despite having a lower silhouette and smaller frontal area, the fully aero-loaded Corvette race car needs about 35 more horses to maintain 130 mph than the production Vette. Even so, the downforce is worth that power penalty.

Windtunnel work showed that the air used to cool the race car's water, oil, and brakes was best taken in through the grille nostrils—those areas normally occupied by turn-signal and driving lamps. Air for engine carburetion, though, had to be brought in through a special raised section atop the hood.

This 3-inch-high hood section had to be constructed for two reasons. First, with the lower body profile, the engine would have poked up through the hood without it. Second, the aero engineers wanted a high-pressure area at the base of the windshield to bring intake air into the carburetor. In the stock Corvette, with its very steep

windshield rake and hood slope, there simply isn't enough of a high-pressure area at the windshield base. Actually, this fact constitutes a tribute to Schenkel and the aero development engineers who windtunnel-tuned the original car. But they had to undo some of that work for the race car.

To take care of the Trans Am Corvette's air requirements and to help control airflow into the ground-effects area, the aero engineers designed special ducting panels to guide the spent cooling air into the venturi entrance. The stock Corvette, of course, takes in all its cooling air from underneath the nose. This does tend to create a certain amount of front-end lift at higher speeds. But the race car is designed to eliminate all uncontrolled airflow from entering the body undersurface. The very low-riding airdam thus helps avoid any disruption of the ground-effects action.

Front Airdam Critical. The front airdam not only comes within 2.17 inches of touching the ground, but it also extends outward, toward the sides of the car, to direct air around the front tires. The purpose here is to help reduce drag, because the tires present a big frontal aspect. The airdam then goes on to push uncontrolled air away from the sides of the car body.

At the same time, the engine exhaust system exits out behind the front tires and into twin, square collector pipes on either side of the car. These collectors were aero-tested not only for lift and drag but also to see whether they could double as a "ground seal" for the lower body edges. The idea was to bring them as close as possible to the road surface, thus forming the side seals for the "ground effects" enclosure. And in another way, the exhausts serve as an extension of the airdam.

Concurrent with the tunnel work, Corvette designers Jerry Palmer and Randy Wittine constantly fed in ideas to keep the race car looking as much as possible like a production Corvette. It's not hard to get off on aerodynamic tangents. Often a

PPG Industries commissioned many-time champion George Follmer to build them a pace roadster at the same time he was putting together his own '84 Vette race car.

racing design veers further and further away from its street identity as it becomes more aerodynamic. The SCCA, of course, mandates that cars competing in the Trans Am series have to look as much as possible like their showroom brethren. Every race car entered has to be approved by the SCCA Trans Am technical staff before it's allowed to run.

Using SCCA Trans Am guidelines, the designers came up with a number of different shapes and sizes of rear spoilers. These were tunnel-tested on the quarter-scale model to see how they affected drag and downforce. The effects of the spoilers had to be pitted against the action of the floorpan venturi cavity. Schenkel finally decided that the best all-around rear spoiler had to be the biggest one allowed under SCCA rules, but he added that an even larger spoiler would have been better, because it would have helped create a stronger low-pressure area behind the body to help pull out more air from underneath the car.

The Body in Glass. With tunnel testing finished, the final quarter-scale model was shipped from Chevrolet to Bob Birchmeier at Diversified Glass Products, Inc., in

Pontiac, Mich. Birchmeier and Diversified (DGP) were chosen to transform the clay model into the final, full-sized lightweight race-car body panels.

DGP had created and built bodies for such notable racing cars as the Roger Penske's PC-series Indy cars, the Pat Patrick cars of Mario Andretti, and Bob Tullius' GTP Jaguar. Birchmeier and his crew of fabricators stand out among the world's best, so in mid-Oct. 1982, Piggins arranged to send over a stock 1984 Corvette fiberglass shell. This shell would be used as the base for subsequent clay modeling, with clay applied directly over it.

The final design and clay modeling were directed by none other than Jerry Palmer and Randy Wittine. Clay was applied to a stock body shell after it had been blocked up at the angle determined to be best for the race car. Setting the shell at the proper angle of air attack let the designers measure and build spoilers and airdams to SCCA rules from the start.

They wanted to avoid mistakes at all costs. The process of transforming the stock fiberglass shell to the final clay race-car model took about 10 working weeks.

At that point, Palmer approved the full-scale clay model. He asked Randy

Follmer's designer, Martin Waide, went for short-trackers' rugged construction, and instead of making everything himself, he used mostly off-the-shelf parts.

Kerry Hitt's Spirit of America kit lets racers update their 1963-82 competition Corvettes to new standards. Optional front spindles (bottom photo) eliminate power steering. The basic kit costs $7995.

Kerry Hitt's Kits

Kerry Hitt, a race-car designer from Harrisburg, Penna., has come up with a novel way for owners of 1963-81 IMSA and SCCA competition Corvettes to update their cars. As you probably know, SCCA (Sports Car Club of America) rules exclude any car older than five years from racing.

With Hitt's kit, though, you can update your veteran Vette to 1984 (or beyond) standards and performance. The kit, sold under the Spirit of America Racing Products banner, costs $7995 and includes everything you'll need to bring your older Corvette racer up to new-generation regs. Included are all the chassis, suspension, and body panels you'll need, plus complete assembly instructions.

Spirit of America, a division of Advanced Composite Products, supplies a MIG-welded tubular chassis with 2-inch square bottom rails, a main cage of 1.75-inch tubing, all front suspension pieces from the spindles outward, and an all-new rear suspension. In other words, you'll be able to use your older front spindles, hubs, bearings, rotors, and calipers. Same for the rear from the

bearing carrier outward.

The kit's rear-suspension geometry has been around for some time. It was originally designed by Bob Riley for the Greenwood Corvette program. The hub carriers have been lightened, and some attachments have changed, but the geometry is still the Riley design. The kit adapts an Oldsmobile constant-velocity joint to the Vette halfshaft to create a plunging halfshaft, as in many European formula cars.

Differential mounting brackets are for quick-change rears, but an optional mount permits adaptation of a conventional "built-up" Corvette rear end.

Body panels emulate the 1984 Corvette, but with aero fixes around the wheelwells for less turbulence. Included are a one-piece rear clip, full hood, spoilers, fenders, doors, etc. Advanced Composite Products make the panels, which can be ordered optionally in Kevlar.

Spirit of America also has an optional suspension kit, designed by Hank Kleban, which features Kleban's new 4.5°-inclination spindle. This allows a 2.5-inch tire scrub radius on a 10-inch-wide

wheel. The car thus doesn't need horse-stealing power steering. Additional Kleban suspension goodies include super-light carbon-fiber filament driveshaft and halfshafts, carbon-carbon disc brake rotors, titanium coil-over springs, Bilstein shocks and, most amazing of all, a set of beavertail-adjustable swaybars front and rear.

"The advantage of these adjustable swaybars," says Kerry Hitt, "is this. When you set up a car for a specific course, you usually sacrifice handling in one or two turns to maximize performance over the rest of the track. You do this on the basis of over- or understeer.

"What Hank's adjustment does is let the driver pick the swaybar settings he wants from inside the car. He can change them anywhere, under any road conditions. Suppose it starts to rain. He can change the roll rate by moving a lever, allowing the car to lean for better traction."

The price of the Stage II kit hadn't been established at presstime. Get further information from Spirit of America Racing Products, 5320 Paxton St., Harrisburg PA 17111. □

Wittine to phone Blaine Ferguson at Brassfield's shop in California to tell him the body was ready. Wittine also called SCCA technical manager John Timanus in Colorado, asking him to come view the finished clay and give his approval before Bob Birchmeier made the final molds.

John Timanus, a 25-year veteran of all types of auto racing, has seen most of the world's best competition vehicles. His reaction and words on seeing the finished Corvette clay model made all the work and effort worthwhile. He told Ferguson that he was "shocked" by the sleekness of this car and its advanced design. Timanus hadn't, of course, seen the standard version of the 1984 Corvette at that time.

SCCA approval released the clay model to be transformed into actual fiberglass panels. This transformation becomes critical, not only because it's the final purpose of this whole exercise but because Birchmeier and his fabricators would have only one shot at copying the full-sized clay's shape. They had to get it right the first time, because the clay model ends up totally destroyed when the female fiberglass molds come off the clay's surface. As it turned out, of course, the job *was* done right the first time, and the panels ended up beautifully faithful to the clay model.

Up to this point, all development costs for the race-car body, including the making of molds and fabricating the actual panels, were covered by Chevrolet. But then Blaine Ferguson's consortium out in California began to fall apart. A split between Ferguson and Brassfield developed in early Dec. 1982, which put the project on hold for a short time.

After a series of phone calls between various parties and some politics that I don't understand, Chevrolet decided that the best way to keep the Corvette race-car project moving would be to transfer the rights to the body to PPG Industries. PPG agreed to buy the tools to produce the body for their Corvette Indy Car Series pace car for the 1983 CART season. The agreement called for DGP to produce and sell the body panels. These arrangements were handled quickly and smoothly, and bodies are now available to all contenders through DPG. The finished racing shells weigh about 150 pounds and, at this writing, cost less than $3000 a copy.

The Premier Teams. Chevrolet's role in the initial race-car development process ended at this point, and it was now up to the individual racing teams to continue. What follows is a recap of the first four serious teams that campaigned—or planned to campaign—1984 Corvettes in the SCCA Trans Am and IMSA GTO series.

The original team—the one that led to the body's specifications—continued with Lee Dykstra, John Bright, Jerry and Darin Brassfield, but without Blaine Ferguson. Lee chose to design his Corvette racer from the ground up. He conceived and produced nearly every element of the finished car. Such pieces as hubs, hub carriers, suspension arms, the chassis, rollcage, and many other items that most builders order off the shelf came directly from Dykstra's drawingboard. He and John Bright certainly didn't take any easy ways out.

The Dykstra-conceived Corvette resulted in using a computer-designed space frame with integral rollcage, all aluminum interior body panels and floor, and an engine front mounting plate with provisions for an external oil pump and alternator. The front suspension used twin A-arms, tubular control arms, tubular stabilizer bar, aluminum hubs, and coils over Koni double-adjustable shocks. Front tires were 25.5 x 11 x 16 Goodyears on BBS knockoff 3-piece 16 x 10-inch wheels.

Rear suspension stayed with the stock Corvette rear axle, the major change being adjustable Konis. Brakes were Lockheed 13-inchers front and rear. Dykstra went with a Weismann 5-speed gearbox behind a Borg & Beck 3-plate clutch and aluminum flywheel. The car used newly designed steering and a 32-gallon ATL fuel

On George Follmer's race car and the PPG pacer, proprietary items in front suspension came from Speedway Engineering, including spindles, hub carriers.

Follmer planned to sell complete chassis to other racers for about $25,000, with finished cars going for $65,000 f.o.b. his dealership in Pomona, California.

cell. For power, Dykstra specified a Ryan Falconer-modified V-8. Output dynoed at around 525 bhp from 305 cubes.

Faithfully built to Dykstra designs by John Bright, the finished car was expected to cost around $100,000 complete, making it one of the most expensive machines in Trans Am competition. Driver for the first Trans Am race was rookie Darin Brassfield.

The Follmer Effort. Another team, this one headed by George Follmer, took a different tack. Follmer, unlike Dykstra, decided to use proven, relatively inexpensive, off-the-shelf parts instead of designing everything himself. As his designer, Follmer hired W. Martin Waide, formerly with Lotus, and instructed Waide to "keep the car simple, keep costs down, and please do it all quickly."

George Follmer's formidable driving background includes winning the U.S. Road Racing championship (1965) and the SCCA's Trans Am championship twice (1972 and '76). He also became Can Am champ in 1972. Follmer has raced Grand Prix Formula One, Formula 5000, IROC, USAC, and NASCAR, always doing extremely well. His credentials make George a heavy contender going into the 1983 season.

As I write this, part of Follmer's chances hinged on his Dennis Fischer-built, 520-bhp, 305-cid V-8. They also depended on ending up with a chassis that could match Dykstra's tour de force—plus his ability to put together sponsorship to help pay his way to more than just West Coast events.

Follmer's econo-racer aimed at a start-up price of around $25,000 for the chassis. This excluded the drivetrain, fuel system, and brakes. For a complete, ready-to-race version, the pricetag was projected at approximately $65,000.

Martin Waide's chassis dimensions tended to be quite similar to Lee Dykstra's, which they had to be to fit underneath the DGP-produced body. Waide likewise chose to go the modified ground-effects route worked out by GM; in fact, he learned some ground-effects tricks of his own when he was with Colin Chapman at Lotus. Waide plans to use a 9-inch Ford rear axle assembly and a Weismann 5-speed

gearbox. The Ford rear end, taken from a ¾-ton pickup, accomodates Porsche constant-velocity output joints.

His car's suspension arms are special designs based on the types commonly used by short-track racers. Off-the-shelf items—many from Speedway Engineering—include hubs, hub carriers, and spindles, all of which have proved strong and reliable in short-track duty and cost a fraction of the handbuilt variety. Rear suspension arms had to be custom fabricated, though, since independent rears aren't favored by short trackers.

At this writing, Follmer is also busy building a replica of his 1984 Corvette competition car for the tamer duty of pacing the 1983-84 PPG Indy-car series. Follmer's PPG car uses a twin-turbocharged V-6 and an open (roadster) body. Engineering is basically the same as the race car's, but with a beefed chassis to compensate for the lost roof structure. Too, the engine and manual 5-speed GM gearbox are mounted in rubber as a concession to comfort. The PPG pace Vette's fuel cell stands behind a Speedway quick-change rear end.

Beyond that, Follmer hopes to sell copies—or at least parts—of his car to other competitors. His plan is to fill the need for quality race cars at reasonable prices. If he succeeds, he'll surely boost the number of Corvette racers on the nation's tracks and will also increase Chevy's chances of winning.

Ducking and Weaving. 1978 Trans Am champion Greg Pickett figures as another serious contender in forthcoming SCCA and IMSA events. Pickett and Jim McCrocklin redesigned their 1982 Corvette, bringing it up to 1984 specifications. They did this partly by making the wheelbase adjustable so they could compare the 1982 version to the '84 car, but they've also been experimenting with broader and narrower track widths.

A car's track is the distance between tire centers as seen from dead ahead or behind. Pickett had been running a narrow front track in his '82 Corvette but felt the '84 car would do better with a wider track—certainly wider than specified by

The Dennis Fischer-built 305 delivered upwards of 520 bhp. Follmer's racer also used Weismann 5-speed gearbox, DGP body, Ford or Speedway rear end.

Ruggedness of Waide's design shows up in the factory-like rocker sections. Like Dykstra's car, these floorboard contours make maximum use of ground airflow.

Follmer's rollcage combined tubular with square-section steel, all welded up in jigs that aided series production. Body was planned to allow easy removal.

Like so many other Corvette race-car builders, Waide chose coil-over front springs and fully adjustable, gas-filled shock absorbers for the Follmer effort.

Follmer's PPG pace roadster required more reinforcement through mid-section to compensate for loss of the rollcage. Roadster did have a rollbar, however.

This is Tom Nehl's Auriga Racing Corvette, which again used rugged, off-the-shelf items in the front suspension plus a hefty, short-tracker-like chassis.

Franklin quick-change rear axle in Auriga Racing's Vette rested ahead of fuel cell that mounted twin pumps. Tommy Riggins oversaw construction of this car.

Rolla Vollstedt's rear suspension for the Auriga car stuck with twin trailing links (adjustable for length), had full-floating axles and Airheart disc brakes.

Dykstra's initial specifications. Should this prove true, Greg's race body will have to be widened to accommodate his car's suspension system and tires.

Pickett has also elected to go with Firestone rather than Goodyear. Pickett participated with Firestone in tire testing during the winter of 1982 and plans to continue race-car development into the future. He feels confident that with his current financial resources plus Firestone's R&D assistance, he and his Doug Gillespie-managed team have a winning combination that can run the entire season. And to bring home the points, it's more important to make and finish all the races than to win just a few.

Auriga Racing. The fourth and least known of the new Corvette teams is headed by Tom Nehl, a GMC truck dealer in Jacksonville, Fla. Nehl commissioned short-track driver/builder/road racer Tommy Riggins to superintend the construction of his new car.

Unlike the other Corvette efforts, Nehl's Auriga Racing team, as it's called, is made up strictly of volunteers; people from his GMC dealership. They're in the professional league, but they don't claim to be pro's. "We race for fun, not for money," Nehl told me in a telephone interview.

Auriga Racing builds its own engines. Their Corvette's suspension system was designed by former Indy-car owner Rolla Vollstedt, whose 20-odd years of racing experience put him on good terms with the majority of independent rears. Nehl hopes his old friend Rolla can help design a suspension that will make his 2520-pound,

560-bhp, 355-cid-powered car competitive in IMSA GTO. And with Auriga's 530-bhp 305 V-8 plus added weight, the car can also compete in the SCCA's Trans Am series. The idea is to run whenever either series makes a swing through the Southeast.

Auriga Racing had hoped—as had several other Corvette teams—to run at Sebring for 1983. None of these cars, though, was finished in time.

The first race where any 1984 Corvette ran was West Palm Beach, Fla., in an SCCA Trans Am event on May Day 1983. The only '84 to make the field was the Dykstra/Brassfield car, with Darin Brassfield driving. Darin started in sixth position, pushed his way up to third, and was passing another car on the 12th lap at the end of the long straight before the hairpins. The other car veered wide, though, putting Brassfield into the dirt, and the rough stuff sheared a bolt in his front suspension. The Vette sat out the rest of the race.

The Dykstra/Brassfield car appeared at West Palm Beach with Ford Motorsports emblems painted onto various parts of its anatomy. This was apparently a slap at Chevrolet for some slight, perceived or real. Chevrolet wasn't talking. Nor was Brassfield. I phoned Paul Preuss at Ford Motorsports, and he told me the Corvette certainly did not have Ford's support. Whatever the reasons for this inglorious debut of the '84 to racing, the incident left a bad flavor in everyone's mouth.

The West Palm Beach race was just over when I sat down to write a finish to this book. I'd hoped to end on a happier note. But I'm sure things will brighten up as the season progresses, and I will bring the newest Corvette's racing record up to date in future editions.

□

Just before we went to press, word arrived of the mid-engined GTP Corvette. This car is destined to run in IMSA's GT series and uses a 3.8 liter (229 cid) turbocharged V-6 placed amidship. The chassis is by Lola, the body by Diversified Glass Products, and the engine by Ryan Falconer. The engine uses aluminum heads and crankcase and puts out 725 bhp at 8500 rpm on methanol. Palmer and Wittine designed the body, aided by PPG Industries.

Component Sources & Materials

Item	Source	Material
Front crossmember	Dana-Parrish	Aluminized steel.
Upper control arms	Imperial Clevite[1]	Forged aluminum.
Lower control arms	Imperial Clevite[1]	Forged aluminum.
Upper control arm shaft	Imperial Clevite[1]	Cold-headed aluminum.
Front knuckles	Alcoa	Forged aluminum.
Front brake calipers	Girlock	Cast aluminum & iron.
Front brake splash shields	Tool Producers	Stamped aluminum.
Front brake rotors	Dayton-Walther	Cast iron.
Front shock absorbers	Delco Prod Div	Tube steel.
Front lower shock brackets	Stolle	Stamped aluminum.
Front leaf spring	Inland Div	Fiberglass/plastic.
Front stabilizer bar	Detroit Forge	Steel.
Front spring protector	Riverside Stpg	Stamped aluminum.
Front stabilizer shaft insulator assembly	Cooper Rubber	Cast aluminum.
Channel beam	CS Ohm	Stamped aluminum.
Prop shaft, base	Chevrolet Div	Steel.
Prop shaft, opt	Dana	Aluminum tubing & forging.
Rear-axle carrier	Dana	Cast aluminum.
Rear-axle cover beam	Dana	Cast aluminum.
Rear upper trailing links	General Tire	Forged aluminum.
Rear lower trailing links	General Tire	Forged aluminum.
Rear camber struts	General Tire	Forged aluminum.
Rear tie-rod assy	TRW	Steel.
Rear tie-rod socket assy	TRW	Aluminum[2].
Rear wheel driveshafts	Dana	Aluminum[2].
Rear knuckles	Alcoa	Forged aluminum.
Rear shock absorbers	Delco Products Div	Tube steel.
Rear spindle yokes	Dana	Forged steel.
Rear brake calipers	Girlock	Cast aluminum & iron.
Rear brake dust shields	N&N Stampings	Stamped aluminum.
Rear parking brake assy	Girlock	Cast aluminum.
Rear brake rotors	Dayton-Walther	Cast iron.
Rear leaf spring	Inland Div	Fiberglass & plastic.
Rear spring bracket	Master Cast	Cast aluminum.
Rear stabilizer bar	Rockwell	Steel.
Rear spring spacers	Motor City Stpg	Sheet aluminum.
Brake master cylinder	Girlock	Cast aluminum.
Brake vacuum booster	Girlock	Stamped steel.
Brake pedal support	Stolle	Stamped aluminum.
Parking brake lever	Gulf + Western	Stamped steel[3].
Parking brake cables	Orscheln & Acco	Plastic-coated & stainless steel.
Engine mounts	Inland Div	Steel & rubber.
Engine rocker covers	Auburn Die Cast	Cast magnesium.
Engine air cleaner	AC Spark Plug Div	Cast magnesium.
Engine water pump	Essex	Cast aluminum.
Coolant gooseneck	Yoder Die Cast	Cast aluminum.
Alternator housing	Delco Prods Div	Cast aluminum.
Alternator mtg bracket	Tool Producers	Stamped aluminum.
Alternator housing	Delco Prods Div	Stamped aluminum.
AIR pump mtg. bracket	Yoder Casting	Cast aluminum.
AIR pump housing	Saginaw Div	Cast aluminum.
Air conditioner bracket	Doehler-Jarvis	Cast aluminum.
Power strng. mtg bracket	Monroe City	Cast aluminum.
Power-strng pump housing	Saginaw Div	Cast iron
Oil filler cap	Stant	Steel & plastic.
Distributor ignition shield	Dynaplast	Molded nylon.
TBI intake cover	Rochester Div	Cast aluminum.
Exhaust manifolds	Benteler	Stainless steel.
Exhaust front Y-pipe	Quanex	Stainless steel.
Catalytic converter	AC Spark Plug Div	Stainless steel.
Catalytic converter shield	Magna	Stamped aluminum.
Exhaust rear Y-pipe	Walker Mfg	Aluminized steel.
Transmission, manual	Doug Nash Engineering	Aluminum case.
Overdrive unit	Doug Nash Engineering	Aluminum case.
Manual transmission shifter	Inland Tool & Mfg	Stamped steel.
Clutch master cylinder	Lucas	Cast aluminum.
Clutch slave cylinder	Lucas	Cast aluminum.
Clutch pedal bracket	Tool Producers	Stamped steel.
Transmission, automatic	Hydramatic Div	Aluminum case.
Torque-converter cover	Tool Producers	Stamped aluminum.
Automatic trans extn	Doehler-Jarvis	Cast aluminum.
Automatic trans shifter	Kent Products	Stamped steel.
Steering rack	Saginaw Div	Steel.
Steering gear housing	Saginaw Div	Steel & aluminum.
Steering gear clamp	Dajaco	Stamped aluminum.
Wheels, 15-inch	Western Wheel	Cast aluminum.
Wheels, 15-inch	Modern Wheel	Cast aluminum.
Wheels, 16-inch	Modern Wheel	Cast aluminum.
Uniframe	GMAD	Steel & HSLA.
Front skegs	Hayes Albion	Aluminum.
Bumper extensions	Modern Tool	Aluminum.
Bumpers	Guideflex	Steel.
Front bumper beam	LOF Plastics	HMC plastic.
Front bumper fascia	Olds Div	RRIM.
Front energy absorber	Guide Div	Plastic.
Front license holder	C&F Stamping	FRP.
Lamps, park & turn	Guide Div	Plastic.
Headlight doors	LOF Plastics	SMC.
Headlamp modules	Guide Div	FRP.
Headlamp bezel	Buffalo Molded	Plastic.
Hood panel, assy	General Tire	SMC.
Front fenders	General Tire	SMC.
Upper fr wheelhouses	Chevrolet Div	FRP.
Lower fr wheelhouses	Rockwell	SMC.
Fr wheelhouse lower rear	LOF Plastics	SMC.
Fr wheelhouse lower cntr.	LOF Plastics	SMC.
Radiator grille panel	Buffalo Molded	Plastic.
Upper radiator baffle	Budd Co	SMC.
Upper radiator support	Budd Co	SMC.
Lower radiator baffle	C&F Stamping	FRP.
Battery tray	Marysville Plastics	FRP.
Lower radiator support	Budd Co	SMC.
Plenum	General Tire	SMC.
Plenum endcaps	Trans Plastic	SMC.
Dash panel	General Tire	SMC.
Front floor panel	General Tire	SMC.
Intermed floor panel	Lobdell Emery	Steel.
Rear underbody	Chevrolet Div	SMC.
Rear closeout panel	Chevrolet Div	SMC.
Rear wheelhouse	Almac	FRP.
Rear underbody fr clsout	Budd Co	SMC.
Lift-out roof, std	Rockwell	SMC.
Lift-out roof, opt	Almac	Acrylic.
Rear upper body assy	General Tire	SMC.
Rear bumper fascia	Olds Div	RRIM.
Lower rear body panel	Budd Co	SMC.
Rear energy absorber	Guide Div	Plastic.
Rocker panels	Magna	RRIM.
Side door assys	General Tire	SMC.
Door opening panel	Rockwell	SMC.
Lock pillar support ext	Trans Plastic	SMC.
I.p. carrier assy	Kusan	Polycarbonate.
I.p. upper braces	Concord Tool	Aluminum.
I.p. lower center bracket	Bopp-Busch	Steel.
I.p. bracket	Newell	Aluminum.
I.p. reinforcement bracket	Bopp-Busch	Steel.
I.p. passenger bolster	Davidson Rubber	Vinyl over urethane.
I.p. lower trim pads	Davidson Rubber	Carpet/foam/plastic.
I.p. rh supports	Concord Tool	Aluminum.
I.p. rh trim plate	Kusan	Polycarbonate.
I.p. fuse box cover	Dynaplast	Polycarbonate.
I.p. center trim plate	Kusan	Polycarbonate.
Instrument trim plate	Kusan	Polycarbonate.
I.p. upper deck	GM Inland Div	Vinyl over foam.
I.p. bottom insulators	Superior Plastics	Foam & ABS.
I.p. reinforcement assy	Modern Tool	Aluminum.
Console trim plate	Kusan	Polycarbonate.
Console side trim panel	C&F Stamping	Azdel & carpet.
Console bins	Kusan	Polyphenoloxide.
Console tape tray	Universal	Polycarbonate.
Shift boot assy	Greenfield Res	Leather.
Automatic shift quadrant	Universal	Polycarbonate.
Console door/armrest	Davidson Rubber	Vinyl/foam/ABS.
Console door hinge	E.R. Wagner	Steel.
Rh dash air outlet	Kusan	ABS.
Steering wheel	GM Inland Div	Steel/vinyl/leather.
Hood release bezel	Dynaplast	ABS.
Hood release handle	Dynaplast	Fiber-reinforced nylon.
LCD instrument cluster	AC Spark Plug Div	Various.
Windshield	LOF	Laminated glass.
Side windows	PPG	Tempered glass.
Rear hatch	PPG	Tempered glass.
Fuel tank	Brisken	Terne-coated steel, poly-ethylene liner.

[1] Subcontractors: Alcoa, Metal Forge, Inland.
[2] Steel with automatic transmission except RPO A-42.
[3] Plastic-coated grip on base car; leather with 16-inch wheels.

Notes: ABS = acrylonitrile, butadiene & styrene plastic; FRP = fiberglass reinforced polyester; HMC = high-glass molding compound; RRIM = reinforced reaction injection molding; SMC = sheet-molding compound.

Standard Equipment

ID	Item	Comment
—	Air conditioning.	Side window defoggers.
—	LCD instrumentation	Includes trip computer, graphic plus digital displays in either metric or English readouts.
UM-7	AM/FM Delco radio	New 2000 ETR series. Includes power rear antenna, 4 speakers; delete for credit.
—	Digital clock	Built into radio receiver.
U-81	Dual rear speakers	Delco Electronics Div.
—	Full-length console	Contains double storage compartment, coin tray, lighter, ashtray, radio, air controls.
—	Power windows	Switches on console.
A-51	Bucket seats	Lear-Siegler.
DG-7	Dual outside mirrors	Electric remote control.
—	Day/night inside mirror	
—	Rack & pinion power steering	
—	Tilt/telescope column	Easily adjustable.
—	Leather-wrapped wheel rim	
—	Full carpeting	On floor, rear deck, bottom of instrument panel.
—	Twin rear storage bins	With false bottoms.
—	Concealing roller shade	For rear deck.
—	Top retainer brackets	Atop rear fender wells.
—	Frameless glass hatch	Three inside releases.
—	One-piece removable roof	See-through panel optional.
—	Top removal wrench	To unbolt roof panel.
—	Theft-deterrent system	With starter interrupt.

ID	Item	Comment
—	Lamp group	Includes high-intensity lamps on door and B-pillar, underdash lamps, underhood lamps, headlight reminder.
—	Illuminated vanity	On right visor.
—	Intermittent wipers	Switch on driver's door; hidden wipers.
—	Acoustical insulation	
L-83	350-cid ohv V-8	With twin TBI.
—	Engine dressup	Magnesium rocker covers and aircleaner top.
YA-7	Calif. assy.-line test	Includes YF-5.
YF-5	Calif. emission eqpt.	Consists of NB-2, VJ-9, YA-7.
VJ-9	Calif. emissions info.	Required by law.
Z-49	Canadian modifications	Required by law.
K-99	97-amp alternator	Std. equipment.
MK-2	7-speed manual trans	Doug Nash T-10 w/overdrive, or THM 700-R4 automatic available at no extra cost.
HE-3	Positraction 3.07:1 axle	Std. axle and ratio.
N-90	15-inch alloy wheels	Listed early but not offered.
QYZ	P215/65R-15 tires	Goodyear Eagle GT blackwalls.
U-75	Power antenna	Automatic lowering.
VK-3	Front license bracket	Replaces RPO BY-8.
—	Quartz-halogen headlights	Retractable.
—	Exterior lamp group	Front & rear cornering lamps, halogen fog lamps.
—	4-wheel disc brakes	Girlock, power assisted.
—	Tinted glass	Including liftback.
—	Full body side molding	Black rubber rub strip.

Regular Production Options

RPO	Item	Description
AG-9	6-way power seat control	Driver's side only ($210).
AQ-9	Sport seats	Cloth trim, fully adjustable ($625).
AU-3	Power door locks	Central locking ($165).
BY-8	"Corvette" front license	Decor panel.
B-16	Leather seat trim	Requires A-51 ($400).
CC-3	Transparent roof panel	Interim for 1984 ($595).
C-49	Rear window defogger	Part of RPO Z-6A only.
DL-8	Dual sport mirrors	Heated, electric remote control, RH convex. Part of RPO Z-6A only.
D-60	Non-recommended color combinations	
D-84	Two-tone paint	See RPO O-1L & O-1U ($428).
FE-7	Sport suspension	Sold only as part of RPO Z-51. Includes HD LCA bushings, HD front & rear springs & stabibizer bars, 13:1 steering, aluminum prop shaft, aluminum axle shafts, aluminum spare wheel, PX-2 alloy 16 x 8½-inch front wheels, PX-2 alloy 16 x 9½-inch rear wheels, GW-4 Positraction rear axle with 3.31:1 ratio.
F-51	HD fr/rear shocks	Sold only in RPO Z-51.
G-92	Performance axle ratio	($22).
GW-4	Positraction 3.31:1 axle	Sold only in RPO Z-51.
K-34	Cruise control	Available both transmissions ($185).
KC-4	Engine oil cooler	Available with Z-51 ($158).
L-83	V-8 engine (std.)	5.7-liter with twin TBI.
MD-8	Turbo Hydramatic 700-R4	No-cost option. 4-speed automatic with 2500-rpm stall speed, lock-up torque converter.
MM-4	7-speed transmission	No-cost option.
MX-0	Merchandising number for MD-8, no-cost THM.	
NA-5	Emissions system, V-8	Federal.
NB-2	Emissions system, V-8	California.
NEW	Wheel & tire package	Export only. Includes RPO's QZD & PX-2 with 8½-inch 16-inch wheels front & rear.

RPO	Item	Description
O-1L	Two-tone paint	Lower body only.
O-1U	Two-tone paint	Upper body only.
PX-2	16-inch alloy wheels	Domestic uses wider rear rims. Included in RPO Z-51.
QZD	16-inch tires & wheels	Goodyear Eagle VR50 blackwalls and alloy wheels, included in RPO Z-51 or $561.20 additional.
UL-5	Delete base radio	Applies credit toward an optional sound system.
UM-6	AM/FM radio with tape player	New 2000 ETR series. Includes power rear antenna, 4 speakers ($153).
UN-8	Universal CB radio	Includes RPO U-83. Separate LH instrument panel speaker provision if ordered with 4-speaker Bose system ($215).
UU-8	Delco-Bose sound system	Specific AM/FM stereo radio w/cassette player, special tone & balance control integrated into speaker design; 2 door & 2 rear Bose direct-reflecting speakers with integral power amplifiers; Dolby DNR & automatic supression system ($895).
U-83	Tri-band power antenna	For CB radio only.
VO-1	Heavy-duty radiator	Included in RPO Z-51 or $57.
Z-51	Performance handling pkg.	Costs $600.20. Combines RPO's FE-7, F-51, VO-1, & QZD. Specifically, it includes HD LCA bushings, HD front & rear springs, stabilizer bars, shock absorbers, 13:1 steering, aluminum prop shaft, aluminum axle shafts, aluminum spare wheel, PX-2 alloy 16 x 8½-inch front wheels, PX-2 alloy 16 x 9½-inch rear wheels, GW-4 Positraction rear axle with 3.31:1 ratio, Goodyear VR50 blackwalls.
Z-6A	Defogger package	Consists of RPO C-49 & DL-8 ($160).

Note: Base price of a new Corvette at the car's California introduction on 3/24/83 was $21,800 plus $475 destination charge and $75 emissions equipment, for a total of $22,350. Prices listed above in parentheses are also from the initial California introduction date.

Comparative Specifications

	Ferrari 308 GTS	Porsche 928S	Mercedes 380SL	1963 Corvette	1968 Corvette	1984 Corvette
Base Price	$59,295	$43,800	$40,030	$ 4,394	$ 4,663	$21,800
Curb Weight, lbs.	3250	3351	3495	3150	3375	3117
Wt. Distribution	42/58	50/50	52/48	53/47	50/50	50/50
Wheelbase, in.	92.1	98.4	96.9	98.0	98.0	96.2
Track, fr/rear, in.	57.8/57.8	61.1/60.2	57.2/56.7	56.3/57.0	58.3/59.0	59.6/60.4
Overall Length, in.	174.2	175.7	182.3	175.3	182.1	176.5
Overall Width, in.	67.7	72.3	70.5	69.6	69.2	71.0
Overall Height, in.	44.1	50.5	50.8	49.8	47.8	46.7
Cargo Cap. cu. ft.	5.3	16.0 approx.	6.6	10.5	8.4[1]	17.9
Fuel Cap. gal.	18.5	22.4	25.5	20.0	20.0	20.0
Engine Type	Midship dohc V-8.	Front sohc V-8, alum. block.	Front sohc V-8, alum. block.	Front ohv V-8, iron block.	Front ohv V-8, iron block.	Front ohv V-8, iron block.
Displacement cu. in.	179	285	234	327	327	350
SAE bhp @ rpm	205/6600	234/5500	155/4750	360/6000	300/5000	200/4200
SAE Torque @ rpm	181/5000	263/4000	196/2750	352/4000	360/3400	290/2800
Induction System	port injexn	port injexn	port injexn	port injexn	4-bbl carb	2 TBI
Auto. Trans.	N/A	Mercedes alum. case	Mercedes	THM	THM	THM 700-R4
Ratios: 1st.	—	3.68	3.68	1.76	2.48	3.06
2nd.	—	2.41	2.41	1.00	1.48	1.63
3rd.	—	1.43	1.44	—	1.00	1.00
4th.	—	1.00	1.00	—	—	0.70
Rev.	—	5.14	5.14	1.76	3.70	2.29
Auto. final drive	—	2.20	2.47	3.36	3.08	2.73
Man. trans.	5-sp	5-spd	N/A	4-spd	4-spd	o.d.
Ratios: 1st.	3.58	4.27	—	2.20	2.20	2.88
2nd.	2.35	2.85	—	1.64	1.64	1.91
3rd.	1.69	2.03	—	1.27	1.27	1.33
4th.	1.24	1.54	—	1.00	1.00	1.00
o.d.or 5th.	.095	1.00	—	—	—	0.67
Rev.	N/A	3.75	—	2.26	2.26	2.78
Manual final drive	3.71	2.27	—	3.70	3.55	2.73
Frame Type	Tubular steel.	Unitized steel.	Unitized steel.	Ladder type, 5 x-members, steel birdcage bolted to frame.	Ladder type, 5 x-members, steel birdcage bolted to frame.	Steel uniframe with integral birdcage.
Body Material	Steel.	Steel; alum. fenders, doors, hood.	Steel	Fiberglass	Fiberglass	Fiberglass

	Ferrari 308 GTS	Porsche 928S	Mercedes 380SL	1963 Corvette	1968 Corvette	1984 Corvette
Front Suspension	SLA, coil springs, tube shocks, stab. bar.	Upper A-Arms, lower trailing arms, coils, tube shocks, stabilizer.	SLA, coil springs, tube shocks, stab. bar.	SLA, coil springs, tube shocks, stab. bar.	SLA, coil springs, tube shocks, stab. bar.	SLA, fiberglass mono-leaf spring, tube shocks, stab. bar.
Rear Suspension	SLA, coil springs, tube shocks, stab. bar.	Upper transverse links, lower trailing arms, coils, tube shocks, stab. bar.	Semi-trailing arms, coil springs, tube shocks, stab. bar.	LCA, 2 trailing arms, fixed-length axle shafts, transverse 9-leaf spring, tube shocks, stab. bar.	LCA, 2 trailing arms, fixed-length axle shafts, transverse 9-leaf spring, tube shocks, stab. bar.	5-link, fixed differential, upper & lower longitudinal control arms, lateral strut, tube shocks, monoleaf fiberglass spring, stab. bar.
Brakes, type	4-whl discs	4-whl discs	4-whl discs	4-whl drums[2]	4-whl discs	4-whl discs
Rotor diam. fr/rear	10.7/10.9	11.1/11.4	10.8/11.0	11.0/11.0[2]	11.75/11.75	11.5/11.5
Steering, type	r & p	r & p	recirc ball	recirc ball	recirc ball	r & p
Steering ratio	N/A	17.75:1	15.59:1	20.2:1[3]	17.6:1	15.5:1[4]
Wheels, front	390 x 190 alloy	16 x 7J alloy	14 x 6½J alloy	15 x 5½K steel	15 x 7JK steel	15 x 7 alloy, 16 x 8.5 alloy opt.
Wheels, rear	390 x 190 alloy	16 x 7J alloy	14 x 6½J alloy	15 x 5½K steel	15 x 7JK steel	15 x 7.5 alloy, 16 x 9.5 alloy opt.
Tires, Standard	Michelin TRX 220/55VR-390	Pirelli P7 225/50VR-16	Michelin XVS 205/70HR-14	Various 6.70 x 15	Various F70 x 15	Goodyear Eagle GT P215/65R-15
Performance Max. lat. acceleration	0.810g	N/A	0.700g	N/A	N/A	0.950g
Braking from 60 mph. ft.	154	150	155	134	N/A	133
0-60 mph, sec.	7.9	6.8	10.9	5.8	8.6	7.1
¼ mile accln.	16.1/88.0	15.2	18.8/75.0	14.5/102.0	15.8/89.4[6]	15.5/88
Top speed, mph	140	146	110	130	128[7]	142

[1] 1982 model.
[2] drum brakes
[3] 17.6:1 opt'l.
[4] 13.1:1 opt'l.
[5] 6.5 sec. w/427.
[6] 13.4/109.5 w/427.
[7] 142 mph w/427.

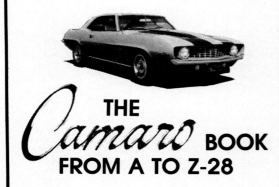

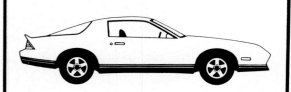

Alphabetical Index

Credits & acknowledgements. Special thanks to the following individuals and institutions: AC Spark Plug Div., Herb Adams VSE, John Amgwert, George Angersbach, Michael B. Antonick, Zora Arkus-Duntov, Jurgen Bauer, Ed Bayless, David G. Beyerlein, Robert Birchmeier, Becky Bodnar, Lisa Borman, Dr. Amar G. Bose, the Bose Corp., David Brady, Harry Bentley Bradley, Gordon Burleigh, Ronald N. Burns, Robert C. Burwitz, John Cafaro, Campbell-Ewald Co., John A. Carol, Ceco Publishing Co., Clark Chapin, Chevrolet Engineering, Chevrolet Public Relations, Larry Colwell, *Corvette News,* Rick Darling, Brian M. Decker, Tom Delano, Billie Delevich, Joseph J. Dell'Ario, Delco Electronics Div., John V. Dinan Jr., Diversified Glass Products Inc., Doug Nash Engineering, William B. Draper, Cheryl Dunkle, Jim Dunne, Douglas J. Ego, John C. Engelman, Blaine Ferguson, Firestone Tire and Rubber Co., V.F. Fishtahler, George Follmer, Roy Fowler, Steve France, Pat Furey, Russell F. Gee, the GM Aero Lab, GM Assembly Div., GM Design Staff, GM Photographic, F.J. Gerbic, General Tire & Rubber Co., William C. Gill Jr., Goodyear Tire & Rubber Co., Don Gould, Marilyn Y. Grant, Robert A. Grimm, Marcia Harmon, Dave Harrison, Jack Hatfield, Gary Hedges, David M. Holls, Charles N. Hughes, Roger Hughet, Jack Humbert, Paul H. Huzzard, James N. Ingle, Walter Jaeger, Karen Kanar, Bill Konopacke, Floyd Joliet, Charles M. Jordan, Daniel M. Kenny, Paul J. King, Ralph Kramer, William A. Lagermann, William R. Lawless, Lear-Siegler General Seating Div., Scott Leon, Andrea Lighthall, William Locke, Robert MacMillan, Gene McCrickard, John F. McGee, Floyd McKee, David R. McLellan, Mercedes-Benz of North America Inc., Ed Miller, Kenneth T. Milne Jr., George Moon, Tom Morrissey, National Corvette Restorers Society Inc., Tom Nehl, William Ott, Jerry P. Palmer, Robert R. Parks, Steve Perry, John Pierce, Vince Piggins, Duane E. Poole, Porsche-Audi of North America Inc., Fred C. Porter, PPG Industries, Arthur E. Pryde, James K. Reinker, Lloyd Reuss, *Road & Track Magazine,* Erwin M. Rosen, Dick Ross, Irwin Rybicki, F.J. Schaafsma, Max Schenkel, Carl W. Schmid Jr., Stuart Schuster, William D. Scott, John Shettler, Bob Stella, Robert C. Stempel, Edwin Stutzman, Gene Sullivan, Donald W. Thomsen, Thompson Advertising Productions Inc., Charles Torner, Paul van Valkenburgh, *Vette Vues Magazine,* Russ von Sauers, Robert A. Vogelei, Cathy Wagner, Glenn A. Walkush, Kay Ward, Bill Warner, Al B. Williams, Don Williams, James J. Williams, Randy Wittine, Stanley J. Worky, Chao-Hsi Wu, Thomas R. Zimmer, John Zwerner. Typesetting by Keen Graphics and Cliff Typographers. Graphic Design by Dick Hanson. Printed by Kingsport Press, a division of Arcata Graphics Co.